THE
EVERYTHING
RAW FOOD
RECIPE BOOK

Dear Reader,

My first introduction to raw foods was nine years ago at the Raw and
Living Foods Festival in Portland, Oregon. That day my eyes were
opened to a whole new way of eating and living in harmony with nature.
I was impressed with the incredible health and energy of everyone at the
festival, including the seniors who'd been eating this way for decades.

I knew that I'd discovered something important! I was so excited to
begin my new journey—I started with simple salads but quickly became
bored. I felt deprived of my favorite meals! I had strong cravings for the
comfort foods my Mom used to make. I missed the spaghetti dinners,
meaty burgers, cheesy pizza, and warm cookies.

Then I discovered the secret to success on a raw foods diet—
gourmet cuisine. By combining the right foods and seasonings, I've been
able to recreate my favorite meals and make them taste even better.

I've compiled 300 of my favorite recipes here for you to experiment
with and make your own. Some of the recipes recreate favorite comfort
foods and others introduce new foods and flavors. I hope you find plea-
sure in the book and valuable tools for your journey to optimal health!

Mike Snyder

Welcome to the EVERYTHING® Series!

These handy, accessible books give you all you need to tackle a difficult project, gain a new hobby, comprehend a fascinating topic, prepare for an exam, or even brush up on something you learned back in school but have since forgotten.

You can choose to read an *Everything®* book from cover to cover or just pick out the information you want from our four useful boxes: e-questions, e-facts, e-alerts, and e-ssentials. We give you everything you need to know on the subject, but throw in a lot of fun stuff along the way, too.

We now have more than 400 *Everything®* books in print, spanning such wide-ranging categories as weddings, pregnancy, cooking, music instruction, foreign language, crafts, pets, New Age, and so much more. When you're done reading them all, you can finally say you know *Everything®*!

QUESTION

Answers to
common questions

FACT

Important snippets
of information

ALERT

Urgent
warnings

ESSENTIAL

Quick
handy tips

PUBLISHER Karen Cooper

DIRECTOR OF ACQUISITIONS AND INNOVATION Paula Munier

MANAGING EDITOR, EVERYTHING® SERIES Lisa Laing

COPY CHIEF Casey Ebert

ACQUISITIONS EDITOR Katrina Schroeder

SENIOR DEVELOPMENT EDITOR Brett Palana-Shanahan

EDITORIAL ASSISTANT Hillary Thompson

EVERYTHING® SERIES COVER DESIGNER Erin Alexander

LAYOUT DESIGNERS Colleen Cunningham, Elisabeth Lariviere, Ashley Vierra, Denise Wallace

Visit the entire Everything® series at *www.everything.com*

THE EVERYTHING®

RAW FOOD RECIPE BOOK

Mike Snyder with Nancy Faass, MSW, MPH
and Lorena Novak Bull, RD

Avon, Massachusetts

To my loving wife, Tina. Thank you for your
patience and unwavering support.—Mike

To Harriet, the best cook I've ever met.—Nancy

An Everything® Series Book.
Everything® and everything.com® are registered trademarks of F+W Media, Inc.

Published by Adams Media, a division of F+W Media, Inc.
57 Littlefield Street, Avon, MA 02322 U.S.A.
www.adamsmedia.com

ISBN 10: 1-4405-0011-8
ISBN 13: 978-1-4405-0011-4

Printed in the United States of America.

10   9   8   7   6   5   4   3

Library of Congress Cataloging-in-Publication Data
is available from the publisher.

This book is available at quantity discounts for bulk purchases.
For information, please call 1-800-289-0963.

Contents

Acknowledgments

My heartfelt thanks go out to all the natural health pioneers who have come before me. Thank you to the raw food authors, chefs, doctors, and others in the community who are sharing the message.

Thanks to those in the raw foods community who have inspired me, including Dr. Gabriel Cousens, Viktorus Kulvinskas, Ani Phyo, Cheri Soria, Dr. Brian Clement, David Wolfe, and Ann Wigmore.

Thank you to Thomas and Gabriel Chavez, who have both provided me with a great deal of support, guidance, and encouragement over the years.

My heartfelt thanks and appreciation to my coauthor, Nancy Faass, for all your inspiration, motivation, and encouragement.

Thanks to Katrina Schroeder and the staff at Adams Media for making the publishing process easy and fun.

Special thanks to my loving friends and family who are a never-ending source of inspiration and encouragement and especially to my parents, Bob and Kathy Snyder, and my brother Jeff Snyder, for your unconditional love and support.

Thank you to my wife, Tina, for your love and support, and for making each day together a joy.

—Mike

To the great researchers and doctors of nutritional medicine who've paved the way for this new era, including Jeffrey Bland, PhD, Gladys Block, PhD, Leo Galland, MD, and Walter Willets, MD—and to an entire new generation of nutritional pioneers like Mike who are showing us the way back to the future. Thanks to our editors, Katrina Schroeder and Brett Palana-Shanahan, and the folks at Adams Media for making this book possible.

With gratitude, Nancy

Introduction

WELCOME TO THE WORLD of raw and living foods! The goal of this book is to share with you new ways of preparing fresh vegetarian and vegan cuisine. This is an idea whose time has come.

Celebrities who have become raw foods enthusiasts include comedian Robin Williams; motivational speaker Tony Robbins; designer Donna Karan; musicians David Bowie and Sting; actresses Angela Bassett, Cher, Demi Moore, Alicia Silverstone, Lisa Bonet, Laura Dern, Leslie Bega (of *The Sopranos*), and Susan Sarandon; supermodel Carol Alt; actors Woody Harrelson, James Brolin, Frankie Lane, Andy Dick, and Ben Vereen; Canadian rocker Bif Naked; and chef Charlie Trotter. In addition, CNN and NBC news have both featured stories on the raw food diet phenomenon.

The approach in this book is gourmet vegetarian and vegan, which means the focus is on fresh fruits and vegetables, leafy greens, nuts, seeds, herbs, and spices. This translates into exceptional cuisine interpreted from the great culinary traditions of the world, featuring recipes such as Thai Green Papaya Salad, Sprouted Moroccan Lentil Soup, Italian Crackers, Chinese Kung Pao Almonds with Mung Bean Sprouts, and Indian-Style Curried Noodles.

There are no recipes containing eggs or meat (either cooked or raw). A classic raw foods diet minimizes many of the foods likely to cause allergies (such as dairy products, cooked grains, and shellfish). This approach also avoids numerous foods linked to disease. (For example, junk food and sweets have been confirmed as a factor in diabetes, and red meat has been found to increase cancer risk.)

Yet the raw foods diet is not about deprivation. It's a chance to discover an entire world of fresh new foods and explore their health benefits. From our kitchens to yours, enjoy!

CHAPTER 1

Welcome to Raw Foods Cuisine

Raw gourmet cuisine is one of life's great pleasures. The food is absolutely delicious and can be adapted to the palate and flavors of any culture, from satisfying American comfort foods to zesty Italian sauces and spicy Indian curries. Simply put, a raw foods diet means eating food in its natural state. Raw foods can be defined as those that are uncooked or prepared at temperatures below 115°F. When food is heated above that temperature, vital nutrients and enzymes are destroyed. Although nutritional supplements are available, science has not yet fully recreated the complex and subtle benefits of fresh, unprocessed food.

The Benefits of Raw Foods

Many people find a raw food diet life changing. They are amazed that something so simple could make such a difference in their health, mood, and energy. When you eat a raw diet, the food becomes the medicine, gradually healing the body by providing essential nutrients. Most people experience some difference within a few days.

Keeping Life Simple

Raw cuisine is elegant, nourishing food made with basic kitchen techniques. This chapter will provide you with an introduction to raw foods prep, with checklists to simplify shopping and menu planning. You'll be surprised by how easy this approach is and what it can mean for you, including:

- **Less time in the kitchen**—With these recipes, you can prepare a scrumptious raw gourmet meal in about twenty minutes—equivalent in elegance to a cooked meal that might take an hour to prepare.
- **Faster cleanup**—With this approach, there are no dirty pots or greasy pans to scrub.
- **Lower grocery bills**—Some people report that they've cut their spending at the grocery store by over 25 percent. If you have a discount natural food store in your area or if you buy staples in bulk, you may save even more.

An Ecofriendly Lifestyle

When you eat locally grown foods, you reduce your carbon footprint—you're no longer using processed foods manufactured six months ago, stored in a box or can, and shipped thousands of miles across the country. In contrast, food from local growers provides you with the flavor of fruits and vegetables fresh from the garden. Eating locally grown or homegrown foods also helps you:

- **Be empowered**—You have the option of growing your own sprouts and herbs at home, grinding your own flour, and making your own bread. This enables you to be less involved with food as a consumer and more as a producer.

- **Create less waste**—Whenever you simplify your lifestyle, you consume less packaging, plastic, paper, and aluminum, which means less waste that will end up in the landfills.
- **Conserve water**—A vegetarian diet requires 300 gallons of water a day, whereas a meat-based diet requires more than 4,000 gallons daily: The simpler lifestyle consumes less than 10 percent of the water.

Starting with the Basics

When people visit their doctor, they usually hear the recommendations, "Cut back on the red meat. Lower your salt intake. Stop eating fried foods." You'd never hear your doctor say, "Cut back on your fruits and vegetables." Most people need to eat more fruits and vegetables, but that raises the question of how to prepare them so that they taste really good. This book will give you hundreds of new ideas, delicious recipes, and a step-by-step guide to eating raw. You can tailor your approach to your lifestyle and your response to the food. Remind yourself that you don't have to eat 100 percent raw to enjoy the health benefits of this wonderful cuisine. Proceed at your own pace.

A Brief Raw Foods History

The raw foods diet is not a new concept. This was the first food eaten by humans before the stove was invented (and even before fire was discovered). There are historical and Biblical references to the raw foods diet. The Essene were a religious group that flourished from the second century B.C. to the first century A.D. Documents from that time report that they ate a diet rich in raw fruits, vegetables, and sprouts. They developed their own form of bread, and a similar bread can be purchased today in most health food stores. Essene bread is made from sprouted grains and seeds, formed into a loaf, and then dehydrated. The Essenes baked their bread directly in the sunlight.

An interesting Biblical reference to the antiaging effects of raw foods is found in the first chapter of Daniel. In this passage, the King gives his servants rich foods and wine, but Daniel refuses to eat them. He persuades the King to agree to a ten-day experiment in which the servants eat only vegetables and water. A quote from Daniel 1:15–16 says "At the end of the ten days they looked healthier and better nourished than any of the young men who ate the royal food. So the guard took away their choice food and the wine they were to drink and gave them vegetables instead."

The Modern Raw Foods Movement

The contemporary raw foods community can trace its roots back to the natural health movement that emerged across the globe in the late nineteenth century. In the United States this movement was led by Dr. Sylvester Graham (innovator of Graham crackers), Dr. Herbert Shelton, and many other health pioneers. These doctors practiced a system of health care known as Natural Hygiene. The philosophy of this approach was to support the body's natural healing process through a raw foods and whole-grain diet, and periodic water fasting. The Natural Hygiene movement is alive today in the natural health communities in the United States and worldwide.

In the mid-twentieth century, natural health doctors began expanding their approach to diet, adding juices, blended foods, cleansing, and detoxification to their programs. These raw food pioneers have included Dr. Ann Wigmore, Dr. Brian Clement, Dr. Max Gerson, Dr. Bernard Jensen, and Dr. Gabriel Cousens.

Raw Gourmet Cuisine

The concept of raw gourmet food emerged about this time, introducing the world to a whole new lifestyle and way of eating. Today, raw gourmet foods are everywhere. Most major cities have restaurants with raw foods cuisine featured on their menus. Examples include the Café Gratitude restaurants in the San Francisco Bay Area (*www.cafegratitude.com*) and Quintessence in New York (*www.raw-q.com*). Most health food stores carry a variety of packaged raw foods including nuts, cookies, crackers, and energy bars, as well as fermented products like sauerkraut. It has never been easier to eat healthy!

The Benefits of a Raw Food Diet

Many people who adopt a raw foods diet experience health benefits in a matter of days or weeks. Deeper changes seem to take up to about six months. Raw foods enthusiasts report increased energy, beautiful skin, greater mental clarity, and better stamina.

Reduced Risk of Cancer and Heart Disease

The following research bears out the benefits of a diet rich in fruits and vegetables:

- Researchers at Harvard Medical School tracked the health of more than 22,000 physicians. The study found those who ate at least 2½ servings of vegetables a day lowered their risk of heart disease by almost 25 percent.
- At the University of California, Berkeley, researchers found that a high intake of fruits and vegetables also reduces the risk of cancer on average by 50 percent.
- A recent study on diabetes at the University of North Carolina reported that a vegan diet rich in vegetables reduces diabetes indicators.
- In Stockholm at a Swedish university hospital, researchers found that a vegan diet also increases immune protection against arthritis.

ALERT

A diet that emphasizes fresh vegetables makes it easier to sidestep certain food allergies. For example, almost 1 percent of the U.S. population has a gluten allergy or celiac disease. Eating raw makes it much easier to avoid wheat products. Dairy allergies are also fairly common, and elements of dairy such as casein (the protein in milk) crop up everywhere, from soy cheese to canned tuna and deli meat. Typically raw foods contain no dairy products.

Looking and Feeling Younger

As impressive as the research data is, it pales in comparison with the feeling of waking up without aches and pains—and being able to look in the mirror and see your own natural beauty re-emerging. Eating raw foods also aids in:

- **Improved health.** Many people who transition to raw foods report improvement in chronic health conditions. If you have a chronic illness, you may want to explore the health benefits of this type of diet.

As with any medical condition, be sure to check with your health care provider.

- **Weight mastery.** People eating raw foods find that it's easier to achieve their optimal weight. They report weight loss and increased muscle mass with only moderate exercise. When you receive true nourishment, food cravings and addictions tend to disappear. Your hunger is satisfied because the body has the essential nutrients it needs.
- **Providing essential vitamins and minerals.** Foods in their raw state are much higher in vitamins and minerals.
- **Protecting the immune system.** A raw food diet also conserves energy for the immune system. Studies by a Swiss researcher in 1930 showed that eating cooked food activates immune function (calling out the white blood cells and putting the body in a state of red alert). Raw food doesn't have this effect, so the body remains in a state of balance.
- **Working in sync with your genetic blueprint.** Your genetic code is hard wired for raw foods. When you eat in sync with your genetics, your body will work better and you will feel better.

Transitioning to Raw Foods

This diet is not an all-or-nothing proposition. You can begin gradually, see how your body responds, and proceed at your own pace. Here are some ideas for transitioning to raw foods.

QUESTION

Why does protein matter?
You need to get enough protein to fuel your body for the day since protein is the raw material that becomes your infection fighters, neurotransmitters, and your enzymes. There are twenty amino acids that combine to make protein. Of these, twelve are essential but need to be obtained from food because the human body cannot make them. Good protein sources include nuts and seeds; green essences like algae, chlorella, and spirulina; bee pollen; hemp seed; and maca.

Start with Smoothies

One good place to begin your quest for better health is the daily green smoothie. Green smoothies are blender drinks made from fresh fruits and leafy greens, which add important nutrients to your diet. This is a great way to increase your intake of leafy green vegetables. Delicious combinations include leafy greens with pears and lemon juice, romaine and mint with bananas, and spring greens with strawberries.

Just this single addition to your diet can create a dramatic improvement in your health and energy. The best time to make these smoothies is in the morning when you first wake up. You can have one for breakfast and take an extra serving with you in a thermos for a snack or an appetizer before lunch.

QUESTION

How can I be sure I'm getting enough protein?
If you have a lean, wiry body type or an athletic metabolism, you may burn a great deal of protein. In that case, you may want to supplement your protein intake with eggs, dairy, or protein powders and bars, based on your own values and requirements. You can get useful feedback from your body by monitoring your energy to see how much protein you need to be at your best.

Progress Slowly

If you find that you like the green smoothie and you want to increase the amount of raw food you're eating, the next step would be to learn some basic food prep techniques. The goal is to practice one food technique until you get the hang of it before moving on to another. For example, you might want to practice creating nori rolls or burrito wraps. Another good option would be to try making vegetable pasta with sauce—ribboned pasta made from zucchini, carrots, jicama, or daikon radish topped with tomato-basil marinara, pesto, or yellow curry.

Another approach is to select one meal a day when you'd like to have raw food. It could be lunch, with a great salad and some form of protein. On the other hand, you may prefer to do the food prep in the evening when you have a little more time to try new entrées and side dishes.

Essential Nutrients

If you give up eggs, you need to replace the nutrients that you used to obtain through this food. These nutrients can be supplied through the good fats and proteins in foods like avocados, nuts, and seeds such as flax.

ALERT

If you are not accustomed to eating a high-fiber diet, you'll probably find these tips helpful: Eat melons and other fruits alone or at least twenty minutes before other foods. Do not combine fruits with nuts, seeds, vegetables, or grains. Do not combine starchy foods with protein-rich foods. Do not combine avocado with nuts. Do not combine sugar with oil. Following these rules can promote better digestion.

Getting Started in the Kitchen

To develop the skills of a fresh chef, explore the techniques and tools that will bring these recipes to life. As you master each technique and move on to the next, you'll continue to broaden your repertoire of gourmet raw foods.

Basic Tools

You can make many of the recipes in this book with just a blender and a good kitchen knife. For about $100, you can purchase all the essential basic equipment you'll need to get started, including:

- Conventional blender or cup-style blender
- Good, sharp knives of different sizes
- Spiral slicer
- A potato peeler for shredding carrots
- An inexpensive mandolin grater
- Citrus juicer—a hand juicer is fine for one to three people
- Miniprep (food) processor
- Garlic press
- Nut milk bag (similar to a cheesecloth, this is a nylon mesh bag that allows you to strain liquid from pulp)

- Measuring cups and spoons
- Melon baller
- Bamboo mat for making sushi/nori rolls

Presentation

Making a delicious and satisfying meal involves more than just mixing a few ingredients together. You want your food to have pleasing colors, textures, aromas, and garnishes so that the meal stimulates all five senses. When food looks great, that tends to increase your enjoyment of the meal.

Beautiful Vegetables

There are a number of simple, manual tools that you can use to create wonderful shapes and designs with the food and very creative presentations. With a spiral slicer, you can make colorful ribbon slices and noodlelike shapes from carrots, zucchini, beets, or apples. Another useful inexpensive little tool is the mandolin grater, which you can use to quickly slice vegetables such as cabbages, zucchini, or portobello mushrooms. A potato peeler is handy for grating carrots into slender ribbons that are attractive and easy to eat. These three simple kitchen tools really speed up prep time, making it possible to prepare elegant salads in just a few minutes.

ESSENTIAL

The ideal pH for your body is slightly alkaline at 7.4 on the pH scale. This balance can be achieved by eating a general diet of around 80 percent alkaline foods and 20 percent acidic foods. Lemons are classified as an acidic fruit, but they actually create an alkaline environment inside the body. Chlorophyll has a similar nutrient profile as the human blood and is a perfect 7.4 pH. This is probably why a diet high in fresh greens tends to promote a good acid-alkaline balance.

Little Power Tools

At times you'll want to grind nuts or grate firm vegetables such as carrots. These denser foods can destroy almost any slow-speed blender—even a really good one. If you're not ready to invest in a high-speed blender, a mini food processor is a good inexpensive solution. You'll be able to grind nuts and harder vegetables in the food processor using the low gear.

Basic Food Prep

Becoming skilled at the preparation of raw entrées involves learning some new techniques. You don't have to master them all at once. For example, one of the staples of raw cuisine is vegan pâté. This versatile food is prepared by grinding nuts and blending them with a mixture of vegetables, seeds, herbs, and spices. The pâté keeps nicely in the fridge for four to seven days, and you can use it over and over in different recipes, including burrito wraps, nori rolls, and salads.

Use fresh herbs whenever possible. They're easy to grow indoors all year round, and they have more flavor than dried herbs. If you grow extra, you can harvest and dry them in your kitchen or in the dehydrator. To grind whole dried herbs into powder, use a coffee grinder or a spice mill, or hand grind them with a mortar and pestle.

ESSENTIAL

Antioxidants are nutrients that help to slow down and prevent premature aging and degenerative diseases such as cancer. Antioxidants are molecules that neutralize harmful free radicals in the body that result from pollution and infection. Most raw foods contain high amounts of antioxidants. The foods at the top of the antioxidant list include goji berries, raw cacao, prunes, acai berry, green tea, blueberries, algae, and mangosteen.

Advanced Food Prep

As you transition into gourmet raw food, you'll probably want to learn more sophisticated food prep techniques. If you enjoy preparing the advanced recipes, you'll want to upgrade to powerful, heavy-duty kitchen equipment. These appliances will save you time and enable you to be more creative.

There are a number of ways to keep the cost down. Many people buy inexpensive equipment online or at yard sales—for example, dehydrators and Vita-Mix blenders in good condition turn up periodically on sites such as Craigslist and eBay.

Tools of the Trade

Kitchen appliances used by fresh chefs and raw foods enthusiasts include:

- Dehydrator
- Sprouter
- High-speed blender
- Electric juicer for fruits and vegetables
- Wheatgrass juicer
- Soy milk and nut milk maker
- Spice mill or coffee grinder
- Sauerkraut slow cooker

Prepare Comfort Foods

Raw gourmet techniques can be used to create meals with the tastes, textures, and aromas that you're used to. These foods satisfy your emotional need for the comforting foods your parents made. For example, when you want a pick-me-up, you could have raw chocolate chip cookies with home-made almond milk. On a cold winter day, you might prepare a comforting bowl of warm soup. Warm foods (heated to about 115°F) are definitely part of the raw food repertoire.

Make Tasty Snacks

If you want to recreate classic comfort foods, the right tool for the job is a dehydrator. All you need is one of these compact appliances and a little advanced planning. Normally, when most folks get hungry they just reach for a bag of chips or crackers or some other type of convenience food. But with raw foods, you have to plan ahead. Slow-baked crackers made in a dehydrator are the best there is, but they take about eleven hours to prepare. Food prep can become an issue when you're hungry and you want some-thing to eat right away! The solution is to prepare healthy snack foods in advance (like crackers, chips, and trail mix), so you always have something ready to eat when you get hungry. That will prevent you from caving in and resorting to junk food.

Bake Your Own Bread

The dehydrator is a useful tool for preparing foods that satisfy the emotional aspects of cuisine, such as baked goods (breads), snack food (chips to serve with guacamole or salsa), warm foods (soups and chilis), and sweets (cookies and snack bars). The foods you create with this slow-cook method are mainly complex carbohydrates, full of good carbs that won't cause weight gain.

The dehydrator can be used to warm foods within a moderate temperature range (up to a maximum of 116°F) that retain nutrients and enzymes. You can use the dehydrator to prepare a variety of foods including:

- Dried fruit and trail mix
- Seasoned or spicy nuts
- Crackers, chips, and energy bars
- Cookies and pie crust
- Tortillas and chapattis
- Essene sprouted-grain breads
- Broth, soups, stews, and chili

Grow Organic Sprouts

Sprouts are considered a true superfood—they may be the single most nutritious food on the planet and one of the least expensive. They typically have about ten to thirty times more nutrients than the best organic vegetables. Most sprouts are also 35 to 50 percent protein.

This amazing food plays a key role in the living foods diet because it's actually alive. Living foods are more nutritious and have more usable proteins, vitamins, minerals, and enzymes. The seed contains all the nutrients needed to grow into a full plant.

You can grow them all year round inside in your own kitchen, and you'll save money at the grocery store because you will actually be growing some of your own organic produce. You can sprout almost any type of seed, grain, bean, or legume. Some popular sprouts include alfalfa, broccoli, clover, fenugreek, lentil, mung bean, mustard, quinoa, and sunflower. Sunflower sprouts are one of the few plant sources of vitamin D for vegans and vegetarians.

Grind Your Own Flour

You can make nut meal and seed flour fresh for all your recipes using a small electric coffee grinder or a spice mill. Having the ability to prepare nuts as you need them maximizes flavor and freshness, and minimizes the loss of nutrients. This fresh flour can be used in many creative ways to add protein, nutrients, and flavor to your food, including:

- **Toppings**—Finely ground seeds can be sprinkled on salads or entrées, or added to smoothies. Seeds such as flax, sesame, sunflower, and hemp do very nicely.
- **Spreads**—A delicious spread can be created by simply mixing nut flour with olive oil. This type of spread has the texture of a nut butter and is delicious on crackers or bread.
- **Dips**—The key to a flavorful dip is starting with the right basic ingredient and seasonings, then pair it with great snack food. For example, to create a good pesto sauce, grind up green pumpkin seeds and mix them with a little olive oil, crushed garlic, and basil. This dip goes well with sliced zucchini, carrots, raw crackers, and chips.
- **Pie crust and torte**—Nut flours can also be used in delicious creations such as a torte, which is a type of layer cake traditionally made in Europe with pecan, almond, walnut, or hazelnut flour (often layered with cream). Interesting variations include chocolate-macadamia torte, coconut-almond torte, and Oregon pistachio torte.

Make Nut Milks, Creams, and Cheeses

Rich, creamy foods can be made with healthy, high-fat vegetables, nuts, and seeds. You can create foods that are incredibly creamy and similar to butter or cream. Start with an avocado, young coconut, or some macadamia nuts, pine nuts, or cashews. Grind the food in a mini food processor, and then gradually add liquid (such as water, coconut water, or juice) to make it creamier, until it reaches the consistency you want.

Popular nut milks are made with almonds or sunflower seeds. First, grind the nuts in a mini food processor. Then add liquid to the mix and process until smooth. Pour the mixture into a nut milk bag and strain out the pulp. You can condense this into one step by using a powerful high-speed blender or a soy milk machine.

Key Ingredients

Fresh cuisine covers an amazing range of delicious ingredients. First you will need some basics to begin with, including:

- Fresh vegetables
- Leafy greens
- Root vegetables
- Cooking herbs and spices
- Sea vegetables
- Fresh fruits
- Dried fruits
- Raw grains and sprouting seeds
- Raw cacao and chocolate
- Raw nuts and seeds
- Young coconut
- Raw unprocessed oils
- Algae
- Herbal tea
- Unprocessed salt
- Raw soy sauce (nama shoyu)

Staples

In addition to the basic ingredients, here are some raw food staples you should always have on hand:

- **Sprouts**—Have one or two trays of sprouts, such as alfalfa, chick peas, lentils, or mung beans, going in a rotation so there are always fresh sprouts available. You may also want to grow leafy green sprouts, such as sunflower greens or wheatgrass.

- **Dried bulk foods**—Dried foods store well and last for a long time, so you can buy a pound of each type of nut and seed that you use, such as almonds, green pumpkin seeds, sunflower, and sesame seeds. To prepare them for the coming day, just start them soaking before you go to bed at night and they'll be ready to use in the morning. Other dried bulk items include unprocessed salt such as Celtic sea salt, Himalayan salt, and Utah Real Salt. Algae can be purchased in a number of forms—spirulina is available in powder, chlorella comes in tablets, and Klamath blue-green algae is sold in powder and capsules. Other pantry staples include herbs and spices, hemp protein powder, green superfood powder, and sea vegetables.
- **Pâté**—Ideally, make vegan pâté about once a week and store it in the fridge. You'll probably find that you use it daily, so each time you prepare it you can mix in different herbs and spices to change the flavor and give you variety.
- **Homemade sauerkraut**—This traditional cultured food is another good staple because it lasts for a long time: it will keep for up to six months in the fridge. It takes about half an hour to prepare and then about five days to ferment.
- **Miso and other fermented foods**—Miso is available at most all natural foods markets and is an excellent ingredient in soups, salad dressings, and pâtés.

Fresh Produce

To keep your fresh produce restocked, you'll want to develop a comfortable shopping routine. If you shop twice a week, you can stay stocked with the following essentials:

- **Leafy greens**—Greens are essential. You want to have a good variety of green vegetables on hand for salads and smoothies. Each time you go to the store, pick up a different type of produce. Good choices include lettuces and baby greens, beet greens, bok choy, cabbages, chard, cilantro, dandelion greens, endive, kale, parsley, radicchio, spinach, watercress, and fresh herbs.
- **Fresh vegetables**—Good choices include young asparagus, celery, chives, cucumbers, fennel, peas in the pod, peppers of all kinds,

scallions, snow peas, string beans, tomatoes, yellow squash, and zucchini.

- **Root vegetables**—These vegetables store well even without refrigeration and will last quite a while in the fridge. Favorites include beets, carrots, parsnips, turnips, sweet potatoes and yams, as well as celery root, daikon and other radishes, fennel, ginger, Jerusalem artichokes, jicama, maca, and water chestnuts.
- **Fresh fruits**—Fruits that are in season are preferable; you don't really need to buy produce that has been shipped halfway around the world. Familiar fruits that are delicious but not overly sweet include apples and pears; berries such as blackberries, blueberries, raspberries, and strawberries; citrus such as oranges and grapefruit; kiwis and mangoes; and stone fruits such as cherries, nectarines, peaches, and plums.
- **Dried fruits**—Good choices include apricots, currants, dates, figs, goji berries, and raisins. Soak them for about a half-hour to reconstitute the fruit.

Coconut Oil

You'll find coconut oil as an ingredient in a number of recipes in this book. Coconut oil is solid at temperatures below 76°F. To use in recipes, the coconut oil must first be in liquid form. You can turn the coconut oil into liquid by placing the jar in warm water for a couple of minutes.

FACT

The only scientifically proven way to extend lifespan is through calorie restriction. Scientists have studied mice and monkeys over a number of years. They found that the animals eating a low-calorie diet live longer and have less disease than their well-fed peers. Eating predominately raw foods is an easy way to gain the benefits of a calorie-restricted diet. Raw foods are naturally low in calories while high in nutrients.

Shortcuts

As you get more involved in raw cuisine, you'll want to develop habits that fit your lifestyle. For example, you'll probably want to have a large salad every night for dinner using fresh ingredients. Many people also make their gourmet entrée at that time. When you're preparing dinner, you can make the food in quantity so you'll have enough for lunch the next day. (Add in a little lemon juice and salt to help keep the food fresh for a day or two. Then store your lunch in a container in the fridge so it will be ready to go in the morning.) This is a good way to take care of two meals at one time.

A simple fruit salad or a green smoothie is a great way to start the day. If you want something more substantial, you can make a blended shake that has higher protein foods in it, like flaxseed or soaked almonds. Nuts or seeds also complement the fruit salad nicely and provide some protein. (Have the fruit about twenty minutes before the nuts so that you digest well and start your day comfortable and happy.) Adding that protein early in the day can help sustain your energy through the morning.

You are about to embark on a true culinary adventure, an exploration of the great cuisines of the world, expressed in raw and living foods. The focus is on a kaleidoscope of succulent fruits, aromatic herbs, pungent spices, tasty nuts and seeds, exotic chocolates, and vibrantly colored vegetables brimming with nutrients.

Superfood Smoothies

recipes continued on next page

recipes continued

———————

Berry Banana Smoothie

This smoothie can be enjoyed year round. It is best in the summertime when fresh berries are abundant. Frozen or dried berries are great substitutions in the off-season.

INGREDIENTS | SERVES 2

1 banana
1 cup strawberries
1 cup blueberries
1 cup ice
1 cup water

1. Place all the ingredients except the water in a blender, adding the fruit in first and putting the ice on top.

2. Pour in ½ cup of the water and blend.

3. Gradually add in remaining water until all the ingredients are blended smooth.

PER SERVING:
Calories: 118 | Fat: 1 g | Protein: 2 g | Sodium: 7 mg | Fiber: 5 g

Berry Smoothies

Because the berries used in this smoothie can be fresh, frozen, or dried, you can enjoy it as a year-round treat. You can use any type of berry you have on hand, including superfoods like goji berries, acai berries, or marion berries, as well as blackberries, blueberries, raspberries, or strawberries.

Almond Milk

Homemade almond milk has a surprisingly rich, delicious flavor. This basic recipe can be used to make different types of nut milk for smoothies, soups, and sauces. The leftover pulp can be dehydrated and used as flour in breads, cookies, and cakes.

INGREDIENTS | SERVES 2

1 cup raw almonds
3 cups water
Pulp from ½ vanilla bean or 1 teaspoon vanilla extract

1. Soak the almonds in the water for 6 to 12 hours. Blend almonds, water, and vanilla together in a food processor or blender (until the rattling noise stops), approximately 1 minute in a high-speed blender.

2. Put a nut milk bag in a bowl and strain through the bag to separate the milk from the pulp. Discard the pulp and place milk in a refrigerated airtight container until ready to use. Can be kept for up to 3 days.

3. An alternate method is to pour ingredients into a soy milk machine, which blends and strains the milk.

PER SERVING:
Calories: 274 | Fat: 24 g | Protein: 10 g | Sodium: 5 mg | Fiber: 0 g

Nut Milk

One of the staples in a raw foods diet is milk made from nuts, seeds, or grains, rather than soy or dairy products. In place of the almonds in this recipe, try cashews, hazelnuts, macadamia nuts, or oats.

Vanilla Almond Milk Smoothie

This is a delicious smoothie that can be served with fresh or frozen cherries.

INGREDIENTS | SERVES 2

2 cups Almond Milk (page 21)
2 cups pear, chopped with peel on
1 cup banana, sliced
½ cup cherries, pitted and chopped
1 teaspoon nutmeg
½ vanilla bean, or 1 teaspoon vanilla extract

1. Add the almond milk, pears, banana, cherries, and nutmeg to the blender. Blend until smooth.

2. Cut the vanilla bean open. Scoop out the inside pulp from the bean and add to blender. Discard the vanilla bean pod. Blend again to incorporate vanilla for another 20 seconds.

PER SERVING:
Calories: 422 | Fat: 22 g | Protein: 10 g | Sodium: 13 mg | Fiber: 7 g

Chocolate Almond Milk Smoothie

This sweet and creamy milkshake has a good balance of seasonings. The carob creates a rich chocolate flavor, and the cayenne gives a hint of heat without making it hot.

INGREDIENTS | SERVES 2

2 cups Almond Milk (page 21)
1 banana
2 dates, pitted
1 tablespoon raw carob powder
¼ teaspoon cayenne pepper powder
Pulp from ½ vanilla bean, or 1 teaspoon vanilla extract

Place all the ingredients into blender and blend until smooth.

PER SERVING:
Calories: 371 | Fat: 21 g | Protein: 9 g | Sodium: 13 mg | Fiber: 4 g

Fresh Vanilla

To use fresh vanilla beans, simply slice open the pod, scoop out the seeds with a spoon, and add them to the recipe. If you're using a high-power blender, you can add the whole vanilla bean and the machine will break it down. If you are using a low-power blender, first slice open the vanilla bean and scoop out the seeds.

Herbal Tea Smoothie

Herbal tea provides the liquid base. You can use green tea, hibiscus, rooibos, pu-erh, chamomile, lavender, pau d'arco, nettle, echinacea, gingko, peppermint, ho shou wu, chai, or darjeeling. Alternatives for the seasoning include cinnamon, pumpkin pie spice, a pinch of cayenne, or chai spices.

INGREDIENTS | SERVES 2

¼ cup dried goji berries or other berries

2 cups water

1 cup herbal tea blend of your choice, brewed for three minutes

¼ cup cashews, soaked

1 tablespoon raw honey

1 tablespoon raw cacao or carob powder (optional)

1 teaspoon nutmeg (optional)

1 cup ice

1. Soak the dried goji berries in 1 cup water for 20 minutes.

2. Add remaining ingredients into the blender. As mixture is blending, gradually add in the goji berries and their soak water and continue blending until smooth.

PER SERVING:

Calories: 169 | Fat: 7 g | Protein: 5 g | Sodium: 6 mg | Fiber: 3 g

Citrus and Berry Smoothie

The citrus juice in this smoothie is a good complement to the berries.

INGREDIENTS | SERVES 2

2 cups fresh orange juice

1 cup strawberries

1 cup blueberries

Pour the juice, strawberries, and blueberries into a blender and blend until smooth.

PER SERVING:

Calories: 178 | Fat: 1 g | Protein: 3 g | Sodium: 4 mg | Fiber: 4 g

Peach Strawberry Smoothie

Strawberries are one of the foods you should buy organic. The fruit is delicate, so nonorganic strawberries are typically sprayed with about 300 pounds of pesticide per acre.

INGREDIENTS | SERVES 2

2 cups peaches, pitted and chopped
1 cup strawberries
½ cup orange juice
½ tablespoon gingerroot, peeled and grated
Juice of ½ lime (1–2 tablespoons)

Blend the ingredients in a blender until smooth, approximately 2 minutes.

PER SERVING:

Calories: 90 | Fat: 1 g | Protein: 2 g | Sodium: 1 mg | Fiber: 4 g

Peaches

Peaches are a stone fruit low on the glycemic index, so they don't trigger insulin or weight gain. They are high in the antioxidant vitamins A and C, and also rich in niacin and potassium.

Apple Ginger Smoothie

*This is a simple and delicious smoothie.
Try adding a pinch of cinnamon or nutmeg for extra seasoning.*

INGREDIENTS | SERVES 2

2 apples, chopped
1 tablespoon gingerroot, peeled and minced
2 cups water

Blend all ingredients except for water until smooth—a regular blender will be able to handle the apple chunks. Start with 1 cup of water, and gradually pour in the second cup of water until the desired consistency is reached.

PER SERVING:

Calories: 97 | Fat: 0 g | Protein: 1 g | Sodium: 7 mg | Fiber: 4 g

Making Ginger Juice

Ginger is a warming spice that improves circulation and digestion. A little ginger adds a lot of flavor. Many of these recipes call for ginger juice, which can be made by pressing a small piece of ginger in a garlic press. In this recipe, the ginger and apples are a match made in heaven!

Basic Green Smoothie with Pears

*This is an easy and delicious way to get your
daily requirement of fresh green vegetables.*

INGREDIENTS | SERVES 2

4 cups pear, chopped

6 tablespoons lemon juice

2 cups water

4 cups lettuce, chopped

1 tablespoon mint (optional)

1. Place pears, lemon juice, and water into the blender. Blend for a short time until ingredients are mixed well.

2. Gradually add in the lettuce and continue blending until smooth. Add the chopped mint last and pulse until blended. If you blend herbs such as mint for too long, they become bitter.

PER SERVING:

Calories: 213 | Fat: 1 g | Protein: 3 g | Sodium: 16 mg | Fiber: 12 g

More about Green Smoothies

The concept of blending leafy greens was popularized by raw food pioneers Ann Wigmore and Victoria Boutenko. Greens are high in protein, chlorophyll, and minerals.

Pineapple Juice and Berry Smoothie

*Acai berries are a superfood from South America known for their high level of
antioxidants and trace minerals. They are found in most health food stores.*

INGREDIENTS | SERVES 2

1 cup fresh pineapple juice

2 cups acai berries, frozen or dried, or any other favorite berry

½ cup young coconut meat

Pulp from ½ vanilla bean or ½ teaspoon vanilla extract

½ cup frozen banana

Place all ingredients into a blender and blend until smooth.

PER SERVING:

Calories: 212 | Fat: 6 g | Protein: 5 g | Sodium: 17 mg | Fiber: 1 g

An Easy Smoothie

This is a smoothie that goes down easy. The pineapple and young coconut are foods that are easy to digest.

Pineapple Apricot Yogurt Smoothie

Yogurt is a traditional ingredient in smoothies.
This recipe uses creamy blended cashews in place of yogurt.

INGREDIENTS | SERVES 2

2 fresh apricots or 5 dried apricots
2 plums, pitted
1 cup soaked cashews
1 cup water
2 cups fresh pineapple juice

Preparing Dried Fruits

Dried fruits that are popular in raw foods cuisine include apricots, figs, plums, raisins, currants, and berries. Soak them in water for about 20 minutes to reconstitute them. You can use them as both a sweetener and a thickener in your recipes.

1. Wash the fresh apricots or soak the dried apricots in water from 1 to 4 hours.

2. Blend together the soaked cashews with 1 cup of water until it becomes smooth and creamy.

3. Place all ingredients into the blender and blend together until smooth.

PER SERVING:

Calories: 392 | Fat: 18 g | Protein: 9 g | Sodium: 11 mg | Fiber: 3 g

Coconut Banana Shake

The almond yogurt gives this shake a creamy texture. This recipe is best in summer when cherries are ripe. Frozen or dried cherries are great during the off season.

INGREDIENTS | SERVES 2

¼ cup Almond Yogurt (page 157)
½ cup frozen banana
¼ cup young coconut meat
1 cup young coconut water
½ cup cherries, pitted and chopped
¼ teaspoon cayenne
¼ teaspoon cinnamon

1. Prepare Almond Yogurt recipe from page 157.

2. Place all ingredients into a blender and blend until smooth.

PER SERVING:

Calories: 103 | Fat: 1 g | Protein: 2 g | Sodium: 127 mg | Fiber: 4 g

Cherries

This delicious stone fruit can be used fresh, dried, or frozen. Cherries are high in vitamins A and C, and their rich pigment is a good source of phytonutrients and antioxidants.

Mint, Ginger, and Pineapple Smoothie

The pineapple juice and spicy chocolate flavors are a delicious combination.

INGREDIENTS | SERVES 2

1 teaspoon ginger juice

2 tablespoons fresh mint

1 cup fresh pineapple juice

2 frozen or fresh bananas

2 tablespoons raw cacao powder

¼ teaspoon cayenne pepper powder

1 tablespoon mesquite pod meal (optional)

1. Peel a small piece of gingerroot and press it in a garlic press to make juice. If you don't have a garlic press, you can chop 1 teaspoon of gingerroot and toss it into the blender.

2. Place all the ingredients into a blender and blend until smooth.

PER SERVING:

Calories: 235 | Fat: 3 g | Protein: 5 g | Sodium: 9 mg | Fiber: 8 g

Mesquite Pod Meal

This unique spice is a nutrient-dense food with a sweet flavor, similar to molasses. Mesquite powder is often used in desserts as a low glycemic sweetener.

Mango Green Smoothie

This is a nutritious smoothie to make in the morning for breakfast. Almond milk is a good substitute for the liquid. You can use any mix of leafy greens you have on hand, such as romaine, baby greens, spring mix, spinach, arugula, or watercress.

INGREDIENTS | SERVES 2

2 cups mango, peeled and chopped into chunks

1 cup leafy greens of your choice

1 cup orange juice

Water as needed

Place all ingredients into a blender and blend together until smooth.

PER SERVING:

Calories: 167 | Fat: 1 g | Protein: 2 g | Sodium: 6 mg | Fiber: 4 g

Breakfast Smoothies

Smoothies are an excellent fast food to make for breakfast. It takes just a couple of minutes to blend the smoothie and clean the blender. A 32-ounce Wide Mouth Nalgene water bottle makes the perfect travel container for smoothies.

Kiwi Mango Smoothie

This is a delicious way to eat tropical fruits. The kiwi skin is very nutritious and can be blended right into the smoothie.

INGREDIENTS | SERVES 2

4 kiwi fruits (about ½ cup chopped)
2 oranges
2 mangos, peeled and pitted (about 1 cup chopped)
½ cup ice

1. Cut off the two ends of each kiwi and discard.

2. Juice two oranges with a citrus juicer.

3. Place all the ingredients into a blender and blend together until smooth.

PER SERVING:
Calories: 283 | Fat: 2 g | Protein: 4 g | Sodium: 11 mg | Fiber: 9 g

Orange Juice

Try this smoothie with different types of oranges. Blood oranges, tangerines, tangelos, and mandarins all work well in this recipe.

Mayan Chocolate Spice Shake

This is a delicious beverage combining almond milk with raw chocolate. Carob is a good substitute for the cacao, and honey is a good substitute for the agave nectar.

INGREDIENTS | SERVES 2

2 cups Almond Milk (page 21)
2 tablespoons agave nectar
2 frozen bananas
1 tablespoon raw cacao powder
1 teaspoon cinnamon powder
1 teaspoon maca powder
½ teaspoon salt
¼ teaspoon cayenne pepper powder

Simply blend all ingredients until you reach a smooth, milkshake texture.

PER SERVING:
Calories: 381 | Fat: 22 g | Protein: 11 g | Sodium: 598 mg | Fiber: 7 g

Chocolate and Maca

The ancient Mayans loved their chocolate beverages mixed with hot chili peppers. The cayenne and cinnamon give this drink a little spice, and the agave nectar balances it out with a sweet, honeylike flavor. The maca root is a nutrient-dense superfood, known for its high protein level, so it can be useful for sustaining energy.

Black Sesame Milkshake, Version 1

*You can make this recipe in about 5 minutes,
using either black, white, or brown sesame seeds.*

INGREDIENTS | SERVES 2

1 cup black sesame seeds

2 cups water

¾ cup banana

2 tablespoons chopped, pitted dates

1. Make a seed milk by blending the sesame seeds on high with 2 cups of water.

2. Pour through a nut milk bag and squeeze out the liquid. Discard pulp.

3. Blend this liquid mixture with the banana and dates until smooth.

PER SERVING:

Calories: 478 | Fat: 36 g | Protein: 13 g | Sodium: 18 mg | Fiber: 10 g

Black Sesame Milkshake, Version 2

*This variation is made with soaked or sprouted sesame seeds, so it requires a little advanced prep.
The milk is a good liquid base for smoothies, soups, and desserts. Some additional sweeteners
that can be used include dates, raisins, apricots, agave nectar, honey, maple syrup, and berries.*

INGREDIENTS | SERVES 2

1 cup black sesame seeds, soaked or sprouted

2 cups water

2 tablespoons chopped fig

½ cup banana

1. Using the soaked or sprouted seeds, make a seed milk by blending them on high speed with 2 cups of water. Pour through a nut milk bag and squeeze out the liquid.

2. Place the liquid back into the blender with the fig and banana. Blend until smooth.

PER SERVING:

Calories: 478 | Fat: 36 g | Protein: 13 g | Sodium: 18 mg | Fiber: 10 g

Soaking Sesame Seeds

Soak the sesame seeds in 3 cups water for 4 to 8 hours. Drain and rinse. If you would like to increase the nutritional content, sprout the seeds for one day in a sprouter. Rinse and drain every 4 to 6 hours.

Cherry Pomegranate Smoothie

This is a refreshing breakfast during the winter.
It contains extra protein to help sustain your energy levels.

INGREDIENTS | SERVES 2

1 cup pomegranate juice,
fresh or bottled

1 cup orange juice

1 banana, fresh or frozen

2 cups frozen or fresh cherries

2 tablespoons raw protein powder

Place all the ingredients in a blender and blend together until smooth.

PER SERVING:

Calories: 260 | Fat: 2 g | Protein: 8 g | Sodium: 13 mg | Fiber: 5 g

Why Freeze Bananas?

If you want to create the texture of a milkshake, use a frozen banana. Just peel a ripe banana and place in a zip-top plastic bag. Freeze overnight.

Red Bliss Pomegranate Smoothie

This beautiful dark red smoothie is high in antioxidants and phytonutrients.
Fresh pomegranate juice is preferred, or you may use the bottled juice found in stores.

INGREDIENTS | SERVES 2

2 pomegranates (enough for 1 cup juice)
½ cup hibiscus tea, brewed for 2 minutes
1 cup strawberries
1 cup raspberries
½ cup frozen banana

Benefits of Pomegranate

Pomegranates are recognized for high antioxidant levels, apparently two or three times those of red wine and green tea.

1. Slice two pomegranates in half and use a spoon to remove the seeds.

2. Run the pomegranate seeds through a juicer until you have 1 cup juice.

3. Place all the ingredients in a blender and blend together until smooth.

PER SERVING:

Calories: 174 | Fat: 1 g | Protein: 2 g | Sodium: 17 mg | Fiber: 7 g

Persimmon Pineapple Smoothie

This smoothie has a rich, candylike flavor.
Carob or mesquite powder is a good substitute for the cacao.

INGREDIENTS | SERVES 2

1 cup pineapple, cubed
2 persimmons (approximately ½ cup fruit)
½ cup banana
Pulp from ½ vanilla bean
1 tablespoon cacao powder

Lemon Water

A great way to start the morning is with a pint of drinking water mixed with a tablespoon of fresh lemon juice. The lemon gives the water a refreshing taste. It also helps create a more alkaline pH in your body.

1. Place the pineapple in the blender. Cut open the persimmon, scoop out the fruit, and add to the blender.

2. Place all remaining ingredients into the blender and blend until smooth. Add just enough water to reach desired consistency.

PER SERVING:

Calories: 106 | Fat: 1 g | Protein: 2 g | Sodium: 2 mg | Fiber: 3 g

Sweet Brazil Nut Milk

*This is a good recipe to serve with a bowl of breakfast cereal or oatmeal.
The milk makes a good liquid base for smoothies and sauces. The leftover
pulp can be used to make cookies, crackers, and breads.*

INGREDIENTS | SERVES 2

1 cup Brazil nuts
3 cups water
¼ cup dates, pitted
¼ teaspoon salt
½ teaspoon pumpkin pie spice

1. Blend the Brazil nuts with 3 cups water until smooth.

2. Pour the blended Brazil nuts through a nut milk bag and into a bowl. Squeeze the nut milk bag to get all the milk out.

3. Pour the milk back into the blender.

4. Add the dates, salt, and pumpkin pie spice to the blender and blend until smooth.

PER SERVING:

Calories: 605 | Fat: 44 g | Protein: 11 g | Sodium: 301 mg | Fiber: 5 g

Strawberry Rhubarb Smoothie

*This is a great way to eat fresh summer rhubarb, which combines well with
strawberries. To use these ingredients as the basis for a sauce or pie filling,
just omit the liquid and blend the ingredients together.*

INGREDIENTS | SERVES 2

3 small rhubarb stalks, chopped into pieces
2 cups strawberries, with green tops discarded
2 cups Almond Milk (page 21)
1 teaspoon cinnamon
2 tablespoons agave nectar
1 tablespoon maca root powder (optional)

Place all the ingredients into a blender and blend until smooth.

PER SERVING:

Calories: 367 | Fat: 22 g | Protein: 10 g | Sodium: 16 mg | Fiber: 5 g

Rhubarb

Rhubarb is a delicious vegetable, but it has such a tart flavor that it is normally prepared with a great deal of sugar. Combining rhubarb with strawberries or dates achieves the right flavor without so much sweetener. Note that only the stalks are eaten. The leaves and roots have toxins that should not be consumed.

Sweet Veggie Smoothie

This is an easy way to eat your veggies! You get a whole salad in one smoothie, with seven different types of fresh vegetables. The flax oil helps make it creamy and adds extra nutrition with high omega-3 fat content.

INGREDIENTS | SERVES 4

1 cup chopped tomatoes

8 large or 12 medium carrots

1 beet, medium or large

½ teaspoon-size chunk of ginger

2 stalks of celery

¼ cup cilantro

1 cup spinach

1 cup loosely chopped red bell pepper

1 tablespoon flaxseed oil (optional)

You can make this recipe with a juicer or a high-speed blender. If you're blending the ingredients, place the chopped tomatoes in the blender first. Add in the remaining ingredients and process until smooth.

PER SERVING:
Calories: 84 | Fat: 0 g | Protein: 3 g | Sodium: 42 mg | Fiber: 2 g

Flaxseed

Flaxseeds are an excellent source of essential omega-3 fats, now widely recognized for their many therapeutic health benefits. They can be used whole or ground in recipes for pâté, burgers, pie crusts, bars, crackers, and breads. Flaxseed tastes good served as a porridge, after being soaked in water for 30 minutes.

Peach Parsley Smoothie

This recipe is good with any type of mild greens such as baby spring mix, romaine, or red leaf lettuce. You can also make it with ripe apricots or pears when they are in season.

INGREDIENTS | SERVES 2

2 ripe peaches, pitted and chopped

1 cup mild greens of your choice

⅛ cup parsley or cilantro

2 cups water

2 tablespoons lemon juice

Parsley

Parsley is a mineral-rich, leafy green vegetable. One of the world's most popular herbs, it is high in iron, chlorophyll, folate, and vitamins A, C, and K. Parsley is intense, so like other nutrient-rich foods, a little bit goes a long way.

1. Place all ingredients, except the water, in a blender and blend until smooth. This recipe is also delicious made in a juicer; in that case, add water at the end as needed.

2. Start with 1 cup of water and gradually add second cup until the desired consistency is reached.

PER SERVING:

Calories: 68 | Fat: 0 g | Protein: 2 g | Sodium: 9 mg | Fiber: 3 g

Green Smoothie with
Wild Dandelion, Arugula, and Pineapple

The taste of the bitter greens is balanced by the sweet fruits, acidic lemon, and spicy cayenne.

INGREDIENTS | SERVES 1–2

½ cup dandelion greens

½ cup each arugula and stinging nettle
(or any of your favorite leafy greens)

1 cup pineapple juice or 1 cup fresh
cubed pineapple

2 tablespoons lemon juice

1 cup water

¼ teaspoon cayenne pepper powder

Place all the ingredients into a blender and blend until smooth. You may want to blend in a few ice cubes to chill the smoothie.

PER SERVING:

Calories: 172 | Fat: 1 g | Protein: 5 g | Sodium: 34 mg | Fiber: 2 g

Stinging Nettle

Stinging nettle leaves are a nutritious wild food. They are high in potassium, iron, chlorophyll, and many other minerals. They have medicinal uses and may be beneficial in cases of anemia or respiratory problems. Handle the nettles carefully so you do not get stung. You may want to wear gloves or use tongs. The nettles will not sting your mouth or tongue. You can roll up the leaves and eat them fresh, or blend them into a green smoothie.

Herbal Detox Smoothie

*This is a bitter smoothie and may take some getting used to.
The greens and herbs are prized for their ability to cleanse the liver.*

INGREDIENTS | SERVES 2

1 cup dandelion greens

½ cup beet greens

2 cups carrot juice

½ cup apple juice

1 teaspoon burdock root

½ teaspoon cayenne pepper

1 teaspoon milk thistle

2 tablespoons lemon juice

Place all the ingredients into a blender and blend with a few ice cubes until smooth.

PER SERVING:

Calories: 114 | Fat: 1 g | Protein: 3 g | Sodium: 45 mg | Fiber: 2 g

The Liver

The liver plays many vital roles in your health. As one of your primary protective barriers, it cleans the blood by removing a broad range of toxins. However, too many alcoholic beverages and processed foods can overburden this vital organ. The nutrients and herbs in this smoothie can assist in cleansing the liver and restoring it to optimal health.

Coconut and Brazil Nut Smoothie

This is a nutritious, protein-rich smoothie that will satisfy your hunger.

INGREDIENTS | SERVES 2

¼ cup Brazil nuts

1 cup young coconut water

2 cups young coconut meat

1 cup orange juice

1 cup mango, peeled and chopped

2 teaspoons maca powder or
1 teaspoon blue-green algae

1. Grind the Brazil nuts in the coconut water, using an S-blade food processor. (You can also use a high-speed blender, but nuts can destroy a less-powerful conventional blender.)

2. Add remaining ingredients and blend until smooth.

PER SERVING:
Calories: 577 | Fat: 47 g | Protein: 13 g | Sodium: 142 mg | Fiber: 8 g

Maca Powder

Maca is a root vegetable native to South America. It is considered a superfood because of its high concentration of nutrients, including selenium, calcium, magnesium, iron, B vitamins, and vitamin C. It is rich in protein and contains nineteen amino acids. Maca is considered an aphrodisiac and is noted for its ability to heighten libido. Smoothies are the perfect way to take maca because the fruits hide the taste of the powder.

Bee Pollen and Herb Smoothie

You may substitute other ripe fruits in season for the peaches.
This recipe works well using different types of herb tea as the base, such as
chai, pau d'arco, cat's claw, green tea, pu-erh tea, hibiscus, chamomile, or kombucha.

INGREDIENTS | SERVES 4

1 cup herbal tea, brewed for 5 minutes and cooled to room temperature

1 teaspoon bee pollen, powdered

1 cup peaches, pitted and chopped

1 cup frozen mangoes

½ cup ice cubes

¼ teaspoon cayenne pepper powder

Place all the ingredients in a blender and blend until smooth.

PER SERVING:

Calories: 49 | Fat: 0 g | Protein: 1 g | Sodium: 9 mg | Fiber: 2 g

Medicinal Herbs

Pau d'arco and cat's claw are found in the Amazon rain forest. Pau d'arco is reported to boost the immune system, fight parasites, improve the lymphatics, and help to eliminate various skin conditions. Cat's claw is said to be an antiviral and contains alkaloids that nutritionally support the immune system. Horsetail builds and strengthens bone and connective tissue. It is high in the mineral silica, which the body uses to make calcium. Silica is reported to be better than calcium for supporting bone strength.

Raw Hemp Protein Shake with Papaya

This is a delicious, protein-rich shake that supplies all the essential amino acids. The almond milk may be replaced with orange juice, water, or water with a tablespoon of almond butter. Good protein-rich substitutes for the hemp include green superfood powders, maca, and bee pollen.

INGREDIENTS | SERVES 2

1 vanilla bean

1 cup Almond Milk (page 21)

1 cup frozen or fresh banana, mango, or papaya

2 tablespoons hemp seed or other protein powder

¼ cup dates, pitted

1. Slice the vanilla bean in half. Using a knife, scrape out the seeds into a blender.

2. Place remaining ingredients into the blender and blend together until smooth.

PER SERVING:

Calories: 404 | Fat: 12 g | Protein: 11 g | Sodium: 8 mg | Fiber: 8 g

Blue-Green Blast with
Klamath Algae, Lemon, and Cayenne

This is a powerful tonic. Wheatgrass juice is a good substitute for the blue-green algae.

INGREDIENTS | **SERVES 4**

1 cup apple juice
1 teaspoon gingerroot juice
2 tablespoons lemon juice
½ teaspoon cayenne pepper powder
1 tablespoon Klamath blue-green algae

Blue-Green Blast

This recipe was inspired by Lou Corona's Lemon Ginger Blast recipe. Cayenne pepper and ginger are two excellent foods for improving blood circulation. You can feel these herbs begin working immediately, because the blood will warm your face, fingers, and toes, bringing back color and a healthy glow to your skin. The blast will also help you stay warm during the winter, especially when combined with exercise.

1. Combine the juices.

2. Stir in the cayenne powder and blue-green algae.

3. Pour it into a shot glass, (1.5 ounces, which equals 1½ tablespoons) which is about 1 serving. Store the remaining beverage in the refrigerator and take small sips throughout the day.

PER SERVING:
Calories: 38 | Fat: 0 g | Protein: 1 g | Sodium: 21 mg | Fiber: 0 g

CHAPTER 3

Fresh Juices and Beverages

Lemonade

This is a refreshing beverage that uses agave nectar instead of processed white sugar. The stevia is optional and helps add a sweet flavor without extra sugar. Liquid stevia can be replaced with ¼ teaspoon stevia power. This recipe is good with a little added vanilla, mint, raspberry, or grated ginger.

INGREDIENTS | SERVES 2

¼ cup lemon juice

2–4 tablespoons agave nectar

2 drops liquid stevia (optional)

1½ cups sparkling mineral water

½ cup ice cubes

Agave Nectar

Agave is a cactus that produces a honeylike nectar. It is one of the more popular sweeteners in raw food cuisine because it is nutritious and has a similar taste and texture to honey. Agave is also well known as a primary ingredient in top-shelf brands of tequila.

1. In a blender place the lemon juice, agave nectar, stevia, and sparkling mineral water and blend until smooth.

2. Add the ice cubes to the blender and briefly pulse until slightly chunky. Serve in tall glasses with a garnish of fresh mint.

PER SERVING:

Calories: 68 | Fat: 0 g | Protein: 0 g | Sodium: 3 mg | Fiber: 0 g

Basic Green Juice

This juice is served daily at most raw food health retreats. You may substitute other leafy vegetables in place of the sunflower greens, but these greens are recommended.

INGREDIENTS | SERVES 2

1½ cups cucumber chunks

4 celery sticks

2 cups sunflower green sprouts or other leafy greens

1. Chop up the veggies so they will fit through your juicer.

2. Juice all ingredients with a juicer, or blend in a blender and strain out the pulp with a nut milk bag.

PER SERVING:

Calories: 38 | Fat: 1 g | Protein: 2 g | Sodium: 66 mg | Fiber: 0 g

Green Juice with Blue-Green Algae and Apples

This is a nutritious alkaline juice rich in minerals and chlorophyll. This is an excellent drink to start your day with, and it's also good for a midday energy boost. You can also substitute pineapple juice for the apple juice. If you're new to Blue-Green Algae, start with a small amount such as a half-teaspoon.

INGREDIENTS | SERVES 2

Juice of 2 large apples

Juice made from 2 cups of greens: use any combination of cucumber, celery, kale, parsley, spinach, or other leafy greens

2 tablespoons lemon juice

1 tablespoon Klamath blue-green algae

Mix juices together. Add extra apple juice if you require a sweeter flavor. Stir in the blue-green algae.

PER SERVING:

Calories: 184 | Fat: 2 g | Protein: 10 g | Sodium: 199 mg | Fiber: 0 g

An Excellent Source of Minerals

Kale supplies some of the essential nutrients missing from the standard American diet. It is high in trace minerals, electrolytes, and the natural sodium that is so important for optimal health.

Wheatgrass Lemon Juice

Most people prefer to balance the bitter flavor of wheatgrass juice with an acidic flavor like lemon.

INGREDIENTS | SERVES 1

½ lemon

1 cup fresh wheatgrass

Wheatgrass Miracle

Wheatgrass is one of the most nutritious and mineral-rich foods on earth. There are so many benefits that whole books have been written about it. Check out the resources section in Appendix A for more information. If grown with the OceanGrown Solution fertilizer, wheatgrass contains up to ninety minerals!

1. Juice lemon with a citrus juicer, or simply squeeze out the juice.

2. Juice the wheatgrass using a wheatgrass juicer. You should have about 2 ounces (¼ cups) of juice.

3. You can either mix the lemon juice and wheatgrass juice together, or take a shot of wheatgrass juice and chase it with a shot of lemon juice.

PER SERVING:

Calories: 21 | Fat: 0 g | Protein: 0 g | Sodium: 10 mg | Fiber: 0

Master Cleanser

This is a popular beverage used for cleansing, detoxification, and weight loss. Master Cleanser is one of the key components of a juice fast cleanse.

INGREDIENTS | SERVES 1

¾ cup water

2 tablespoons Grade B maple syrup, to taste

2 tablespoons lemon juice

¼ teaspoon powdered cayenne pepper

Combine the ingredients in a blender and blend. You can prepare the juice right before you drink it or prepare it in advance to consume throughout the day.

PER SERVING:

Calories: 115 | Fat: 0 g | Protein: 0 g | Sodium: 8 mg | Fiber: 0

Master Cleanse

The Master Cleanse is used in a regimen sometimes called the Lemonade Diet. This approach was developed in 1941 by Stanley Burroughs and published in his book *The Master Cleanser*. The Master Cleanse fast has become popular because it helps with detoxification and weight loss. The full cleanse involves drinking only the Master Cleanser recipe and water for a week or two. You will want to consult a medical professional before starting the full cleanse, and also read Burroughs's book.

Pineapple Grape Juice

Both red and green grapes work well in this recipe. Organic grapes are preferred because nonorganic grape juice may have too many concentrated pesticides. This is a fairly sweet drink, so this recipe isn't intended for daily consumption.

INGREDIENTS | SERVES 1

½ cup pineapple chunks

½ cup grapes of your choice

Run all ingredients through a juicer, or blend in a blender and strain through a nut milk bag.

PER SERVING:

Calories: 89 | Fat: 0 g | Protein: 1 g | Sodium: 2 mg | Fiber: 0 g

Fresh Fruit Juice

As a general rule, blend the whole fruits into a smoothie, complete with fiber, to slow down the sugar absorption. Since fruit juice is high in sugars, it should just be consumed periodically as a special treat. On a day-to-day basis, opt for whole fruit rather than fruit juices. Vegetable juice is another good option, since it's usually lower in natural sugars.

Apple Ginger Juice

Another great apple-ginger combo!
You can also add a tiny pinch of cayenne for a little heat.

INGREDIENTS | SERVES 1

2 apples, cored and chopped
1 tablespoon gingerroot, peeled and minced
¼ teaspoon cinnamon

Run apples and ginger through a juice extractor, or blend in a blender and strain through a nut milk bag. Stir in the cinnamon powder, and serve.

PER SERVING:
Calories: 196 | Fat: 1 g | Protein: 1 g | Sodium: 4 mg | Fiber: 0

Honeydew Spritzer

Fizzy spritzers are very popular in Europe. Sparkling mineral water gives
this juice the taste of a fizzy soda. Fresh mint is a pretty garnish.

INGREDIENTS | SERVES 2

3 cups honeydew melon, sliced into chunks
1 cup watermelon, sliced into chunks
¼ cup orange juice
¼ cup sparkling mineral water

Juice the melons and mix with orange juice and sparkling water. Serve over crushed ice.

PER SERVING:
Calories: 129 | Fat: 1 g | Protein: 2 g | Sodium: 47 mg | Fiber: 0

Watermelon

Watermelon is rich in lycopene and vitamin C. Many of the nutrients are actually found in the rind, so you can also juice the rind along with the flesh to get the full nutritional value.

Lemon Lime Spritzer

Pear juice is a good substitute for the apple juice.

INGREDIENTS | SERVES 2

½ cup lemon juice
¼ cup lime juice
2 tablespoons agave nectar
1 cup apple juice
½ cup sparkling mineral water
½ teaspoon stevia powder

Stir all ingredients together and serve in wine glasses.

PER SERVING:
Calories: 136 | Fat: 0 g | Protein: 0 g | Sodium: 6 mg | Fiber: 1 g

Stevia
The stevia plant has a very sweet taste and is low on the glycemic index (it doesn't raise your blood sugar so it's helpful in minimizing weight gain). It can be used fresh, dried as a powder, or as a liquid extract. It is an excellent substitute for other sweeteners in desserts and beverages.

Orange Pomegranate Juice

When preparing pomegranate, to avoid a bitter taste, remove the white inner fiber between the seeds.

INGREDIENTS | SERVES 2

2 pomegranate fruits
3 oranges

Pomegranate Seeds
While the whole seed is edible, the juice inside the seed is where the flavor lies. The juice is prized for its unusually high levels of antioxidants and phytonutrients.

1. Slice open both pomegranates and scoop out the seeds with a spoon.

2. Peel the oranges.

3. Run the oranges and pomegranate seeds through the juicer. Serve over ice.

PER SERVING:
Calories: 180 | Fat: 1 g | Protein: 3 g | Sodium: 8 mg | Fiber: 0 g

Orange, Pineapple, and Kiwi Juice

Pineapple contains a powerful enzyme, bromelain, known for its ability to break down protein. Fresh pineapple juice contains a high quantity of bromelain, so this is a good complement to a protein-rich meal.

INGREDIENTS | SERVES 2

1 orange
4 kiwi fruits
1 cup pineapple

1. Remove skin from the orange and discard. Remove ends from kiwi and discard.

2. Juice all ingredients and serve over ice.

PER SERVING:

Calories: 173 | Fat: 1 g | Protein: 3 g | Sodium: 5 mg | Fiber: 0 g

Cranberry Grape Juice

This is a delicious beverage to make fresh during cranberry season.

INGREDIENTS | SERVES 2

3 cups grapes (red or green)
2 cups fresh cranberries

Juice all the ingredients and serve over ice. The grapes are sweet but essential in this recipe to balance out the tartness of the cranberries.

PER SERVING:

Calories: 202 | Fat: 0 g | Protein: 2 g | Sodium: 7 mg | Fiber: 0 g

Cranberry

The cranberry is rich in antioxidants, especially proanthocyanins, a nutrient that has been found beneficial in preventing and treating urinary tract infections. Cranberry juice is recommended by a broad spectrum of health professionals.

Thai Iced Tea

This is a good beverage served with Thai Green Papaya Salad (page 86),
and Pad Thai with Almond Sauce (page 212)

INGREDIENTS | SERVES 2

4 tablespoons agave nectar
1½ cups black tea, brewed
1 cup Almond Milk (page 21)
2 tablespoons orange juice
¼ teaspoon star anise powder
2 teaspoons vanilla extract
1 teaspoon cinnamon
2 cups ice

1. Pour agave nectar into the black tea.

2. Stir in the almond milk, orange juice, star anise, vanilla, and cinnamon.

3. Serve in two tall glasses. Put 1 cup of ice in each glass and pour the tea mixture over the ice cubes.

PER SERVING:

Calories: 204 | Fat: 11 g | Protein: 4 g | Sodium: 9 mg | Fiber: 1 g

Star Anise

This is a pretty star-shaped spice that is gathered from evergreen trees in southwest China. Anise is a popular seasoning throughout Asia and India.

Mimosas with Fresh Mint and Oranges

This beverage is just the right thing for Sunday morning brunch.

INGREDIENTS | SERVES 2

1 orange
2 cups fresh orange juice
1 cup sparkling mineral water
4 fresh mint leaves, for garnish

Mimosa

These drinks are usually made with bubbly champagne. The sparkling mineral water gives the same light, refreshing effect without the alcohol.

1. Slice orange in half. Cut two thin slices of the orange (shaped like a wheel) and save them to use as a garnish.

2. Stir orange juice together with the sparkling water.

3. Serve in champagne flutes and garnish each glass with two mint leaves and one thin orange wheel slice.

PER SERVING:

Calories: 112 | Fat: 0 g | Protein: 2 g | Sodium: 4 mg | Fiber: 0 g

Cabernet Mix with Plums and Blackberries

This juice is rich with a dark red color and hints of plum and blackberry.

INGREDIENTS | SERVES 2

1 cup concord grapes
1 cup sliced ripe plums
1 cup blackberries
2 tablespoons lemon juice

Juice all ingredients and serve in wine glasses.

PER SERVING:
Calories: 104 | Fat: 1 g | Protein: 2 g | Sodium: 2 mg | Fiber: 0 g

Blackberries

The blackberry is a nutritious fruit that grows on thorny shrubs and occurs in thousands of varieties. One of the most popular is the Marion blackberry, which is a sweet hybrid developed in Oregon. Blackberries are rich in pigments and phytonutrients and are an excellent source of vitamin C, potassium, copper, and magnesium.

Carrot, Beet, Spinach, and Ginger Juice

You can adapt this recipe in a number of ways, making it simply with carrot, beets, and ginger; emphasizing the greens; or making it with the carrot juice and spices.

INGREDIENTS | SERVES 2

2 cups carrot, chopped
1 cup beets, chopped
½ cup beet greens
1 cup spinach
1 tablespoon gingerroot, minced
⅛ teaspoon cayenne pepper powder

Juice all the vegetables and ginger and then stir in the cayenne powder.

PER SERVING:
Calories: 90 | Fat: 1 g | Protein: 3 g | Sodium: 175 mg | Fiber: 0 g

Beet Greens

Beet are considered a good food to support liver health, but the greens are also healthful and an excellent source of iron and folic acid.

Cabbage, Carrot, and Ginger Juice

Cabbage is a very nutritious food. Many doctors recommend drinking cabbage juice daily to speed up the healing process and support digestive health.

INGREDIENTS | **SERVES 1**

1 cup green cabbage
1 cup carrot, chopped
1 celery stick
1 tablespoon gingerroot, peeled

Juice all the ingredients and serve.

PER SERVING:

Calories: 43 | Fat: 0 g | Protein: 1 g | Sodium: 69 mg | Fiber: 0

Bloody Mary with Fresh Tomatoes and Spices

This is a delicious, nonalcoholic version of the popular cocktail. Some optional garnishes include pickle spears or lemon slices.

INGREDIENTS | **SERVES 2**

5 large tomatoes
½ teaspoon fresh horseradish (optional)
1 teaspoon ground black pepper
½ teaspoon cayenne pepper powder
1 tablespoon lemon juice
1 teaspoon celery salt (optional)
2 cups ice
2 celery sticks
6 olives

1. Juice tomatoes and horseradish if using, and mix with black pepper, cayenne pepper, lemon juice, and salt (optional).

2. Fill 2 pint glasses with 1 cup of ice each and put 1 celery stick into each glass.

3. Fill pint glasses with tomato mixture and garnish with olives.

PER SERVING:

Calories: 110 | Fat: 2 g | Protein: 5 g | Sodium: 1,329 mg | Fiber: 3 g

Asian Bubble Tea

This is a sweet beverage reminiscent of the bubble tea drinks popular in Asia. The chia seeds grow larger as they are soaked and have a similar texture to tapioca. The blueberries resemble the big tapioca balls in the bubble tea.

INGREDIENTS | SERVES 1

¼ cup chia seeds

1½ cups Almond Milk (page 21)

1 cup green tea

½ cup ice

1 tablespoon agave nectar

2 tablespoons blueberries

Asian Bubble Tea

Bubble tea is a sweet tea beverage served with large tapioca balls, which are also called tapioca pearls. It comes with a thick straw that is big enough to suck up the tapioca balls. This recipe was created in Asia and is now gaining popularity in the United States. Bubble tea cafés are abundant in Taiwan and Hong Kong. They are gaining popularity in many major U.S. cities. The bubble refers to the foam created in the drink by shaking it with ice. The tea can be made sweeter by preparing the almond milk with dates. The green tea can be replaced with your favorite herbal tea.

1. In a small bowl, soak the chia seeds in the Almond Milk. Stir the seeds occasionally during the first 10 minutes. Cover the bowl and continue soaking in the refrigerator for 6 to 8 hours.

2. Brew a cup of your favorite green tea. Allow it to cool down to room temperature.

3. In a large shaker cup with a lid, place the ice, tea, agave nectar, and Almond Milk with chia seeds. Tighten the lid and shake vigorously. Alternatively, use a Tupperware container with lid to shake the ingredients. The shaking motion creates the air bubbles.

4. Place the blueberries at the bottom of a pint glass. Pour the mixture from the shaker over the blueberries and serve.

PER SERVING:

Calories: 284 | Fat: 20 g | Protein: 8 g | Sodium: 12 mg | Fiber: 5 g

CHAPTER 4

Fruit Salads, Parfaits, and Other Treats

Melon Melody Salad

This is a perfect recipe for hot weather because it contains several foods that are naturally cooling to the body, including melon, lemon, and mint.

INGREDIENTS | SERVES 2

¼ cup lemon juice
2 cups honeydew melon, in balls (using a melon baller)
1 cup cantaloupe, in balls
1 cup watermelon, in balls
¼ cup fresh mint

1. Pour the lemon juice over the melon balls.

2. Garnish with mint leaves and serve in a big bowl.

PER SERVING:
Calories: 98 | Fat: 0 g | Protein: 2 g | Sodium: 35 mg | Fiber: 3 g

Mint

This aromatic green leafy herb is a popular seasoning available in many different varieties, including peppermint and spearmint. It can be used fresh, dried, juiced, frozen, and as a liquid extract or tincture. Other culinary herbs in the mint family include basil, marjoram, oregano, rosemary, sage, savory, and thyme.

Citrus Fruit Salad

This recipe is high in vitamin C, provided by all these fruits. You can use any fruits that have a little bite, and this tangy combination can be served with or without sweetener.

INGREDIENTS | SERVES 2

½ cup grapefruit, peeled and sliced
½ cup oranges, peeled and sliced
½ cup tangerines, peeled and sliced
½ cup strawberries, sliced
½ cup blackberries
½ cup kiwi, peeled and sliced
2–4 tablespoons agave nectar (to taste)

Mix all fruits together in a serving bowl. Drizzle the agave nectar on top to garnish.

PER SERVING:
Calories: 201 | Fat: 1 g | Protein: 4 g | Sodium: 4 mg | Fiber: 8 g

Grapefruit

Grapefruit is a tasty but bitter citrus fruit, high in vitamins, minerals, antioxidants, and phytonutrients including vitamin C, B5, B6, and folate. Research has found that it promotes stable blood sugar and that it is a mild natural appetite suppressant that promotes weight loss. Be sure to remove the bitter inner white rind when preparing the grapefruit for this salad.

Sweet Fruit Salad

Cherimoya is a delicious sweet fruit, native to Ecuador and Peru. It has a soft custardlike texture with a tropical flavor, reminiscent of bubblegum with hints of coconut, pineapple, strawberry, and banana. Since this recipe is based on sweet dates and tropical fruits, consider it a special (and occasional) treat.

INGREDIENTS | SERVES 4

1 cup dates or figs, seeded and chopped

1 cup cherimoya (optional), peeled and chopped

1 cup papaya, peeled and chopped

½ cup mango, peeled and chopped

1 cup banana, peeled and chopped

1 cup young coconut water

1 tablespoon raw carob powder

1. If the dates or figs are dried, soak them in water for one hour. Combine cherimoya, papaya, mango, ⅔ cup banana, ¾ cup dates in a bowl.

2. In a blender add ⅓ cup banana, ¼ cup dates, coconut water, and the carob powder. Blend until smooth to make a dressing.

3. Drizzle the dressing over fruits and serve.

PER SERVING:

Calories: 159 | Fat: 0 g | Protein: 2 g | Sodium: 66 mg | Fiber: 5 g

Fruit Fondue

Ideal fruits for fondue include large berries such as strawberries, slices of peaches or plums, cherries, or chunks of apple, pear, or banana.

INGREDIENTS | SERVES 2

1 cup raw or soaked cashews

1 cup Almond Milk (page 21) or water

¼ cup dates, chopped

1 tablespoon raw cacao powder

Fresh fruit for dipping

1. Begin by blending the cashews with ½ cup Almond Milk or water. Then add the dates and cacao powder and blend until smooth. Continue blending until you achieve a thick sauce that will adhere to the fruit, gradually adding liquid little by little as needed.

2. Dice equal amounts of fresh fruit. Arrange on a plate with fondue forks or toothpicks in each piece. Pour prepared sauce into a bowl and dip the fruit pieces into the sauce. If you're having guests, you can provide each person with their own sauce dish.

PER SERVING:

Calories: 561 | Fat: 40 g | Protein: 17 g | Sodium: 15 mg | Fiber: 5 g

Banana Berry Salad

This is a great salad to share at a potluck or picnic.

INGREDIENTS | SERVES 6

4 cups sliced banana
3 cups sliced strawberries
3 cups kiwi, peeled and sliced
1 cup dried coconut

1. Place the banana, strawberries, and kiwi in a large bowl.

2. Sprinkle the dried coconut on top. Stir well to evenly coat the fruit with the coconut flakes.

PER SERVING:
Calories: 258 | Fat: 10 g | Protein: 4 g | Sodium: 9 mg | Fiber: 9 g

Cherimoya Bliss

When cheirmoyas are not in season, some good substitutions include papaya, peaches, pears, and fresh or frozen mango.

INGREDIENTS | SERVES 2

1 cup cherimoya, peeled and chopped
1 cup young coconut water
½ cup young coconut meat
1 cup banana, sliced
1 pint strawberries, sliced

1. Place cherimoya, coconut water, and coconut meat in a blender and blend until creamy.

2. Arrange banana and strawberries on a serving plate, and pour the cherimoya cream over the fruit.

PER SERVING:
Calories: 214 | Fat: 2 g | Protein: 4 g | Sodium: 132 mg | Fiber: 9 g

Bananas

There are hundreds of types of bananas, although usually we only see one type, the yellow cavendish, which is popular because of its long shelf life. Bananas are used in the raw foods diet because they are high in calories. This tropical fruit also contains high levels of vitamin B6, potassium, vitamin C, and manganese.

Blueberry Cream Salad

This is a simple and delicious dessert for blueberry season.

INGREDIENTS | SERVES 2

1 cup frozen bananas
½ cup pine nuts
1 teaspoon maple syrup
¼ teaspoon vanilla
2 cups blueberries

1. Place the bananas, pine nuts, maple syrup, and vanilla into the blender and blend into a cream. Alternatively, homogenize them through a heavy-duty juicer.

2. Mix together the blueberries and the prepared banana cream.

PER SERVING:

Calories: 388 | Fat: 24 g | Protein: 7 g | Sodium: 3 mg | Fiber: 7 g

Applesauce

This recipe is delicious served warm right out of the dehydrator. With the dehydrator we can duplicate the smells and flavors of hot apple pie and cinnamon, fresh out of the oven! The dehydrator warms and softens the apples, releasing the aroma and essence of the spices.

INGREDIENTS | SERVES 2

2 cups apple, chopped
2 tablespoons agave nectar
¼ cup dates, raisins, or currants
½ teaspoon ground cloves
1–1½ teaspoon cinnamon
2 teaspoons lemon juice
½ teaspoon nutmeg
¼ teaspoon salt
1 cup water

1. Dehydrate the apples in a food dehydrator at 145°F for 2 hours. When the apples are almost done dehydrating, place the remaining ingredients in a blender and blend until smooth.

2. Put the prepared sauce and dehydrated apples into a food mill or food processor with an *S* blade, and process until ingredients are mixed together but still chunky. Place combined mixture back into the food dehydrator for 1 hour and serve warm.

PER SERVING:

Calories: 603 | Fat: 15 g | Protein: 4 g | Sodium: 599 mg | Fiber: 11 g

Persimmon Date Pudding

Be sure that the persimmons are fully ripened. This recipe uses the Japanese persimmon, commonly found in stores. If you want to adapt the recipe for use with the flavorful but astringent American persimmon, you'll need to experiment a little to balance the flavors.

INGREDIENTS | SERVES 2

2 fully ripe persimmons (enough for ½ cup)
¼ cup dates, pitted
½ cup sliced avocado
½ tablespoon raw carob powder
½ teaspoon mint extract, or 1 drop of peppermint essential oil

Persimmons

The persimmon is a soft fruit with a hard outer shell. They have a chalky bitter taste before they are ripe. The Hachiya persimmon must be fully ripened to a soft, jellylike texture before eating. The Fuyu persimmon can be eaten before it is soft.

1. Slice the persimmon in half and scoop out the soft fruit with a spoon.

2. Process all ingredients in a food processor with the *S* blade, or in a high-powered blender, until smooth. Serve immediately or refrigerate up to 3 days.

PER SERVING:
Calories: 126 | Fat: 3 g | Protein: 1 g | Sodium: 3 mg | Fiber: 3 g

Sunny Fruit Parfait

This is a delicious fruit salad to serve for breakfast or a late-night snack. If you'd like, you can add sprouted or soaked buckwheat to give this recipe a nice granola crunch. Good alternatives for the sunflower seeds include cashews, macadamia nuts, or pine nuts.

INGREDIENTS | SERVES 2

½ cup sunflower seeds
1 tablespoon lemon juice
1 teaspoon lemon zest
1 tablespoon agave nectar
½ teaspoon vanilla extract
½ teaspoon cinnamon
½ cup strawberries, sliced
½ cup banana, sliced
½ cup blackberries

1. Soak sunflower seeds for 6 to 8 hours. Drain and rinse.

2. Place the sunflower seeds, the lemon juice, lemon zest, agave nectar, vanilla, and cinnamon in a blender and blend until smooth.

3. Place a layer of strawberries on the bottom of a dessert bowl or glass. Place a layer of the prepared sunflower cream on top of the strawberries. Place a layer of banana and blackberries on top of the cream, followed by a second layer of cream. Top off the parfait with blackberries, strawberries, and bananas.

PER SERVING:
Calories: 163 | Fat: 5 g | Protein: 3 g | Sodium: 2 mg | Fiber: 4 g

Peach Pie Parfait

This is both a satisfying breakfast and a delightful dessert.
If peaches aren't your favorite you could also use plums or pears in this recipe.

INGREDIENTS | SERVES 2

1 cup peaches, peeled and chopped
½ cup strawberries, sliced
2 cups blueberries
1 cup young coconut meat
2 teaspoons cinnamon
1 teaspoon vanilla
1 cup Granola Bars recipe (page 100) or small chunks of pecans or walnuts
¼ cup dried coconut flakes

The Perfect Meal

Parfait is a French word that means "perfect." It is a dessert traditionally arranged in colorful layers and served in a tall, clear glass. Layers commonly used include cream, ice cream, custard, fruit, granola, yogurt, syrup, and a whipped cream topping.

1. Sprinkle the peach and strawberry slices with lemon juice and set aside.

2. Place 1½ cups blueberries and the coconut meat in a blender and blend to create a cream. Add the cinnamon and vanilla. Blend until smooth.

3. In 2 tall, clear glasses, pour a thin layer of the blueberry cream. Top with a thin layer of granola.

4. Place a layer of peaches and strawberries onto the granola.

5. Pour a second layer of cream onto the fruit. Top with another layer of granola, a few more pieces of fruit, and then a thin drizzle of cream on the very top.

6. Garnish with remaining blueberries and coconut flakes.

PER SERVING:

Calories: 624 | Fat: 33 g | Protein: 11 g | Sodium: 12 mg | Fiber: 18 g

Fig and Pecan Cream Parfait

This is a good meal to make with children because of its simplicity and colorful appeal. If you are using dried figs, soak them in water for 30 minutes first to reconstitute them.

INGREDIENTS | SERVES 2

1 vanilla bean
½ cup pecans
½ cup young coconut water
2 tablespoons agave nectar (optional)
½ cup Raw Trail Mix recipe (page 101), or your favorite trail mix or nut pieces
½ cup sliced strawberries or raspberries
½ cup fresh figs, or ¼ cup of dried figs, sliced

Figs

Figs are a nutritious, sweet fruit rich in fiber, potassium, manganese, and calcium. They are delicious snacks both fresh and dried. Figs have a long history and play a prominent role in many different religions and cultural stories. Most notable is Genesis 3:7, when Adam and Eve use fig leaves to make the world's first articles of clothing.

1. Cut open the vanilla bean and scrape out the pulp.

2. Place the pecans into a food processor with an *S* blade. Process the pecans until well blended. Gradually pour in the coconut water, agave nectar, and vanilla pulp until a creamy texture is reached.

3. In 2 tall glasses, place a thin layer of pecan cream on the bottom, topped with a layer of trail mix, and then a layer of berries and figs. Repeat the layers until you reach the top.

4. Garnish with a little cream and berries and serve with a long spoon.

PER SERVING:

Calories: 945 | Fat: 58 g | Protein: 20 g | Sodium: 86 mg | Fiber: 21

Chocolate Mango Parfait

This layered parfait can be served for breakfast or dessert. Good additions include vanilla beans, pumpkin pie spice, and cinnamon. This recipe works with either fresh or frozen mangoes.

INGREDIENTS | SERVES 2

½ cup walnuts

¼ cup dates, chopped

1 tablespoon carob powder

¼ cup pine nuts

½ cup mango, peeled and chopped

½ cup blueberries

Mangoes

The bright yellow color of the mango makes for a beautiful blended sauce or pudding. When blended with a creamy food such as an avocado or cashews, it makes a delicious icing for a cake.

1. In a food processor, process the walnuts, dates, and carob powder together until well mixed and chunky. Set aside.

2. Using a blender or food processor, blend pine nuts and mango until smooth.

3. In a clear glass dessert bowl or wine glass, scoop a layer of the walnut-date mixture onto the bottom, then place a layer of blueberries on top and a layer of the mango-pine nut mixture on top. Continue placing layers until you reach the top. Serve immediately, or place in the freezer for 20 minutes until it hardens up. You can also store the parfait covered in the refrigerator.

PER SERVING:

Calories: 421 | Fat: 31 g | Protein: 8 g | Sodium: 4 mg | Fiber: 7 g

Strawberry Pear Roll-Ups

These fruit roll-ups will stay fresh for a week in the fridge. Use only ripe fruits. This recipe also works well with many other fruits in season. While the dehydrator temperature is set at 135°F, the moisture in the food keeps the actual temperature about 20 degrees cooler, and all the enzymes are preserved.

INGREDIENTS | SERVES 6

4 cups sliced strawberries
1 cup pear, peeled, cored, and chopped

1. Place all the ingredients in a blender and purée until smooth.

2. Pour the purée onto dehydrator trays with nonstick sheets. Dehydrate at 135°F for 4 to 6 hours.

3. Allow the roll-ups to cool, about 10–15 minutes. Peel them off the dehydrator tray, and tightly roll them up in a cylindrical shape. If you will be storing the roll-ups, wrap them tightly in plastic wrap.

PER SERVING:
Calories: 44 | Fat: 0 g | Protein: 1 g | Sodium: 1 mg | Fiber: 3 g

Banana Leathers

These fruit leathers are good plain, or you can make them with seasonings such as raw cacao, carob, or cinnamon, to taste.

INGREDIENTS | SERVES 6

4 cups sliced banana
1 tablespoon agave nectar
½ teaspoon vanilla extract

Fruit Leathers

Fruit leathers can be used as crepes for breakfast or dessert, served with a fresh fruit filling. This is a great way to preserve ripe fruit before it spoils. They can be made with almost any blend of ripe fruits or berries.

1. Place all the ingredients in a blender and purée until smooth.

2. Spread the mixture onto dehydrator trays with nonstick sheets. Dehydrate at 145°F for 2 hours. Turn down the temperature to 115°F and dehydrate for 8 to 12 hours.

3. Allow the leathers to cool, about 10–15 minutes. Peel them off the dehydrator tray, cut them into squares, and roll them tightly into a cylindrical shape. If you will be storing the leathers, wrap them tightly in plastic wrap.

PER SERVING:
Calories: 100 | Fat: 0 g | Protein: 1 g | Sodium: 1 mg | Fiber: 3 g

Almond Butter Banana Leathers

This recipe can also be made by adding 1 tablespoon cacao or carob powder for a hint of chocolate. Another variation uses coconut, blending in ¼ cup young coconut meat, which adds a nice, creamy texture to the leather. Leathers made from fruit and nuts provide the ultimate crepe substitute.

INGREDIENTS | SERVES 6

4 cups sliced banana
1 cup almond butter

1. Place all the ingredients into a blender or food processor and purée until smooth.

2. Pour the purée onto dehydrator trays with nonstick sheets. Dehydrate at 135°F for 4 to 6 hours.

3. Allow the leathers to cool down, about 10–15 minutes. Peel them off the dehydrator tray, and roll them tightly into a cylindrical shape.

4. If you will be storing the leathers, wrap them tightly in plastic wrap.

PER SERVING:
Calories: 353 | Fat: 25 g | Protein: 7 g | Sodium: 6 mg | Fiber: 4 g

CHAPTER 5

Classic Breakfasts

Fresh Fruit Compote

Compotes can be made with a variety of fresh or dried fruits. Fresh fruits that avoid spikes in blood sugar include stoned fruits such as peaches, plums, apricots, and cherries, or berries such as strawberries, blueberries, blackberries, and raspberries, complemented by citrus fruit such as oranges or tangerines.

INGREDIENTS | SERVES 1

1 tablespoon agave nectar, as needed

1 cup chopped fresh fruit (such as plums, apricots, or peaches)

⅛ teaspoon cinnamon

⅛ teaspoon vanilla extract

Drizzle the agave nectar on the fruits if they are tart. Stir in cinnamon and vanilla and enjoy.

PER SERVING:

Calories: 247 | Fat: 0 g | Protein: 4 g | Sodium: 8 mg | Fiber: 5 g

Benefits of Fresh Fruit

Fresh fruit not only tastes good, it helps fight cancer. Researchers at U.C. Berkeley have shown that eating fresh fruits and vegetables cut the risk of cancer by 50 percent.

Blueberry Muffins

These little muffins make great snacks and are easy to travel with. The almond flour is the leftover pulp from making Almond Milk (page 21). Whole almonds ground into a powder can be substituted for the almond flour. These muffins are good topped with a coconut cream icing or strawberry sauce.

INGREDIENTS | SERVES 6

1 cup pecans

½ cup flaxseed

2 cups almond flour

¼ cup liquid coconut oil

3 tablespoons agave nectar

1 teaspoon vanilla

1 cup blueberries

1. Grind the pecans into a powder using a food processor. Grind the flaxseed to a powder in a coffee grinder.

2. Add the almond flour, flaxseed powder, coconut oil, agave nectar, and vanilla to the food processor and continue processing until smooth.

3. Add the blueberries and briefly mix them into the mixture. Form the mixture into little round patties and dehydrate at 145°F for 2 hours. Turn down the temperature to 110°F. Flip over the muffins and continue dehydrating for 2 hours until dry.

PER SERVING:

Calories: 538 | Fat: 47 g | Protein: 11 g | Sodium: 18 mg | Fiber: 11 g

Dried Fruit Compote

This recipe can be served as a dessert or as part of a layered parfait.
It can be used as a spread on crackers and bread, or stirred in with yogurt.

INGREDIENTS | SERVES 4

1 cup dried figs or your favorite dried fruit

1–2 tablespoons agave nectar (to taste)

¼ teaspoon salt

½ teaspoon vanilla extract

½ teaspoon cinnamon

2 tablespoons water

Dried Fruit Compotes

Good options for dried fruit compotes include prunes, currants, raisins, and dates, as well as dried mangos, cherries, and apricots.

1. Soak the whole figs in just enough water to cover them, plus another inch. Soak for 8 to 12 hours in the refrigerator.

2. Remove figs from water, cut and discard stems from the figs. Chop the figs and place in a medium bowl. Pour the agave nectar, salt, vanilla, and cinnamon on top of the figs and stir until they are well coated.

3. In a food processor with the *S* blade, blend ¼ cup figs until they become a thick sauce. Gradually add a small amount of water, 1 teaspoon at a time as needed, to create a thick sauce.

4. In the bowl, combine the prepared sauce with the whole figs. Recipe will stay good for a few days in the refrigerator.

PER SERVING:

Calories: 155 | Fat: 0 g | Protein: 1 g | Sodium: 149 mg | Fiber: 4 g

Raw Swiss Muesli

*This is an easy breakfast that will store for a couple of months in an airtight container.
If you will be storing it, do not add the agave nectar, lemon juice, bananas, or the apples
until you are ready to eat it. This recipe tastes good with tart Granny Smith apples.*

INGREDIENTS | SERVES 2

1 cup rolled oats

¼ cup sunflower seeds, soaked

½ cup walnuts, soaked

2 tablespoons agave nectar

2 tablespoons lemon juice

1 teaspoon carob powder

½ cup sliced banana

½ cup grated apple

4 tablespoons raisins (optional)

2 cups Almond Milk (page 21)

1. Place the oats, sunflower seeds, walnuts, agave nectar, lemon juice, and carob powder into a large bowl. Stir the ingredients until well combined.

2. Add the banana slices and grated apple to the muesli (reserve a few banana slices for garnish).

3. Pour the muesli into breakfast bowls. Garnish with banana rounds, add raisins if desired, and pour in the Almond Milk.

PER SERVING:
Calories: 914 | Fat: 52 g | Protein: 23 g | Sodium: 19 mg | Fiber: 10 g

Sprouted-Grain Cereal

This is a hearty breakfast made with sprouted grains that can be served with Almond Milk (page 21) and a little honey or agave nectar as a sweetener. You can substitute raw carob or raw cacao powder in place of the mesquite. Pumpkin pie spice is a good substitute for the cinnamon.

INGREDIENTS | SERVES 4

2 cups total of grains made up of buckwheat, rye, oats, barley, millet, quinoa, wheat, or sunflower seeds (around ¼ cup each)

1 cup apple, cut into small chunks

½ teaspoon salt

1–2 teaspoons cinnamon (to taste)

½ teaspoon mesquite powder (optional)

1. Soak and sprout all grains according to the sprouting chart (see Appendix B).

2. In a large bowl stir all ingredients together. Serve in cereal bowls with almond milk and garnish with slices of fresh fruit.

PER SERVING:

Calories: 445 | Fat: 4 g | Protein: 16 g | Sodium: 587 mg | Fiber: 15 g

Sprouted Grains

Sprouted grains by definition are living foods and have a high level of vitamins and protein. The enzymes break down the grain, so they're highly nourishing. Sprouted-grain cereals and breads are considered superior to those made with whole-grain flour, because the sprouted form is less processed. That means it's absorbed more slowly, thus supporting stable blood sugar and a steady supply of energy. Using a combination of sprouted grains also provides complete protein.

Cinnamon Oatmeal

This is a delicious, nutritious breakfast that will help maintain your strength and energy level through the morning. The Brazil nut milk is made using the same recipe and techniques as almond milk. Pumpkin pie spice or mesquite powder are good alternatives to the cinnamon.

INGREDIENTS | SERVES 2

1½ cups dried oat groats, sprouted
¼ cup goji berries
2 cups Brazil nut milk
¼ cup fresh or dried blueberries
½ cup banana, sliced into rounds
1 tablespoon cinnamon
2 teaspoons maple syrup (optional)

Oats

The two most popular forms of oats are rolled oats and oat groats, which contain more fiber and are even more nutritious than rolled oats. Oats are an excellent source of manganese, selenium, trypto-phan, antioxidants, and vitamin B1. Some of the health benefits associated with oats include lower cholesterol levels, reduced risk for diabetes, and a reduced risk of car-diovascular disease. Although oats contain small amounts of the protein gluten, stud-ies have shown that some people with glu-ten intolerance and celiac disease can eat oats without negative effects.

1. Soak the oat groats for 24 hours in a bowl of water. (Drain and rinse the oats after the first 12 hours and continue soaking another 12 hours in fresh water.)

2. Drain and rinse the oats again after soaking and allow them to dry in a colander for 30 minutes.

3. Soak the goji berries in water for 20 minutes.

4. Pour the oats into 2 cereal bowls. Add 1 cup Brazil nut milk to each bowl of oats. Garnish with the berries, bananas, cinnamon, and maple syrup (optional).

PER SERVING:
Calories: 806 | Fat: 30 g | Protein: 30 g | Sodium: 32 mg | Fiber: 17 g

Sweet Almond Oat Cereal

This is a great meal for breakfast. It is delicious served with Almond Milk (page 21) and garnished with fresh fruit.

INGREDIENTS | SERVES 2

2 cups steel cut oats

½ cup almonds

1½ cups bananas

1 teaspoon cinnamon or pumpkin pie spice

½ cup blueberries, blackberries, strawberries, or sliced peaches

2 tablespoons agave nectar

Pumpkin Pie Spice

This pleasant blend of spices is typically made with cinnamon, ginger, nutmeg, and allspice or cloves. Some formulas also include mace or salt. Although you'll find dozens of different recipes for the blend, they're all predominantly cinnamon. Pumpkin pie spice is a good match for pie pumpkin, sweet potato, and squash dishes, cereals, and slow-baked muffins, cakes, cookies, and bars. These spices also complement fruit such as apples, pears, or peaches, nuts including walnuts and pecans, and smoothies like those based on almond milk.

1. Soak the oats in 2½ cups water overnight, for 6 to 8 hours. Soak the almonds in 1 cup water for 8 to 12 hours. Rinse and drain.

2. Process the almonds, oats, bananas, and cinnamon in a food processor until they are broken down into big chunks.

3. Transfer the ingredients into serving bowls. Top with blueberries or fruit of your choice, and drizzle the agave nectar on top.

PER SERVING:
Calories: 341 | Fat: 19 g | Protein: 11 g | Sodium: 2 mg | Fiber: 8 g

Pine Nut Crunch Cereal

This recipe uses soaked or sprouted seeds and buckwheat groats and is slow-baked in the dehydrator. It's good as a meal, a quick snack, or food to bring with you when you go traveling.

INGREDIENTS | SERVES 2

½ tablespoon pumpkin pie spice

¼ teaspoon salt

½ cup pine nuts

1 cup buckwheat groats, after soaking or sprouting

¼ cup green pumpkin seeds

½ cup sunflower seeds, soaked

1 to 2 tablespoons maple syrup

1 tablespoon lemon juice

2 cups Almond Milk (page 21)

1. In a bowl, mix together the spices with the pine nuts, buckwheat sprouts, pumpkin seeds, sunflower seeds, and maple syrup and lemon juice.

2. Spread mixture onto dehydrator trays and dehydrate at 115°F for 24 hours until crunchy. Serve in cereal bowls with Almond Milk and slices of fresh fruit.

PER SERVING:

Calories: 732 | Fat: 43 g | Protein: 18 g | Sodium: 106 mg | Fiber: 10 g

Pine Nuts

Pine nuts are the edible seeds of pine trees. They are good sources of both protein and dietary fiber. The shell must be removed before the pine nut can be eaten. Unshelled pine nuts have a fairly long shelf life if kept in a dry, cold place like your refrigerator. Shelled pine nuts can go rancid fairly quickly within the course of a week to a few days depending on heat and humidity. If you do buy shelled pine nuts, be careful in your selection as there is a chance they could be rancid at the time of purchase if they have been improperly stored.

Chia Porridge

This breakfast will sustain your energy through the morning. The prunes can be replaced with other dried fruits: dates, apricots, or figs. The cinnamon may be replaced with maca, nutmeg, vanilla, cardamon, mesquite powder, or freshly grated ginger. Serve this with Almond Milk (page 21) and freshly sliced fruit.

INGREDIENTS | SERVES 2

½ cup buckwheat, sprouted

¼ cup chia seeds, soaked

2 cups sliced banana

¼ cup prunes, pitted

1 teaspoon cinnamon

Prunes

Prunes are plums that have been dehydrated into a wrinkled, chewy, dried fruit. They are great additions to smoothies, jams, compotes, and other sauces. They can be used as a sweetener to replace dates or raisins. Prunes are a great food for breaking a fast; they are a nutritious fruit high in antioxidants, phytonutrients, vitamin A, potassium, iron, and copper.

1. Soak the buckwheat in water at room temperature for 6 to 8 hours. Soak the chia seeds in a separate bowl in ¾ cup water in the refrigerator for 6 to 8 hours. Stir the chia seeds a few times for the first 10 minutes.

2. Rinse and drain the buckwheat a few times, until the water is clear.

3. In a food processor or blender, blend the buckwheat until smooth. Add just enough water, a tablespoon at a time, to help it blend.

4. Add the banana, prunes, and cinnamon to the buckwheat and continue blending until smooth.

5. Stir in the chia seeds. Pour the porridge into serving bowls and serve.

PER SERVING:

Calories: 403 | Fat: 6 g | Protein: 10 g | Sodium: 10 mg | Fiber: 16 g

Cranberry and Butternut Squash Porridge

This recipe is good served with flax crackers. You may substitute other nuts—soaked almonds, walnuts, or pecans—for the macadamia nuts. It also tastes good with a pinch of nutmeg and mesquite.

INGREDIENTS | SERVES 4

2 cups butternut squash, peeled and cut into cubes

1 cup macadamia nuts

½ cup apple

1 tablespoon cinnamon

1 teaspoon vanilla

1 cup young coconut water

1 teaspoon ginger juice

½ cup dried cranberries

Place all the ingredients, with the exception of the cranberries, into a blender and blend until smooth. Serve in breakfast bowls and garnish with dried cranberries.

PER SERVING:

Calories: 317 | Fat: 26 g | Protein: 4 g | Sodium: 68 g | Fiber: 7 g

Porridge

Porridge is a simple dish traditionally prepared with oats. It is popular in Europe and is often made with barley, rice, wheat, grits, or cornmeal. Butternut squash creates a similar taste and texture to porridge and provides a tasty alternative for people who are gluten intolerant.

Kasha Porridge

This is a delicious and satisfying breakfast. If extra liquid is desired, a sweet liquid may be added such as apple juice, young coconut water, or almond milk. This recipe is delicious when garnished with fresh fruit or berries.

INGREDIENTS | SERVES 2

2 cups soaked or sprouted buckwheat groats (soaked for 6 to 8 hours)

1 cup apple, chopped

1 tablespoon cinnamon

½ teaspoon salt

2 teaspoons orange zest

Place all ingredients in a food processor and process with the *S* blade until smooth and creamy.

PER SERVING:

Calories: 627 | Fat: 6 g | Protein: 23 g | Sodium: 584 mg | Fiber: 21 g

Kasha

Kasha is a traditional recipe from Europe using toasted buckwheat. The recipe is over a thousand years old and is a staple dish in Russia and Eastern Europe. There is a Russian proverb that says "Cabbage soup and porridge are all we need to live on."

Fig Porridge

Serve this in the summer, when fresh figs are plenty. Take time the night before to do the prep. If you're using dried figs, soak them in water for 1 or 2 hours. Rolled oats may be substituted for the steel cut oats. Rolled oats are lighter than steel cut oats and only need to be soaked for 1 hour in water.

INGREDIENTS | SERVES 2

1 cup steel cut oats, presoaked for 6 to 8 hours

½ cup walnuts, soaked

½ cup figs, chopped

1 tablespoon honey

1 teaspoon vanilla extract

¼ cup goji berries, soaked (optional)

1. Place the soaked oats and walnuts into a food processor and process until smooth and creamy.

2. Add the remaining ingredients and continue processing until well mixed and chunky.

PER SERVING:

Calories: 427 | Fat: 22 g | Protein: 10 g | Sodium: 4 mg | Fiber: 7 g

Pear Crepes

These are delicious wraps to serve for breakfast.
The pears can be replaced with other fresh fruits in season.

INGREDIENTS | SERVES 4

2 cups young coconut meat

4 cups pear, chopped

2 cups sliced banana

1 cup Strawberry Date Sauce (page 231) or Raspberry Sauce (page 233)

1. Place the coconut meat and pear in a blender and blend until smooth. Spread the blended mixture onto dehydrator trays with nonstick sheets. Dehydrate at 115°F for 4 hours to make fruit leathers. Score leathers into round circles, approximately 8" in diameter.

2. Mash the banana with a fork. Place a round fruit leather on a plate and spread a layer of mashed banana on top. Roll it up into a crepe shape.

3. Place the crepe rolls on a plate and cover with Strawberry Date Sauce.

PER SERVING:

Calories: 209 | Fat: 1 g | Protein: 2 g | Sodium: 3 mg | Fiber: 8 g

Peach Cream Crepes

This is another version of slow-baked crepes using a cashew-based wrap.
Good garnishes for the crepes include fresh fruit or berries, coconut cream, or strawberry sauce.

INGREDIENTS | SERVES 4

2 cups cashews, soaked for 2 to 4 hours
2 tablespoons lemon juice
3 tablespoons agave nectar
¼ teaspoon salt
Filling for Peach Cream Crepes (below)

1. Place the cashews, lemon juice, agave nectar, and salt in a blender and blend until smooth.

2. Spread a thin layer of the mixture on dehydrator trays with nonstick sheets. Dehydrate at 145°F for 1 hour. Turn down heat to 110°F and dehydrate for an additional 12 to 18 hours.

3. Score the crepe wraps into squares. Spread a layer of the filling for Peach Cream Crepes onto one end and roll them up.

PER SERVING:
Calories: 412 | Fat: 29 g | Protein: 12 g | Sodium: 153 | Fiber: 2 g

Filling for Peach Cream Crepes

The carob in this filling can be omitted to vary the flavor.
The peaches can be replaced with other fresh fruits in season.

INGREDIENTS | SERVES 4

2 cups peaches, chopped
½ cup pine nuts
¼ cup dates, chopped
1 tablespoon carob or cacao powder

In a blender, place the peaches, pine nuts, dates, and carob powder and blend together until smooth.

PER SERVING:
Calories: 177 | Fat: 12 g | Protein: 3 g | Sodium: 1 mg | Fiber: 3 g

Banana Crepes

These are delicious wraps to serve for breakfast. Freshly sliced fruits and berries make a good garnish. A good replacement for the banana leathers is the young Coconut Wraps from page 189.

INGREDIENTS | SERVES 2

2 Banana Leathers (page 60)

½ cup Coconut Cream (page 255)

½ cup Strawberry Date Sauce (page 231) or Apricot Jam (page 232)

½ cup sliced strawberries

Crepes

Crepes are the national dish of France where the recipe originated. This classic gourmet fare consists of a thin pancake rolled up with a filling of choice.

1. Begin to make the Banana Leather recipe, but rather than cutting the leather into strips, score it into circles. Lay each banana leather flat on the plate.

2. Spread a layer of coconut cream onto the banana leather.

3. Tightly roll up the banana leather into a crepe.

4. Drizzle the Strawberry Date Sauce over the crepes and garnish each with sliced strawberries.

PER SERVING:

Calories: 505 | Fat: 32 g | Protein: 11 g | Sodium: 16 mg | Fiber: 7 g

CHAPTER 6

Salads and Vegetable Dishes

recipes continued on next page

recipes continued

———————

Arugula with Cranberries and Walnuts

This salad is good served with the Almond Cheese recipe on page 159. You may also add extra diced vegetables for a heartier meal. You can vary this recipe by substituting 1 cup avocado and 1 cup cherry tomatoes in place of the cranberries and walnuts.

INGREDIENTS | SERVES 2

3 tablespoons olive oil

1 tablespoon agave nectar (optional)

2 tablespoons balsamic vinegar

¼ teaspoon cumin

2 cups arugula or chopped head lettuce

½ cup dried cranberries

½ cup walnuts

1. Whisk together the olive oil, agave nectar, balsamic vinegar, and cumin to create the vinaigrette dressing.

2. Combine the remaining ingredients in a mixing bowl and drizzle the vinaigrette on top.

PER SERVING:

Calories: 664 | Fat: 53 g | Protein: 10 g | Sodium: 15 mg | Fiber: 6 g

Oils

Be sure to purchase only high-quality raw oils. Look for olive oil labeled "extra virgin olive oil," or EVOO.

Oranges with Fresh Greens

This is a delicious salad. The sweet and creamy dressing provides a nice contrast to the bitter arugula. In place of the escarole lettuce, you can substitute other types of salad greens. For the fresh mint you can substitute one teaspoon of dried mint or the fresh herbs of your choice.

INGREDIENTS | SERVES 4

1½ cups arugula

1½ cups escarole lettuce

½ cup pine nuts

½ cup orange juice

½ cup olive oil

½ teaspoon salt

¼ teaspoon cayenne pepper powder

1 tablespoon fresh mint, chopped (optional)

¾ cup orange slices

1 cup sliced avocado

1. Rinse the arugula and escarole lettuce under water. Dry the lettuce with a salad spinner or pat dry with a clean paper towel.

2. To create the dressing, use a blender or food processor and blend together pine nuts, orange juice, olive oil, salt, and cayenne pepper until smooth. Add the mint last (optional) and briefly pulse.

3. Arrange the lettuce and arugula on salad plates. Top with orange and avocado slices. Drizzle the dressing over the salad and serve.

PER SERVING:

Calories: 548 | Fat: 51 g | Protein: 12 g | Sodium: 314 mg | Fiber: 7 g

Arugula with Strawberries and Hazelnuts

The balsamic vinegar adds a tangy flavor to the strawberries.
In place of the strawberries, you can substitute other fresh berries in season.

INGREDIENTS | SERVES 2

1 cup strawberries
3 tablespoons olive oil
3 tablespoons lime juice
¼ teaspoon cayenne pepper powder
3 cups arugula
1 cup cucumber, sliced into thin rounds
1 cup hazelnuts

Arugula

Arugula, also called rocket, is a leafy green vegetable with a strong, slightly bitter flavor. It is a great source of vitamins A, C, and K; folate; calcium; iron; and magnesium.

1. Place the strawberries into a blender and blend into a dressing. Gradually add the olive oil, lime juice, and cayenne pepper.

2. Place a bed of arugula on the bottom of a salad bowl. Arrange the cucumber slices on the arugula and garnish with hazelnuts.

3. Drizzle the dressing on top of the salad and serve.

PER SERVING:

Calories: 648 | Fat: 62 g | Protein: 12 g | Sodium: 11 mg | Fiber: 9g

Romaine with Tangerines or Oranges

This salad works well with all types of fresh herbs. Some good substitutions for the basil include mint, oregano, thyme, or rosemary. This salad is also delicious with simply olive oil and lemon juice.

INGREDIENTS | SERVES 2

½ cup orange juice
3 tablespoons extra-virgin olive oil or flax oil
2 tablespoons fresh basil
3–4 cups chopped romaine lettuce
1 cup diced red bell pepper
½ cup walnuts
1 cup orange or tangerine slices

1. Place the orange juice and the olive oil in a blender and blend together well. Add the basil to the blender and pulse briefly to mix.

2. Place romaine lettuce and red bell pepper into a salad bowl and top with walnuts and orange or tangerine slices. Pour on the prepared salad dressing and mix well.

PER SERVING:

Calories: 476 | Fat: 40 g | Protein: 7 g | Sodium: 11 mg | Fiber: 7 g

Herbs

Fresh herbs have more flavor than dried herbs, and they are easy to grow all year round indoors. When blending herbs, add them last because they will become bitter if processed for too long.

Raw Caesar Salad

This is a tasty variation on the traditional Caesar salad. It uses avocado instead of egg for the creamy texture, and the pine nuts replace the Parmesan cheese. In place of croutons, you can use flax crackers or any other favorite dehydrated crackers.

INGREDIENTS | SERVES 2

2–3 cups romaine lettuce

½ cup pine nuts

1 cup avocado

2 tablespoons olive oil

1 clove garlic

1 teaspoon salt

2 tablespoons lemon juice

½ teaspoon black pepper

¼ cup water

1 cup Tomato, Basil, and Flax Crackers (page 107), crumbled

1. Chop up the romaine lettuce and place in a large salad bowl.

2. Process pine nuts briefly in a coffee grinder or food processor and sprinkle on top of the lettuce.

3. In a blender place the remaining ingredients, except the crackers, and blend until creamy.

4. Toss the prepared dressing with the salad and top with cracker crumbs.

PER SERVING:
Calories: 760 | Fat: 67 g | Protein: 17 g | Sodium: 1,848 mg | Fiber: 22 g

History of Caesar Salads

Caesar Cardini, a popular Italian chef, invented this recipe in the early twentieth century. The base of the salad is traditionally romaine, Parmesan cheese, crunchy croutons, garlic, and salty anchovies. This variation uses delicious crunchy crackers made from soaked seeds.

Dandelion Greens with Tart Apples and Italian Dressing

This salad has a good balance of flavors with the bitter dandelion greens and tart apple.
If you can't find dandelion greens, you can use endive, frisée greens, or other fresh greens.
This salad is delicious simply with olive oil and a little salt, or olive oil and lemon juice.

INGREDIENTS | SERVES 2

Salt to taste

2 tablespoons olive oil

3 tablespoons lemon juice

1–2 teaspoons Italian seasoning (optional)

1 small Granny Smith or Braeburn apple, diced with skin on

2 cups dandelion greens

1 cup romaine lettuce

1. To make the Italian dressing, blend together the salt, olive oil, lemon juice, and Italian seasoning until smooth.

2. Put the diced apple in the bottom of a small bowl.

3. Chop greens and lettuce and place over the apple chunks.

4. Drizzle the dressing over the salad and serve.

PER SERVING:
Calories: 193 | Fat: 14 g | Protein: 2 g | Sodium: 93 mg | Fiber: 4 g

Granny Smith Apples

Granny Smith apples are good with salads because they are quite stable and retain their color (rather than turning brown). You could use any tart apple with this recipe if the salad will be eaten quickly or if you sprinkle the apple with a little lemon juice.

Spicy Coleslaw with Cashew Mayonnaise

This is a great side dish for the BBQ Chips (recipe on page 116) or the Spanish Chile (recipe on page 124). For a little more kick add ¼ teaspoon mustard powder.

INGREDIENTS | SERVES 4

½ head red cabbage

½ head green or Napa cabbage

½ cup carrot

½ cup red onion

¼ cup daikon radish

½ teaspoon salt

2 tablespoons raw apple cider vinegar

1 cup Cashew Mayonnaise (page 88)

1 teaspoon black pepper

1. Grate or shred the cabbages, carrot, onion, and radish using a mandolin, cheese grater, or the grater blade on a food processor.

2. Sprinkle the salt onto the shredded vegetables and mix together.

3. Pour on the apple cider vinegar, black pepper, and the cashew mayonnaise and mix everything together.

PER SERVING:

Calories: 328 | Fat: 24 g | Protein: 8 g | Sodium: 460 mg | Fiber: 7 g

Raw Apple Cider Vinegar

There are numerous health and beauty benefits associated with apple cider vinegar (ACV). Whole books have been written about it, the most famous being *Apple Cider Vinegar: Miracle Health System* by natural health pioneer Patricia Bragg. The unpasteurized brands by Bragg or Spectrum are recommended.

Kale and Sea Vegetables with Orange Sesame Dressing

This salad is a great appetizer for an Asian-themed meal.
It is good served with miso soup and nori rolls.

INGREDIENTS | SERVES 4

¼ cup wakame

½ cup sea lettuce

3 cups kale

½ teaspoon salt

¼ cup orange juice

6 tablespoons sesame seeds (additional for garnish)

1 tablespoon kelp powder

Sea Vegetables

Sea vegetables are among the most nutritious and mineral-rich foods on earth. Ocean water contains all the mineral elements known to man. For example, both kelp and dulse are excellent sources of iodine, which is an essential nutrient missing in most diets. Sea vegetables are dried and should be soaked in water to reconstitute before eating. The soak water contains many beneficial minerals and can be used to water your house plants.

1. Soak the wakame and sea lettuce in water for 30 minutes. Rinse and discard the soak water.

2. Remove the stems from the kale. Roll up the kale leaves and chop into small pieces.

3. Sprinkle salt onto the kale and massage it by hand to create a wilting effect.

4. Place the orange juice, sesame seeds, and kelp powder into a blender and blend until smooth.

5. Toss the dressing with the kale and sea vegetables in a large bowl until well covered. Sprinkle about 1 teaspoon sesame seeds on top.

PER SERVING:

Calories: 90 | Fat: 5 g | Protein: 4 g | Sodium: 380 mg | Fiber: 2 g

Marinated Kale and Avocado Salad

This delicious salad uses wilted and marinated kale, and it has a good balance of flavors to stimulate the taste buds.

INGREDIENTS | SERVES 2

1 bunch dinosaur kale (approximately 3 cups kale)

1 teaspoon salt

2 tablespoons lemon juice

2 tablespoons olive oil

1 tablespoon nama shoyu

1½ cup diced avocado

1 cup cherry tomatoes, chopped

1 tablespoon dulse flakes

Kale

Kale is a vegetable in the cabbage family. It is very strong and hearty and will grow in all soil types and most climates. It is considered a superfood because of the high quantity of concentrated nutrients, including carotenoids and other antioxidants, iron, and calcium.

1. Peel the stems off the kale leaves. Roll the leaves and chop into small pieces.

2. Place the chopped kale into a large bowl and sprinkle with salt. Massage the salt into the kale by hand and let it sit for 10 minutes so the kale will become soft and wilt.

3. Pour the lemon juice onto the kale and let it marinate for a few minutes. The acidic lemon juice will further wilt the kale.

4. Pour the olive oil and nama shoyu onto the kale and mix well.

5. Top the kale with avocado, chopped cherry tomatoes, and dulse flakes. Enjoy as a side salad with your entrée of choice.

PER SERVING:
Calories: 378 | Fat: 31 g | Protein: 7 g | Sodium: 1712 mg | Fiber: 12 g

Thai Green Papaya Salad

*Served as a spicy side dish, this salad complements the Pad Thai with
Almond Sauce (page 212) and the Thai Iced Tea (page 46). Garnish with slivered almonds.
A little olive oil and nama shoyu are good condiments to drizzle on top.*

INGREDIENTS | SERVES 2

¼ cup lime juice

1 tablespoon fresh lemongrass, or
1 teaspoon lemongrass powder

2 tablespoons agave nectar

1 teaspoon ginger juice

¼ teaspoon cayenne pepper

1 cup green papaya, peeled and
shredded

½ cup carrot, julienne cut

2 cups red or yellow bell pepper, diced

2 tablespoons fresh cilantro, minced

1. Blend together the lime juice, lemongrass, agave nectar, ginger juice, and cayenne pepper.

2. Mix the papaya, carrot, and bell pepper together in a large bowl with the blended sauce. Top with the cilantro.

PER SERVING:

Calories: 157 | Fat: 1 g | Protein: 2 g | Sodium: 29 mg | Fiber: 5 g

Green Papaya

The papaya fruit is green just before it is ripe. It is high in the papain enzyme, which helps improve digestion and is also used as a meat tenderizer because it breaks down protein.

Pineapple Coconut Coleslaw

This coleslaw has a sweet, tropical twist. Jicama is a good substitute for the carrot. Fresh pineapple juice could be substituted for the water. This is a good side dish to serve with a veggie burger.

INGREDIENTS | SERVES 4

½ teaspoon salt
3 cups grated green cabbage
1 cup grated carrot
1 cup cashews, soaked
¾ cup dried coconut
1 cup pineapple, cut into small chunks
2 tablespoons agave nectar
Water as needed for the blender

Coleslaw

Coleslaw is a traditional side dish of shredded cabbage and carrots. Many restaurants serve this mixed with a little vinegar and mayonnaise.

1. In a medium bowl, sprinkle salt onto the grated cabbage and carrots and stir.

2. Using a food processor or blender, blend together the cashews, ¼ cup dried coconut, ¼ cup pineapple, and agave nectar. Add just enough water so you can blend it.

3. Toss together the remaining pineapple and dried coconut with the grated cabbage and carrot. Stir in the blended dressing and stir until well mixed.

PER SERVING:

Calories: 297 | Fat: 19 g | Protein: 8 g | Sodium: 326 mg | Fiber: 4 g

Spring Greens with Berries

The acid in the lime juice breaks down the fat in the olive oil to make a flavorful dressing. You can make this as a fresh salad focused on the greens and fruit, or add some spice by including the onion, jalapeño, and cumin.

INGREDIENTS | SERVES 2

1 jalapeño pepper
4 tablespoons lime juice
4 tablespoons olive oil
¼ teaspoon cumin
4 cups mixed baby spring greens
1 pint fresh blackberries or raspberries
¼ cup red onion, sliced paper thin

1. Slice the jalapeño pepper and remove the seeds and stem.

2. Place the lime juice, olive oil, cumin, and 2 teaspoons of the jalapeño pepper in a blender and blend together.

3. Toss the dressing with the greens, berries, and onions and serve as a side salad.

PER SERVING:

Calories: 327 | Fat: 28 g | Protein: 3 g | Sodium: 19 mg | Fiber: 9 g

Cashew Mayonnaise

Serve this condiment with the Jicama "Potato" Salad recipe (page 91) and the Mock-Tuna Salad Sandwich (page 194). Blending in ¼ teaspoon fresh horseradish adds some heat to the recipe. This recipe works great with almond milk, macadamia nuts, pine nuts, avocado, or young coconut in place of the cashews.

INGREDIENTS | SERVES 2

1 cup cashews, soaked for 3–6 hours

1 cup water

¼ cup coconut oil

2 tablespoons olive oil

¼ teaspoon ground mustard seeds or mustard powder

2 teaspoons lemon juice

¼ teaspoon salt

¼ teaspoon minced garlic (optional)

1. In a food processor or blender, blend cashews with 1 cup water until smooth.

2. Add remaining ingredients to the blender or food processor and mix until smooth.

PER SERVING:

Calories: 724 | Fat: 70 g | Protein: 12 g | Sodium: 299 mg | Fiber: 2 g

Carrot and Red Cabbage Salad with Cashew Mayonnaise

This is a delicious, simple salad. Some good additions to this recipe include red bell pepper and beets, or red apples and lemon juice.

INGREDIENTS | SERVES 2

1½ cups sliced red cabbage

1½ cups carrots (or more), sliced into thin ribbons

¾ cup Cashew Mayonnaise (above)

3 tablespoons sesame seeds (to taste)

Mix the vegetables together with the cashew mayonnaise until they are well coated. Sprinkle the sesame seeds on top and serve in a salad bowl.

PER SERVING:

Calories: 489 | Fat: 42 g | Protein: 10 g | Sodium: 222 mg | Fiber: 6 g

Classic Cucumber Salad

This is a good salad to serve with miso soup and spring rolls.

INGREDIENTS | SERVES 2

2 tablespoons dill, or diced fresh rosemary, oregano, thyme

3 tablespoons lemon juice

2 tablespoons balsamic vinegar

1 teaspoon sesame seeds

1 teaspoon sesame oil

1 tablespoon agave nectar

2 cups cucumber, sliced into thin rounds

1. In a small bowl, combine the dill, lemon juice, balsamic vinegar, sesame seeds, sesame oil, and agave nectar.

2. Toss cucumbers with the sesame mixture and serve.

PER SERVING:

Calories: 94 | Fat: 3 g | Protein: 1 g | Sodium: 6 mg | Fiber: 1 g

Cool Cucumbers

A member of the melon family, cucumbers are inexpensive, nutritious, and easy to grow, with low sugar and high water content that helps you stay hydrated. They are a great kidney cleanser, acting as a diuretic to help clean the kidney and bladder of debris. Cukes are the perfect summer salad vegetable—cooling, refreshing, alkaline, and rich in nutrients.

Savory Green Beans

This is a great way to prepare green beans. Herbamare is a blend of fourteen different savory dried herbs. The Herbamare may be replaced with your favorite blend of dried herbs. Use a curry powder or oriental seasoning blend to spice up the beans.

INGREDIENTS | SERVES 4

1 teaspoon Herbamare or savory herb seasoning blend

2 tablespoons lemon juice

2 tablespoons olive oil

¼ teaspoon salt

2 cups green beans

1. Stir together the Herbamare, lemon juice, olive oil, and salt.

2. Place the green beans in a large bowl. Pour the sauce onto the beans and stir to coat the beans. Marinate for 3 hours at room temperature or overnight in the refrigerator.

3. To speed up the marinating process, you can put the beans in a dehydrator for 2 hours at 110°F.

PER SERVING:

Calories: 80 | Fat: 7 g | Protein: 1 g | Sodium: 294 mg | Fiber: 2 g

Green Beans

Green beans, sometimes called string beans or snap beans, are nutritious vegetables rich in vitamins A, C, and K and folate, and they are great sources of the minerals potassium and manganese. This is one of the few beans that can be eaten raw.

Spiced Collards Salad

This is a delicious way to eat collard greens. The lemon and olive oil help balance the bitter greens. Macadamia nuts, cashews, or avocado are good replacements for the pine nuts. You can use any fresh herb you have on hand to change the flavor. This salad will stay fresh in the refrigerator for a couple of days.

INGREDIENTS | SERVES 2

3 cups tender young collard greens

1 teaspoon salt

3 tablespoons lemon juice

½ cup pine nuts

2 tablespoons olive oil

½ teaspoon garlic powder

½ tablespoon fresh basil or ¼ teaspoon dried basil

½ tablespoon fresh oregano or ¼ teaspoon dried oregano

2 cups diced tomatoes

¼ cup diced scallions

1 cup diced red bell pepper

Collard Greens

Collard greens and kale are the two most nutrient-rich foods in the leafy green category. They belong in the cruciferous and brassica family, along with cabbage, broccoli, and bok choy. Collard greens are excellent sources of antioxidants; phytochemicals; chlorophyll; vitamins A, C, and K; manganese; folate; calcium; zinc; and a number of other nutrients. Numerous scientific studies have revealed that the phytonutrients found in the brassica vegetables help prevent cancer.

1. Remove the stems from the collard greens. Roll up the greens and chop them into small pieces.

2. Sprinkle the salt onto the collards. Massage the collards by hand to work the salt into the greens so they begin to wilt.

3. Pour 2 tablespoons lemon juice on greens and mix. Let them sit for a couple minutes to wilt.

4. Blend the pine nuts, olive oil, garlic powder, and 1 tablespoon lemon juice until smooth. Put the basil and oregano in the blender and briefly pulse until the herbs are mixed in and still chunky.

5. Dice the tomato, onion, and red bell pepper and place on top of the collard greens. Toss the salad with the blended dressing and serve.

PER SERVING:

Calories: 431 | Fat: 37 g | Protein: 9 g | Sodium: 1,189 mg | Fiber: 7 g

Creamy Avocado Salad

This is a perfect summer salad. The red leaf lettuce balances the tang of the spinach, and the cayenne adds sweet and spicy flavors.

INGREDIENTS | SERVES 4

2 cups red leaf lettuce
1 cup spinach
1½ cups sliced avocado
1½ cups diced tomatoes
2 tablespoons lemon juice
¼ teaspoon cayenne pepper powder
2 tablespoons basil, minced (optional)
½ cup scallions

1. Wash and dry the lettuce and spinach.

2. To make the dressing, use a food processor or blender and blend together 1 cup avocado with 1 cup tomato, lemon juice, and cayenne until smooth. Add the basil and briefly pulse.

3. Place the remaining avocado, lettuce, and spinach in a salad bowl. Top with diced tomato and scallions.

4. Drizzle the dressing over the salad.

PER SERVING:

Calories: 108 | Fat: 8 g | Protein: 2 g | Sodium: 18 mg | Fiber: 5 g

Jicama "Potato" Salad

For presentation, sprinkle a little paprika on top. Tasty ingredients you could add include red bell peppers, scallions, add celery seed, mustard powder, or fresh or dried dill to taste. Serve with the Veggie Burgers (recipe on page 199).

INGREDIENTS | SERVES 2

2 cups jicama, peeled and cut into cubes
½ cup Cashew Mayonnaise (page 88) (to taste)
½ cup red onion, sliced thin
½ cup hearts of celery, sliced thin
1 tablespoon capers or olives
Salt and pepper to taste

1. Mix the jicama and mayonnaise together until the jicama is well covered. Stir in onion, celery, and capers or olives, and mix well.

2. Add the salt and freshly ground black pepper to taste.

PER SERVING:

Calories: 299 | Fat: 14 g | Protein: 6 g | Sodium: 252 mg | Fiber: 8 g

Jicama

This root vegetable is also called a Mexican potato. It's found in most grocery stores and is used in many raw food recipes because of its pleasing crunchy texture and a balanced light, sweet, and starchy flavor. It resembles a potato but doesn't need to be cooked.

Jicama Fennel Slaw

This is a creamy and crunchy slaw that is great for picnics and road trips.
Good substitutes for the lime juice include apple cider vinegar, lemon juice, or orange juice.
Good substitutes for the poppy seeds include sesame seeds or hemp seeds.

INGREDIENTS | SERVES 2

½ cup cashews
3 tablespoons lime juice
1 teaspoon lime zest
¼ teaspoon salt
Water for the sauce
1 cup jicama, peeled and grated
1 cup fennel bulb, peeled and grated
1 cup green cabbage, shredded
¼ cup poppy seeds

1. In a blender place the cashews, lime juice, lime zest, and salt and blend. Slowly add the water until it blends to the consistency of whipped cream.

2. Toss the jicama, fennel, and cabbage with the prepared cashew cream and poppy seeds. This recipe will stay fresh for up to three days in the refrigerator.

PER SERVING:
Calories: 326 | Fat: 22 g | Protein: 11 g | Sodium: 332 mg | Fiber: 10 g

Orange Cashew Salad Dressing

This is a delicious dressing made with a base of cashews.
Olive oil may be used in place of the sesame oil.

INGREDIENTS | SERVES 2

4 tablespoons cashews, soaked
2 tablespoons extra-virgin sesame oil
½ cup orange juice

Place all the ingredients into a blender and blend until smooth. Continue to blend until the cashews are fully emulsified.

PER SERVING:
Calories: 239 | Fat: 21 g | Protein: 3 g | Sodium: 3 mg | Fiber: 1 g

Unrefined Oils

A majority of these recipes use unrefined extra-virgin olive oil because it is readily available. There are other types of unrefined oils that you may use in place of olive oil. A health food store should have a good selection. Be sure to check the label to make sure the oils are cold pressed, raw, and extra virgin. Some raw oils include sesame, sunflower, almond, evening primrose, flax, hemp, poppy seed, and coconut.

Cauliflower Couscous Salad

Couscous is a staple in Middle Eastern cuisine. It compliments the Fresh Falafels (page 192), the Tabouli Salad (page 94), and the Marinated Kale (page 85). Good substitutes for the hemp oil include flax oil, olive oil, sesame oil, or Udo's oil.

INGREDIENTS | SERVES 2

2 cups cauliflower

2 tablespoons lemon juice

1 tablespoon olive oil

½ teaspoon salt

1 tablespoon fresh parsley, or 1 teaspoon dried

1 tablespoon fresh mint, or 1 teaspoon dried

1 tablespoon fresh cilantro, or 1 teaspoon dried

½ teaspoon cumin

¼ cup chopped olives

1. Process the cauliflower in a food processor with the *S* blade until it is finely chopped and looks like little spherical granules. This serves as your couscous grain.

2. Pour the cauliflower couscous into a medium bowl and add the lemon juice, olive oil, and salt. Mix well.

3. Finely chop the parsley, mint, and cilantro.

4. Sprinkle the cumin onto the couscous and mix in the herbs.

5. Serve in a salad bowl and garnish with the olives.

PER SERVING:

Calories: 112 | Fat: 9 g | Protein: 2 g | Sodium: 758 mg | Fiber: 3 g

Couscous

Couscous is a tiny grain or pasta of semolina wheat that was traditionally made by hand. It has been used for centuries in northern Africa and the Middle East. Mixing the cauliflower with the lemon juice provides a texture similar to the grain.

Tabouli Salad

This recipe uses cauliflower to replace the traditional bulgur, which is a cooked grain. The lemon juice and salt help to soften up the parsley. It is sometimes served with cinnamon, allspice, oregano, and scallions.

INGREDIENTS | SERVES 2

¼ cup cauliflower

2 tablespoons lemon juice

2 teaspoons dried mint

1 teaspoon salt

1 teaspoon fresh ground black pepper

¼ cup olive oil

¼ cup parsley, finely chopped

2 cups tomato, finely chopped, seeds removed

1 cup cucumber, finely chopped

Tabouli

A popular Middle Eastern side salad found in most Arabic restaurants, tabouli is traditionally served with a platter that includes foods such as hummus, falafel, and baba ganoush.

1. In a food processor with an *S* blade, process the cauliflower into small pieces. It will look like rice.

2. Blend together the lemon juice, mint, salt, pepper, and olive oil until smooth. It can be stirred with a fork in a bowl or blended in a blender.

3. Place the cauliflower, parsley, tomato, and cucumber in a large salad bowl.

4. Pour half of the blended dressing onto salad and mix well by hand. Let it sit for 30 minutes to marinate.

5. When you are ready to serve the salad, mix it with the remaining dressing.

PER SERVING:

Calories: 293 | Fat: 28 g | Protein: 3 g | Sodium: 1,184 mg | Fiber: 3 g

Sunflower Raspberry Dressing

This is a delicious salad dressing to serve with the Arugula with Cranberries and Walnuts salad (page 79) or the Oranges with Fresh Greens salad (page 79). Macadamia nuts or pine nuts are good substitutes for the sunflower seeds.

INGREDIENTS | SERVES 2

½ cup sunflower seeds, soaked for 6 hours

1 cup raspberries

2 tablespoons lemon juice

¼ cup water

Place all the ingredients, except the water, into a blender and blend until smooth. Gradually add the water until the dressing reaches the desired consistency.

PER SERVING:

Calories: 240 | Fat: 18 g | Protein: 8 g | Sodium: 5 mg | Fiber: 7 g

Tarragon Tomato Salad Dressing

*This is a simple and delicious salad dressing.
The salt can be replaced with celery, miso, nama shoyu, or dulse.*

INGREDIENTS | SERVES 2

2 cups tomatoes

½ cup avocado

2 tablespoons fresh minced tarragon

½ teaspoon salt

1 clove garlic

Place all the ingredients into a blender and blend until smooth.

PER SERVING:

Calories: 96 | Fat: 6 g | Protein: 3 g | Sodium: 594 mg | Fiber: 5 g

Garlic Sprouts

Many garlic cloves have a little sprout or root growing in the middle. These sprouts have a bitter taste and may affect the flavor of the recipe. The sprouts can be removed by cutting the garlic clove in half and pulling out the sprout. Some people enjoy the taste of the sprout, while others prefer to toss them in the compost bin.

Cool Cucumber Salad Dressing

The cucumber supplies the liquid to help blend the cashews into a cream. More cucumber can be added for a thinner dressing, or add more cashews for a thicker sauce.

INGREDIENTS | **SERVES 2**

1 cup cucumber
1 cup cashews
2 tablespoons dill
¼ cup celery

Place all ingredients into a blender. Blend until smooth.

PER SERVING:

Calories: 375 | Fat: 29 g | Protein: 12 g | Sodium: 19 mg | Fiber: 3 g

Salad Dressing

Raw salad dressings are easy to prepare. Most of the bottled salad dressings in the grocery store contain unhealthy ingredients such as cooked vegetable oils and processed sugars. The two main ingredients of a salad dressing are the fat content and an acidic ingredient to emulsify the fat. Good choices for healthy fats include avocado, extra-virgin oil, nuts, or seeds. The acidic component may consist of lemon, lime, or orange juice; acidic fruits; apple cider vinegar; balsamic vinegar; or ume plum vinegar.

Ranch-Style Salad Dressing

This is a creamy recipe reminiscent of the popular ranch dressing. It is great as a salad dressing, a dip for vegetables, and a spread on wraps.

INGREDIENTS | **SERVES 4**

1 cup cashews
2 tablespoons lemon juice
2 tablespoons olive oil
2 tablespoons agave nectar
1 clove garlic
1 teaspoon onion powder
1 teaspoon dill
½ teaspoon sea salt

Place all the ingredients into a blender and blend until smooth.

PER SERVING:

Calories: 262 | Fat: 21 g | Protein: 6 g | Sodium: 295 mg | Fiber: 1 g

Dill

Dill is a perennial herb, popular in gourmet cooking, that was used by both the Egyptians and the Romans. It has an appearance similar to fennel, and both the dill seeds and the fresh, slender dill fronds can be used in cooking.

Spicy Sprout Salad Dressing

This can be used as a salad dressing, dip, or soup base. Radish sprouts taste just like radishes, and the sprouts are more nutritious. To create a dip using these ingredients, use less water and more avocado. Substitutes for the avocado include cashews, pine nuts, or macadamia nuts.

INGREDIENTS | SERVES 4

¼ cup radish sprouts

¼ cup alfalfa sprouts

1 tablespoon lemon juice

¼ cup avocado

½ cup red bell pepper

½ cup tomato

2–4 tablespoons water, as needed

Place all the ingredients into a blender and blend together until smooth. Pour over your favorite salad.

PER SERVING:

Calories: 27 | Fat: 2 g | Protein: 1 g | Sodium: 3 g | Fiber: 1 g

Preparing Sprouts

To prepare these sprouts, soak 3 tablespoons alfalfa seeds and radish seeds for 8 to 12 hours. Drain and rinse. Then transfer the seeds to a sprouter. Sprout for 5 days, and rinse the seeds two or three times a day. Rinse the sprouts to remove the hard hulls and they are ready to use.

CHAPTER 7

Breads, Crackers, and Snacks

Granola Bars

These are convenient snacks for traveling. They are good to have on hand when you need a quick bite to eat. They will keep for a month or two when stored in an airtight container at room temperature. Keep in mind, though, that the buckwheat needs to be sprouted for 24 hours first.

INGREDIENTS | SERVES 8

1½ cups dry buckwheat

1 cup almonds, soaked

½ cup dates or raisins, soaked for 1 hour

1 cup flaxseeds, soaked

½ cup young coconut meat

3 tablespoons raw honey or agave nectar

1 tablespoon pumpkin pie spice

2 teaspoons cinnamon

1. Soak the raw buckwheat groats in 4 cups water for 30 minutes. Drain, rinse, and sprout for 24 hours.

2. Using the *S* blade in a food processor, process all ingredients until well mixed. Do not over process—mixture should still be chunky.

3. Form mixture into rectangle bar shapes and place on dehydrator trays with nonstick sheets. Dehydrate at 145°F for 2 to 3 hours. Flip over the bars and continue dehydrating at 110°F for another 12 hours or until dry.

PER SERVING:

Calories: 367 | Fat: 19 g | Protein: 12 g | Sodium: 8 mg | Fiber: 12 g

Raw Trail Mix

This is a high-protein snack that is good when traveling. It will keep for up to two months in an airtight container stored at room temperature.

INGREDIENTS | SERVES 2

¾ cup dry buckwheat groats

1 cup almonds

1 cup green pumpkin seeds

3 tablespoons raw honey or agave

1 tablespoon carob powder

1 teaspoon cinnamon

1 cup dried fruit of your choice—goji berries, dried cherries, currants, and/ or raisins

Pepitas

Pumpkin seeds are also known as pepitas or "little seeds of squash." The seeds are good sources of protein, the essential minerals iron, zinc, manganese, magnesium, phosphorus, copper, and potassium, and provide essential polyunsaturated fatty acids (omega-3 fatty acids). Pumpkin seeds prevent hardening of the arteries and regulate cholesterol in the body. Some studies have found that pumpkin seeds also promote prostate health.

1. Soak the buckwheat for 6 hours and sprout for 1 day. Soak the almonds for 12 hours. Soak the pumpkin seeds for 4 hours.

2. Mix the buckwheat, almonds, and pumpkin seeds together and add the honey, carob, and cinnamon.

3. Spread the mixture onto dehydrator trays and dehydrate at 145°F for 2 hours. Lower temperature to 115°F and continue dehydrating for another 8 hours.

4. Add the dried fruit and mix well.

PER SERVING:
Calories: 1,217 | Fat: 73 g | Protein: 45 g | Sodium: 83 mg | Fiber: 23 g

Protein Nuggets

Spirulina is one of the most protein-rich foods on earth. This recipe is a crunchy snack that will sustain your energy levels for long periods of time. They are easy to travel with and will stay fresh for a few weeks when refrigerated.

INGREDIENTS | SERVES 4

2 cups sprouted buckwheat
1 cup dried coconut
1 cup pistachios
¼ cup dates, pitted and chopped
2 tablespoons honey
1 tablespoon spirulina
1 tablespoon carob

1. Soak the buckwheat for 6 to 8 hours. Drain and rinse until the water is clear.

2. Dehydrate the buckwheat until crunchy, about 6 hours at 110°F.

3. In a coffee grinder, grind the dried coconut to a flour.

4. In a food processor, process all ingredients together until well blended and chunky. Form into little square nuggets.

5. Dehydrate at 145°F for 2 hours. Turn down the temperature to 110°F and flip the nuggets. Continue dehydrating for 12 hours or until dry.

PER SERVING:
Calories: 528 | Fat: 25 g | Protein: 16 g | Sodium: 26 mg | Fiber: 12 g

Nut Crackers with Dip

This meal makes a great appetizer or snack. It is good served with the Sprouted Moroccan Lentil Soup (page 167) and the Jamaican Wrap Filling (page 191).

INGREDIENTS | SERVES 4

2 cups almonds

½ cup flaxseeds

1 teaspoon salt

4 tablespoons lemon juice

½ cup pine nuts

1 cup hazelnuts

¼ cup olive oil

1 clove garlic, minced

½ cup fresh basil, chopped

Garlic

Garlic is among the worlds most popular herbs. It has many culinary and medicinal uses. It is known for its ability to boost the immune system, cleanse the blood, help fight colds and viruses, and help clear the digestive tract of harmful bacteria.

1. Soak the almonds for 12 hours in water. Drain and rinse.

2. Grind the flaxseeds to a powder in a coffee grinder.

3. In a food processor, process the almonds, ground flaxseeds, ½ teaspoon salt, and 2 tablespoons lemon juice until smooth. Spread the cracker batter on dehydrator trays with nonstick sheets. Dehydrate at 115°F for 24 hours.

4. To prepare the dip, place the pine nuts, hazelnuts, olive oil, the remaining 2 tablespoons lemon juice and ½ teaspoon of salt, and the garlic in a food processor and process until smooth. Add the chopped basil and pulse until it is mixed into the dip.

PER SERVING:

Calories: 942 | Fat: 87 g | Protein: 26 g | Sodium: 589 mg | Fiber: 18 g

Grain and Seed Crackers

These are crunchy crackers that are good served with hummus dip, olive tapenade, and/ or pesto. They can be used to make a sandwich or crumbled into pieces to sprinkle on a salad. The crackers will stay fresh in airtight containers for 2 months.

INGREDIENTS | SERVES 6

1 cup buckwheat groats
1 cup sunflower seeds
½ cup flaxseeds
4 tablespoons agave nectar
1 teaspoon salt
2 tablespoons lemon juice
½ jalapeño pepper

1. Soak the buckwheat groats for 30 minutes. Rinse and drain. Soak the sunflower seeds for 1 hour. Rinse and drain. Soak the flaxseeds for 30 minutes in ½ cup water. Do not drain.

2. Place all ingredients in a food processor with an *S* blade and process until well mixed and chunky.

3. Spread the cracker batter on dehydrator trays with nonstick sheets and score into squares. Dehydrate at 145°F for 2 hours. Turn down heat to 110°F and dehydrate for 12 hours or until crunchy.

PER SERVING:
Calories: 330 | Fat: 19 g | Protein: 11 g | Sodium: 394 mg | Fiber: 9 g

Thai Spice Crackers

These crackers complement the Cashew Almond Pâté (page 142) and the Pad Thai with Almond Sauce (page 212) recipes. You can substitute about ¼ cup coconut water for the water and agave nectar.

INGREDIENTS | SERVES 4

2 cups sunflower seeds
½ cup ground flaxseed
½ cup young coconut meat
1 teaspoon curry powder or Thai seasoning blend
2 tablespoons water
2 tablespoons agave nectar
1 clove garlic, minced
½ teaspoon salt

1. Soak the sunflower seeds in water for 4 hours.

2. In a food processor with an *S* blade, blend all ingredients together until well mixed but still chunky.

3. Spread mixture onto dehydrator sheets with nonstick sheets. Dehydrate at 145°F for 2 hours. Flip crackers and continue dehydrating at 115°F for 12 hours until crunchy.

PER SERVING:
Calories: 543 | Fat: 45 g | Protein: 19 g | Sodium: 304 mg | Fiber: 12 g

Curry and Pumpkin Seed Crackers

These crackers are delicious served with the Pad Thai recipe on page 212.

INGREDIENTS | SERVES 8

1 cup flaxseeds

2 cups green pumpkin seeds

1 cup sunflower seeds

2 garlic cloves

1 tablespoon curry powder

¼ cup onion

¼ cup dates, pitted and chopped

1 teaspoon salt

1 cup orange juice

Green Pumpkin Seeds

Pumpkin seeds are highly nutritious and rich in protein, zinc, iron, magnesium, as well as omega-3, and omega-6 fats. There is evidence that pumpkins were raised in Mexico before 5,000 BCE.

1. Grind the flaxseeds into a powder using a coffee grinder.

2. In a food processor with an *S* blade, process together all ingredients into a smooth batter.

3. Spread the batter ¼-inch thick onto dehydrator trays with nonstick sheets. Score the batter with a spatula into square or triangle shapes.

4. Start dehydrating at 145°F. After 2 hours, turn the dehydrator down to 110°F.

5. After 4 hours, remove the nonstick sheet and flip the crackers. Continue dehydrating for an additional 8 to 12 hours.

PER SERVING:

Calories: 436 | Fat: 34 g | Protein: 16 g | Sodium: 306 mg | Fiber: 9 g

Sunflower Onion Crackers

This is a delicious cracker to serve with hummus dip.
It can be used to make a sandwich or crumbled onto a salad.

INGREDIENTS | SERVES 8

2 cups flaxseeds
2 cups sunflower seeds
4 cups sweet onions
½ cup olive oil
¼ cup nama shoyu
2 teaspoons fresh thyme

1. Grind the flaxseeds to a powder in a coffee grinder.

2. Grind the sunflower seeds in a food processor. Pour into a large mixing bowl and set aside.

3. Process the sweet onions in a food processor until they are small pieces.

4. Stir and mix all ingredients together in the mixing bowl.

5. Spread the mixture onto dehydrator trays with nonstick sheets. Dehydrate at 145°F for 2 hours. Lower the temperature to 110°F and continue dehydrating 8 to 12 hours. After 4 hours, flip the crackers onto mesh sheets and remove the nonstick sheets.

PER SERVING:
Calories: 447 | Fat: 40 g | Protein: 12 g | Sodium: 461 mg | Fiber: 9 g

Tomato, Basil, and Flax Crackers

*These crackers are good served with the Cashew Almond Pâté (page 142)
or the hummus recipes in Chapter 8.*

INGREDIENTS | **SERVES 4**

1 cup sunflower seeds

½ cup sun-dried tomatoes

2 cups flaxseeds

1 cup chopped fresh tomatoes

4 tablespoons fresh basil, chopped

½ cup celery, finely chopped

¼ cup dates, pitted and chopped

1 tablespoon jalapeño pepper, seeded and minced

2 tablespoons olive oil

2 teaspoons salt

1. Soak the sunflower seeds in water for 4 hours. Soak the sun-dried tomatoes for 3 hours.

2. Grind the flaxseeds into a coarse powder.

3. Set aside the flaxseeds, fresh tomato, and basil.

4. Process sunflower seeds, celery, sun-dried tomatoes, dates, jalapeño pepper, olive oil, and salt in a food processor with the *S* blade.

5. Add the tomato, basil, and ground flaxseeds into the food processor and pulse until all ingredients are well mixed.

6. Spread the mixture about ¼-inch thick onto dehydrator trays with nonstick sheets. Dehydrate at 145°F for 2 hours. Turn over the crackers and continue dehydrating at 115°F for an additional 8 hours.

PER SERVING:

Calories: 772 | Fat: 61 g | Protein: 24 g | Sodium: 1,345 mg | Fiber: 28 g

Zucchini Crackers

This is a good cracker to serve with a pâté, or use it to make a sandwich with the Veggie Burgers (page 199).

INGREDIENTS | SERVES 8

¾ cup dry buckwheat groats
2 cups flaxseed
½ cup sun-dried tomatoes
4 cups zucchini, peeled and diced
1 cup apple, chopped
½ cup onion, diced
½ cup olive oil
2 tablespoons lemon juice
3 tablespoons basil, minced

1. Soak the buckwheat groats for 30 minutes. Rinse and sprout for 1 day.

2. Grind the flaxseed to a powder with a coffee grinder. Soak the sun-dried tomatoes for 1 hour.

3. In a food processor, process together all ingredients, gradually adding the olive oil and lemon juice as it is processing. Add the basil last.

4. Spread the mixture onto dehydrator trays with nonstick sheets. Score the crackers into square shapes.

5. Dehydrate at 145°F for 2 hours. Turn down the heat to 110°F. After 4 hours, flip over the crackers onto mesh sheets and continue dehydrating for 6 more hours.

PER SERVING:
Calories: 430 | Fat: 32 g | Protein: 11 g | Sodium: 191 mg | Fiber: 15 g

Italian Crackers

These crackers are delicious served with the Raw Pasta with Cream Sauce (page 205).

INGREDIENTS | **SERVES 8**

2 cups flaxseed

½ cup sun-dried tomatoes

2 cups almonds

¼ tablespoon fresh diced cilantro or parsley

4 tablespoons lemon juice

2 tablespoons olive oil

1 tablespoon Italian seasoning

1 teaspoon salt

2 tablespoons fresh diced jalapeño pepper, to taste

Cilantro

Cilantro, also known as coriander, is both a culinary and medicinal herb. The whole plant is edible: the green leaves of cilantro are used in traditional Thai and Mexican cuisine, and the seeds are ground and used as the spice coriander. Natural health doctors report that cilantro has chelating effects, gently supporting the removal of heavy metals from the body.

1. Soak the flaxseed in 2 cups water for 6 to 8 hours. Soak the sun-dried tomatoes in 1 cup water for 2 hours.

2. Set aside the flaxseed. Using a food processor, blender, or heavy-duty juicer, process all the remaining ingredients into a batter. Pour the batter into a large mixing bowl and mix together with the flaxseed.

3. Spread the batter ¼-inch thick on dehydrator trays with nonstick sheets.

4. Start dehydrating at 145°F. After 2 hours, turn down the temperature to 110°F.

5. After 4 hours, remove the nonstick sheet and flip the crackers. Continue dehydrating for an additional 8 to 12 hours.

PER SERVING:

Calories: 472 | Fat: 39 g | Protein: 16 g | Sodium: 375 mg | Fiber: 16 g

Tortillas

This is a delicious Mexican dish that is good served with a scoop of Guacamole with Cilantro and Cumin (page 137) and Cashew Sour Cream (page 163).

INGREDIENTS | SERVES 4

2 cups young coconut meat

¼ cup red bell pepper, chopped

1 tablespoon beet juice

¼ teaspoon salt

½ cup Mexican Pâté (page 146)

1 cup Simple Salsa (page 135)

½ cup iceberg lettuce, shredded

Coconut Wraps

The dehydrated coconut meat mixture makes a soft and pliable tortilla wrap. You can add different colors of juice to change the colors of the wraps. Spinach juice will make green wraps, golden beet juice or turmeric will give them a golden color, and carrot juice will make them orange.

1. Prepare the burrito wraps the day before or the morning of, blending together the young coconut meat, red bell pepper, beet juice, and ¼ teaspoon salt.

2. Spread the burrito wrap mixture onto dehydrator trays with nonstick sheets. Dehydrate at 115°F for 4 hours.

3. Cut the burrito wraps into round tortilla shell shapes and lay flat on a dish.

4. Place 2–4 tablespoons of the Mexican pâté onto each wrap. Place a heaping spoonful of salsa onto each wrap. Top with iceberg lettuce.

5. Lightly moisten one edge of the wrap and roll up the burrito.

PER SERVING:

Calories: 67 | Fat: 3 g | Protein: 2 g | Sodium: 460 mg | Fiber: 2 g

Traditional Sprouted Essene Bread

This is a nutritious bread that can be eaten plain, with a nut butter spread, or used to make sandwiches. You can substitute other sprouted grains such as rye, barley, and kamut. For variation you can mix in fresh herbs or chopped vegetables such as celery, carrots, bell pepper, or beets.

INGREDIENTS | SERVES 4

2 cups wheat berries, sprouted 2 days

1½ cups water

2 tablespoons raw honey or agave nectar

1 tablespoon olive oil

1 teaspoon salt

Essene Bread

The Essenes were a Jewish religious group who lived from 200 BCE to AD 100. They were the first to create this sprouted-grain bread, which was dried in the hot desert sun. The sprouting process activates the enzymes in the grain and makes the grains easier to digest.

1. In a food processor with an *S* blade, grind the sprouted wheat and water together until a dough forms.

2. Mix in the honey, olive oil, and salt. Briefly process until all the ingredients are mixed together.

3. Spread the mixture with a spatula onto dehydrator trays with nonstick sheets. Spread the mixture evenly, about ½-inch thick, and score into squares.

4. Dehydrate at 145°F for 3 hours. Flip the bread over and continue dehydrating at 110°F for 8 hours.

PER SERVING:

Calories: 169 | Fat: 4 g | Protein: 4 g | Sodium: 592 mg | Fiber: 1 g

Apple Flax Bread

You may substitute other nuts and seeds in place of the sunflower seeds. Some good substitutes include green pumpkin seeds, almonds, and soaked buckwheat. A pear is a good replacement for the apple.

INGREDIENTS | SERVES 6

4 cups flaxseed

1 cup sunflower seeds

2 cups apple, chunked

½ cup dates, pitted

4 tablespoons olive oil

3 tablespoons lemon juice

2 tablespoons agave nectar

Flax

Flax is an annual plant with slender stems, green leaves, and most often pale blue flowers with five petals, though the flowers can sometimes be red as well. Flax is grown for its seeds and also for its fibers—parts of the plant have been used to make fabrics, paper, fishing nets, dye, and even soap. Flax is also a beautiful plant that can be grown for decorative purposes in a garden.

1. Grind 2 cups flaxseed into a powder with a coffee grinder. Soak the remaining 2 cups flaxseed for 2 hours in water.

2. In a food processor, blend together the flaxseed (both ground and whole) and all the remaining ingredients until mixed and still chunky. Spread mixture about ¼-inch thick onto dehydrator trays with nonstick sheets. Score the batter into squares with a spatula.

3. Dehydrate at 145°F for 2 hours. Flip over the bread and continue dehydrating at 110°F for 8 to 12 hours.

PER SERVING:

Calories: 898 | Fat: 68 g | Protein: 26 g | Sodium: 37 mg | Fiber: 35 g

Sweet Portuguese Bread

This bread is good with a pumpkin seed spread, and it is a tasty side dish to serve with the Asparagus Soup (page 133).

INGREDIENTS | SERVES 4

1 cup almonds

2 cups flaxseed

1 cup grated apple

2 tablespoons honey

2 tablespoons orange juice

2 teaspoons cardamon

½ teaspoon salt

½ cup Almond Milk (page 21)

Portuguese Holiday Bread

This is a variation on a specialty bread often made during the Easter and Christmas holiday seasons because it symbolizes rebirth. It is traditionally made with milk, sugar, and honey and shaped into round loaves.

1. Soak the almonds in water for 12 hours. Drain and rinse the almonds. Grind the flaxseed into a coarse powder with a coffee grinder.

2. Place all ingredients in a food processor with an *S* blade and process until well mixed. Add the flaxseed last. Mixture should be slightly thick and chunky.

3. Form the mixture into an oval-shaped loaf and slice into round, toast-sized pieces.

4. Place the round slices onto dehydrator trays with nonstick sheets. Dehydrate at 145°F for 3 hours. Flip the bread over and continue dehydrating at 110°F for 2 hours or until the desired texture is reached.

PER SERVING:

Calories: 737 | Fat: 56 g | Protein: 24 g | Sodium: 319 mg | Fiber: 28 g

Banana Bread

This bread makes a good snack and travel food. It can be used to make sandwiches, or with nut butter, eaten for breakfast.

INGREDIENTS | SERVES 6

2 cups ripe bananas

3 cups almond flour

¼ teaspoon salt

2 tablespoons liquid coconut oil

1 teaspoon vanilla extract

1 teaspoon cinnamon

1 cup flaxseed

1. In a food processor with an *S* blade, blend the bananas. Pour in the almond flour, salt, coconut oil, vanilla, and cinnamon and continue processing until well mixed.

2. Grind the flaxseed into a coarse powder with a coffee grinder.

3. Pour the processed mixture into a large bowl and stir in the ground flaxseed.

4. Put half the batter back into the food processor and mix briefly. Then remove and repeat the process with the second half of the mixture.

5. Spread the batter about ¼-inch thick onto dehydrator trays with nonstick sheets. Use a spatula to score the batter into squares.

6. Dehydrate at 145°F. After 2 or 3 hours, flip the bread over. Turn heat down to 110°F and continue dehydrating for 8 hours.

PER SERVING:
Calories: 556 | Fat: 44 g | Protein: 18 g | Sodium: 126 mg | Fiber: 17 g

Marinated Zucchini Strips

These are good snacks eaten alone, and they can also be used as pizza toppings and sandwich fillings. You can experiment using different herbs and spices. You can also marinate other vegetables that will soak up the marinade, such as mushroom, onion, eggplant, and bell peppers.

INGREDIENTS | SERVES 4

4 medium zucchini

6 tablespoons olive oil

1 tablespoon lemon juice

2 teaspoons salt

2 cloves garlic

⅛ teaspoon cayenne pepper

2 tablespoons fresh rosemary

Cayenne Pepper

Hot cayenne pepper is popular for both culinary and medicinal uses. The heat of this spice is rated from 30,000 to 50,000 Scoville units. Many herbalists consider cayenne their favorite herb due to its ability to improve blood circulation through the body, which also supports the delivery of nutrients.

1. Slice the zucchini into small, thin strips using a knife or mandolin slicer.

2. In a blender, process the olive oil, lemon juice, salt, garlic, cayenne pepper, and rosemary together into a sauce.

3. Dip each zucchini strip into the sauce and lay it flat on a dehydrator tray with a nonstick sheet.

4. Dehydrate at 145°F for 1 hour. Turn down the temperature to 115°F and continue dehydrating for 2 hours, until the zucchini is pliable.

PER SERVING:

Calories: 206 | Fat: 21 g | Protein: 2 g | Sodium: 1,176 mg | Fiber: 2 g

Rye Bread

This bread can be used to make sandwiches, served with a salad, or as croutons.
Spread on your favorite sauce or jam for a quick snack. Once dehydrated,
the rye bread will stay fresh in an airtight container for 3 to 4 weeks.

INGREDIENTS | SERVES 4

2 cups rye, sprouted 2 days
Water for blending
1 teaspoon caraway seeds
½ teaspoon coriander

1. In a food processor with an *S* blade, grind the sprouted rye to a dough. Add just enough water to help it blend. Alternatively, homogenize the rye with a heavy-duty juicer.

2. Stir in the caraway seeds and coriander.

3. Form the dough into small, flat, round loafs. Dehydrate at 145°F for 2 hours. Turn down the temperature to 110°F. Flip the bread over and continue dehydrating for 12 hours or until crisp.

PER SERVING:
Calories: 285 | Fat: 2 g | Protein: 13 g | Sodium: 5 mg | Fiber: 13 g

BBQ Chips

This is a great snack that has a flavor reminiscent of barbecue chips. The maple syrup can be replaced with dates, agave nectar, or honey. The vinegar can be replaced with lemon or lime juice. For the seasoning, you have the option of using a tablespoon of premixed barbecue seasoning blend.

INGREDIENTS | SERVES 4

½ cup sun-dried tomatoes
4 cups zucchini, thinly sliced
1 clove garlic
2 tablespoons olive oil
1 tablespoon apple cider vinegar
2 tablespoons maple syrup
½ tablespoon chili powder
2 teaspoons onion powder
1 teaspoon paprika

1. Soak the sun-dried tomatoes in water for 2 hours.

2. Set aside zucchini. Place all the remaining ingredients in a blender and blend together until smooth.

3. Place the zucchini into a casserole dish or large bowl and marinate in the prepared sauce for 2 hours.

4. Dehydrate the zucchini at 110°F for 4 hours or until crunchy.

PER SERVING:
Calories: 131 | Fat: 7 g | Protein: 3 g | Sodium: 164 mg | Fiber: 3 g

Marinated Eggplant Crisps

This is a good way to prepare eggplant—the salt and the dehydration process soften the eggplant and makes it crunchy. It is good served with the Veggie Burgers (page 199), or chopped into small chunks and served with the Raw Caesar Salad (page 81) and Corn Chowder (page 128).

INGREDIENTS | SERVES 6

1 large eggplant

2 teaspoons salt

¼ cup nama shoyu

2 tablespoons apple cider vinegar

2 tablespoons olive oil

2 tablespoons agave nectar

1 teaspoon cumin

½ teaspoon cayenne pepper

½ teaspoon ground allspice

Eggplant

Eggplants, native to India and nearby Southeast Asia, are a member of the nightshade family of plants, related to tomatoes, potatoes, and peppers. The eggplant fruit contains manganese, B vitamins, and folate.

1. Slice the eggplant into thin strips using a mandolin slicer or a sharp knife.

2. Rub salt onto the eggplant strips and let sit on a plate for 30 minutes.

3. In a blender, blend the remaining ingredients together into a sauce.

4. In a large bowl, mix together the eggplant and the prepared sauce. Let it marinate for 1 hour. (Once the eggplant is marinated, you can use the leftover marinade as a salad dressing.)

5. Place the marinated eggplant onto dehydrator trays with nonstick sheets. Dehydrate at 145°F. After 2 hours, flip over the eggplant and turn the dehydrator down to 110°F. The eggplant should be crispy and ready to eat after 12 hours.

PER SERVING:

Calories: 93 | Fat: 5 g | Protein: 2 g | Sodium: 1,378 mg | Fiber: 3 g

French Kale Chips

Kale is low on the glycemic index and rich in minerals.
If you have a garden, this is a great way to use the extra kale.

INGREDIENTS | SERVES 6

6 cups kale
¼ cup olive oil
¼ cup apple cider vinegar
½ teaspoon salt
2 tablespoons lemon juice
1 clove garlic
2 tablespoons herbes de Provence

Spice Blends

Every culture uses unique flavors, herbs, and spices in their cuisine. You can find good herb and spice blends at health food stores and online that reflect the cuisine of each culture, including Oriental, Mexican, Indian, Creole, and Thai cuisine. Spice blends can be used to season a wide variety of foods including soups, stews, sauces, pâtés, marinades, nori roll fillings, veggie burgers, and salad dressings. A flavorful blend can be an effective way to jump-start a good basic recipe.

1. Remove the stems from the kale and tear the leaves into big pieces. Place into a large bowl and set aside.

2. Place all the remaining ingredients, except the herbes de Provence, in a blender and blend until smooth. Add the herbes de Provence last and briefly pulse until well mixed.

3. Mix the sauce with the kale in a bowl. Use your hands to ensure the kale is well coated with the sauce.

4. Place the kale on dehydrator trays. Dehydrate at 115°F for 4 hours until dry.

PER SERVING:
Calories: 121 | Fat: 10 g | Protein: 2 g | Sodium: 224 mg | Fiber: 2 g

Pesto Kale Chips

This sauce is also good on zucchini noodle pasta, and the recipe should stay fresh for a couple weeks in an airtight container or zip-top bag.

INGREDIENTS | SERVES 4

6 cups kale
1 cup pine nuts
¼ cup nama shoyu
¼ cup lemon juice
¼ cup olive oil
1 tablespoon onion powder
1 clove garlic
½ teaspoon salt
¼ cup fresh chopped basil

1. Remove the stems from the kale and tear the leaves into big pieces. Place in a large bowl and set aside.

2. In a blender or food processor, blend all remaining ingredients, except the basil, until smooth. Add the basil last and briefly pulse until well mixed.

3. Mix the sauce with the kale. Use your hands to ensure the kale is well coated with the sauce.

4. Place the kale on dehydrator trays. Dehydrate at 115°F for 4 hours until dry.

PER SERVING:
Calories: 417 | Fat: 37 g | Protein: 9 g | Sodium: 1,235 mg | Fiber: 4 g

Curried Kale Chips

Kale, like broccoli, is a member of the brassicas family and has antioxidant, anti-inflammatory, and potent anticancer properties, particularly when chopped or minced.

INGREDIENTS | SERVES 6

6 cups kale
½ cup cashews, soaked 4 hours
4 tablespoons olive oil
4 tablespoons lemon juice
1 teaspoon curry powder
½ teaspoon turmeric
½ teaspoon salt
1 clove garlic

1. Remove the stems from the kale and tear the leaves into big pieces. Place in a large bowl and set aside.

2. In a blender or food processor, blend all remaining ingredients until smooth. You may need to add 1 tablespoon water to help the cashews blend.

3. Mix the sauce with the kale in a bowl. Use your hands to ensure the kale is well coated with the sauce.

4. Place the kale on dehydrator trays. Dehydrate at 115°F for 4 to 6 hours until crunchy.

PER SERVING:
Calories: 139 | Fat: 10 g | Protein: 4 g | Sodium: 225 mg | Fiber: 2 g

Spicy Marinated Nuts

*These are good snacks to travel with and will stay fresh
in the refrigerator for a couple of weeks.*

INGREDIENTS | SERVES 4

3 cups mixed nuts (Brazil nuts, cashews, walnuts, pecans, or almonds)
4 tablespoons agave nectar
2 tablespoons tamari
1 tablespoon cinnamon
¼ teaspoon cayenne pepper powder

1. Mix all ingredients together in bowl until the nuts are covered.

2. Let the nuts marinate for 3 hours at room temperature.

3. Pour off excess liquid and store nuts in an airtight container in the refrigerator.

PER SERVING:

Calories: 592 | Fat: 48 g | Protein: 18 g | Sodium: 508 mg | Fiber: 8 g

Coriander Chili Cashews

*This is a crunchy snack with a sweet and spicy flavor. It is a good snack
to travel with and will store for a month in airtight containers.*

INGREDIENTS | SERVES 4

2 cups cashews
¼ cup olive oil
3 tablespoons coriander seed powder
4 tablespoons agave nectar
2 teaspoons chili powder
1 teaspoon salt

1. Soak the cashews for 6 to 8 hours. Rinse and drain.

2. In a large mixing bowl, stir all ingredients together.

3. Spread the cashews onto dehydrator trays.

4. Dehydrate at 110°F for 24 hours or until the desired texture is reached.

PER SERVING:

Calories: 341 | Fat: 29 g | Protein: 6 g | Sodium: 599 mg | Fiber: 2 g

Coriander

Coriander is the seed of the cilantro plant. It is available in whole seed or powder form. It has an aromatic flavor with hints of lemon and sage that make it perfect for pâtés and sauces.

Sunflower Crunch

This is a spicy snack that will satisfy your desire for crunchy food. After it is dehydrated, it will stay fresh for a couple weeks when stored in an airtight glass jar. Flavorful seasonings that can be added to the marinade include jalapeño pepper, basil, or minced garlic.

INGREDIENTS | SERVES 6

4 cups sunflower seeds

½ cup olive oil

½ cup nama shoyu

¼ cup water

4 tablespoons lemon juice

Soaking and Sprouting

Many of these recipes require soaking and sprouting. Soaking the nuts and seeds improves the flavor, makes them softer, removes the bitter tannins, and increases the amount of vitamins. Soaking activates the life force and turns raw food into living food. Make it a habit to soak your nuts, seeds, and grains in the evening before you go to bed. They will be ready to use immediately the next morning. Alternatively, they can be stored in the refrigerator until dinner, or left at room temperature to sprout.

1. Soak the sunflower seeds in water for 6 to 8 hours. Drain and rinse.

2. Set aside the sunflower seeds. In a blender, blend all remaining ingredients together until smooth.

3. Place the sunflower seeds into a large bowl. Pour in the prepared marinade and let the seeds soak for 3 hours.

4. Drain the marinade. Spread the seeds in a single layer on dehydrator trays. Dehydrate at 145°F for 2 hours. Turn down heat to 110°F and continue dehydrating for 24 hours or until desired dryness is reached.

PER SERVING:

Calories: 589 | Fat: 53 g | Protein: 20 g | Sodium: 309 mg | Fiber: 8 g

CHAPTER 8

Soups, Salsas, and Dips

Spanish Chile

This recipe is good served with Chipotle Sprout Wraps (page 168) and Tomato, Basil, and Flax Crackers (page 107). You can select your favorite onion for this recipe—red onions, scallion, or sweets onions would work well.

INGREDIENTS | SERVES 4

½ cup soaked sun-dried tomatoes
1 cup red bell pepper, chopped
2 cups tomatoes, diced
1 clove garlic
1 teaspoon cumin
2 teaspoons chili powder
1 teaspoon oregano
¼ cup onion, diced
1 cup lentils, sprouted 2 days

1. Soak the sun-dried tomatoes in 2 cups water for 3 hours. Remove tomatoes and save the soak water.

2. In a blender, blend the sun-dried tomatoes, red bell pepper, 1 cup tomato, garlic, cumin, chili powder, oregano, and 1 cup of the soak water from the sun-dried tomatoes.

3. In a large mixing bowl, mix together the prepared sauce, onion, remaining 1 cup tomato, and lentils. The dish will keep for 2 days in the refrigerator.

PER SERVING:

Calories: 103 | Fat: 1 g | Protein: 7 g | Sodium: 166 mg | Fiber: 3 g

Lentils

Lentils are a small legume popular in Middle Eastern and Indian cuisine, valued by vegetarians as a good, inexpensive source of protein, fiber, B vitamins, iron, magnesium, and phosphorus. They are one of the first cultivated foods and have been found at archeological sites dating back 8,000 years. Lentils are also described in stories and parables found in the Old Testament of the Bible.

Gazpacho Soup

This is a light, refreshing, summertime soup. It is good mixed with diced vegetables such as celery, onion, red bell pepper, zucchini, and avocado.

INGREDIENTS | SERVES 4

3 cups tomatoes, diced
2 cups cucumber, peeled and diced
1 cup red bell pepper, diced
1 tablespoon apple cider vinegar
¼ cup onion, diced
1 clove garlic
2 tablespoons olive oil (or sesame or flaxseed oil)
2 tablespoons lemon juice
2 tablespoons fresh chopped basil
2 tablespoons fresh chopped parsley (for garnish)

1. Set aside the basil and parsley.

2. In a food processor with an *S* blade, process 2 cups tomato, 1 cup cucumber, ½ cup bell pepper, apple cider vinegar, onion, garlic, olive oil, and lemon juice until well blended but still chunky.

3. Add the basil and briefly pulse the food processor.

4. Pour the soup into a bowl and mix with the remaining diced vegetables. Cover the bowl and place in the refrigerator for 2 hours to chill.

5. Pour into soup bowls and garnish with parsley and optional diced vegetables.

PER SERVING:

Calories: 113 | Fat: 7 g | Protein: 2 g | Sodium: 12 mg | Fiber: 3 g

Gazpacho Soup

The recipe for gazpacho originated in Spain. This raw vegetable soup is usually served cold in the summertime. It is especially delicious when tomatoes are in season.

Sea Veggie Energy Soup with Sprouts

This is a nourishing, mineral-rich green soup that will leave you satisfied and full of energy. Whole dulse is one of the more flavorful of the sea vegetables. Use a variety of sea vegetables for extra minerals. The sunflower green sprouts can be substituted with your favorite leafy greens.

INGREDIENTS | SERVES 2

¼ cup whole dulse or 1 tablespoon powdered dulse

1 cup apple, chopped

2 cups sunflower green sprouts

½ cup pine nuts

1 cup water

½ cup avocado, chopped

Sunflower Seeds

Sunflower seeds are a staple in the raw foods diet. They are one of the most widely used foods because they are inexpensive, readily available, nutritious, and easy to use. The unhulled sunflower seeds still have the shell, and they are used to grow baby green lettuce in your sprouter. The hulled seeds have the shell removed and are excellent ingredients to use in sauces, smoothies, pâtés, trail mix, and granola. They tend to have the most flavor if they are soaked for 6 to 8 hours.

1. Soak the whole dulse for 5 minutes in water and drain. If you are using other sea vegetables, most of them needs to be soaked for about 30 minutes. The powder does not need to be soaked.

2. Place all the ingredients, except the avocado, in a blender and blend until smooth. Briefly blend in the avocado last.

PER SERVING:
Calories: 169 | Fat: 7 g | Protein: 5 g | Sodium: 943 mg | Fiber: 6 g

Fresh Vegetable Soup

This is a satisfying soup. The spinach provides the base, and the lemon juice helps balance the taste of the spinach. The tomato and cucumber provide the liquid base, and the avocado makes it creamy. You can make a variation of this soup without the spinach. Garnish with fresh herbs such as basil and/or mint.

INGREDIENTS | SERVES 4

¾ cup tomatoes, chopped

1 cup celery hearts, chopped

1 cup cucumber, chopped

½ cup red bell pepper, chopped

½ cup avocado, chopped

4 tablespoons lemon juice

1 cup spinach

½ teaspoon salt

¼ teaspoon cayenne pepper (optional)

¼ cup water as needed

1 teaspoon paprika

1. Place the tomatoes, celery, cucumber, red bell pepper, avocado, and lemon juice in a high-speed blender or an S-blade food processor. Briefly process for approximately 30 seconds. If you have a conventional blender, juice the celery first or omit it.

2. Add the spinach, salt, cayenne pepper, and water to the blender. Blend until smooth. Serve in soup bowls and garnish with a pinch of paprika.

PER SERVING:
Calories: 57 | Fat: 3 g | Protein: 2 g | Sodium: 322 mg | Fiber: 3 g

Paprika

Paprika is a popular spice made from ground dried bell peppers. It is a great source of vitamin C and antioxidants. The rich color enhances the visual appeal of foods, and it has a sweet spiciness that is great in stews and sauces.

Corn Chowder

This soup is a good appetizer for many of the entrées. You can replace the agave nectar with other sweeteners such as raw honey or dates.

INGREDIENTS | SERVES 4

1 cup raw macadamia nuts

1 cup walnuts, soaked 4 to 6 hours

2–4 tablespoons olive oil

¼ teaspoon cayenne pepper powder

2 tablespoons agave nectar

½ clove garlic

½ teaspoon salt

3 cups water

2 cups fresh corn

1 cup zucchini, peeled and cut into 1½-inch cubes

¼ cup celery, diced

2 tablespoons fresh thyme

1. Create the soup base by blending the macadamia nuts, walnuts, olive oil, cayenne, agave nectar, garlic, salt, and water.

2. Pour the soup base into a large bowl and stir in the corn, zucchini, celery, and thyme.

PER SERVING:

Calories: 596 | Fat: 52 g | Protein: 10 g | Sodium: 317 mg | Fiber: 8 g

Chowder

A chowder is a thick and creamy soup. It is commonly made with potatoes and seafood. There is a variation called Manhattan chowder, which is a red soup base made with tomato. This chowder uses nuts for the cream and zucchini replaces the potatoes.

Creamy Tarragon Soup

This is a satisfying soup that is quick and easy to prepare. The jalapeño pepper can be replaced with other fresh or dried peppers. The tarragon can be replaced with other fresh herbs you have on hand.

INGREDIENTS | SERVES 2

½ cup zucchini, peeled and chopped

1 tablespoons minced jalapeño pepper

1 clove garlic, minced

2 tablespoons fresh tarragon or 1 teaspoon dried tarragon

2 tablespoons lime juice

1 cup water

1 cup avocado, chopped

1. Place all ingredients except the avocado and water in a blender and blend.

2. Gradually add the water, ¼ cup at a time, until it becomes smooth. Add the avocado last and blend until creamy.

PER SERVING:

Calories: 132 | Fat: 11 g | Protein: 2 g | Sodium: 9 mg | Fiber: 6 g

Butternut Curry Soup

This is a delicious soup to serve with the Thai Green Papaya Salad (page 86).
You may substitute ground fenugreek powder for the fenugreek sprouts.
Almond milk or young coconut water are good substitutes for the water.

INGREDIENTS | SERVES 2

1 cup cucumber, chopped

2 cups butternut squash, peeled and chopped

½ cup red bell pepper, chopped

1 cup pine nuts

¼ cup leeks, diced

2 teaspoons fresh minced or grated ginger

1½ teaspoons curry or cumin powder

¼ teaspoon salt

¼ teaspoon cayenne pepper powder

Water for blending

1. In a food processor, blend the cucumber until it's liquefied, and then add the squash.

2. Gradually add the remaining ingredients to the food processor and blend until smooth. Add small amounts of water gradually, if needed.

3. Let the soup sit for 15 minutes before eating, to enhance the flavor.

PER SERVING:

Calories: 577 | Fat: 47 g | Protein: 14 g | Sodium: 311 mg | Fiber: 9 g

Curry

Curry is a blend of spices popular in Southeast Asia and India. It commonly contains warm spices, including red pepper, cumin, and turmeric, a deep orange-yellow powder with many medicinal properties.

Herbed Kohlrabi Soup

Kohlrabi is a vegetable in the cabbage and turnip family. Both the bulbs and leafy greens of the kohlrabi can be eaten raw. The tough outer skin of the bulb can be peeled away to reveal the sweet, delicate, and crunchy texture.

INGREDIENTS | SERVES 6

2 kohlrabi bulbs
¼ cup kohlrabi greens
1 cup Almond Milk (page 21)
3 cups water
2 tablespoons olive oil
1 teaspoon salt
¼ cup scallions, minced
1 tablespoon fresh thyme or 1 teaspoon dried thyme
2 tablespoons fresh tarragon or 1 teaspoon dried tarragon
½ teaspoon nutmeg
¼ cup grated beets for garnish

1. Peel the outer skins of the kohlrabi bulbs with a paring knife. Grate ½ cup of the kohlrabi bulbs and set aside for garnish.

2. Blend all ingredients together except the grated kohlrabi and beets.

3. Pour into soup bowls and garnish with the grated kohlrabi and beets.

PER SERVING:
Calories: 104 | Fat: 8 g | Protein: 3 g | Sodium: 411 mg | Fiber: 3 g

Kohlrabi
The kohlrabi bulb can be eaten whole like an apple, or it can be processed into a recipe. This vegetable is a great source of complex carbohydrates and dietary fiber, thiamin, vitamin C, folate, magnesium, and potassium.

African Cauliflower Soup

This is a spicy soup that is good served with a scoop of nut cream and garnished with fresh herbs. Good substitutions for the avocado include cashews, macadamia nuts, pine nuts, or young coconut meat.

INGREDIENTS | SERVES 4

1 cup jicama, peeled and diced
2 cups cauliflower, chopped
1 cup tomatoes, diced
½ cup cucumber, peeled and chopped
½ cup sweet onions, diced
2 tablespoons olive oil
1 teaspoon cumin
½ teaspoon cinnamon
2 tablespoons lemon juice
½ cup avocado, chopped
1 cup water
½ teaspoon salt
½ tablespoon fresh ginger
3 tablespoons fresh cilantro

1. Set aside ¼ cup jicama and ½ cup cauliflower to add at the end for a chunky texture.

2. Blend all remaining ingredients together until puréed. The avocado will create a creamy texture.

3. Garnish the soup with diced cauliflower and jicama.

PER SERVING:

Calories: 136 | Fat: 10 g | Protein: 2 g | Sodium: 315 mg | Fiber: 5 g

Shchi Cabbage Soup

In this traditional soup, the vegetable juice creates a tasty broth base. If you don't have a juicer, you can simply blend the whole foods in a high-powered blender with extra water. Shchi Soup is often made with sauerkraut blended in.

INGREDIENTS | SERVES 2

1 cup cucumber juice
½ cup celery juice
½ cup cabbage juice
¼ cup daikon radish juice (optional)
4 tablespoons grated onion
½ cup grated green cabbage
with 1 tablespoon lemon juice
or ½ cup chopped tomato with
1 tablespoon miso

1. Pour the cucumber, celery, cabbage, and radish juices into a large bowl. Stir in the miso or lemon juice.

2. Add remaining ingredients to the bowl. Mix the vegetable juices with the chunks of vegetables. Serve in soup bowls.

PER SERVING:

Calories: 41 | Fat: 0 g | Protein: 2 g | Sodium: 31 g | Fiber: 1 g

Shchi Soup

Shchi is a soup that is popular in Russia. It is usually made with winter vegetables and is good warmed up on the stove or in a dehydrator to 110°F.

Ginger, Fennel, and Pear Soup

The avocado gives the soup a rich, creamy texture, which can be complemented nicely with finely chopped fresh herbs and soft vegetables for a garnish. This soup tastes delicious served warm. Drizzle on a little Ranch-Style Salad Dressing (page 96) for a nice presentation.

INGREDIENTS | SERVES 2

2 cups pear, cored and chopped

1 teaspoon ginger, juice or minced

1 cup fennel bulb, chopped

2 tablespoons lemon or lime juice

¼ teaspoon salt

1 clove garlic (optional)

1 teaspoon paprika

1 cup zucchini (optional garnish)

Fennel

Three parts of the fennel plant are used in gourmet cooking: the bulb, the leaves, and the seed. This is a tangy, delicious vegetable, rich in many phytonutrients, vitamins, and minerals including vitamin C, potassium, and folate.

1. Place the pears into a blender or food processor and blend until smooth—the pear provides a liquid base for the soup. Add either 1 teaspoon minced ginger or ginger juice; blend until mixed.

2. Add all the remaining ingredients, except the paprika and zucchini, and blend until smooth. You may need to add a little water to achieve a smooth texture.

3. If you'd like, you can garnish soup with cubes of chopped zucchini. Stir in the zucchini cubes and sprinkle the paprika on top.

PER SERVING:

Calories: 102 | Fat: 0 g | Protein: 1 g | Sodium: 315 mg | Fiber: 6 g

Thick and Chunky Asparagus Soup

This quick recipe can be prepared in just a few minutes (with easy cleanup). You may substitute olive oil, hemp oil, or Udo's oil in place of the flaxseed oil. If you don't have the chipotle powder, you can use a jalapeño or serrano pepper, cayenne pepper powder, or any other type of hot pepper as seasoning.

INGREDIENTS | SERVES 4

1½ cups avocado

2 tablespoons flaxseed oil

1 tablespoon lime juice

2 tablespoons onion, minced

½ tablespoon fresh chopped rosemary or 1 teaspoon dried

½ tablespoon fresh chopped oregano or 1 teaspoon dried

¼ teaspoon chipotle powder

Water to achieve the desired texture

1 cup Roma tomatoes, chopped

½ cup asparagus tips, sliced fine

1. Place avocado, flaxseed oil, lime juice, onion, rosemary, oregano, and chipotle powder in a blender and blend until smooth and creamy. You may need to add a little water to achieve the desired consistency.

2. Pour into 4 soup bowls and garnish with the tomatoes and asparagus.

PER SERVING:

Calories: 165 | Fat: 15 g | Protein: 2 g | Sodium: 7 mg | Fiber: 5 g

Flaxseed Oil

This nutritious oil is one of the best plant sources of omega-3 essential fats. Flaxseed oil should never be used for cooking because it becomes rancid quickly when exposed to heat and oxygen. The least stable of all oils, it must be stored in a dark container in the refrigerator at all times and consumed within a few weeks after opening the bottle. Research has found that combining flaxseed oil with a high-protein food such as cottage cheese, spirulina, or bee pollen provides healing benefits.

Nut and Berry Soup

A delicious soup base can be made with any soft nut such as soaked walnuts or young coconut meat. It is a flavorful, light fruit-based soup with a little heat. If you'd like, garnish with orange or tangerine slices.

INGREDIENTS | SERVES 2

½ cup cashews or walnuts, soaked
1 tablespoon olive oil
1 cup orange juice
1 pint blueberries
¼ teaspoon cayenne pepper powder

1. In a blender or a food processor with an *S* blade, process the nuts and olive oil. Add the orange juice and process once more.

2. Add blueberries and cayenne and process until mixture is smooth.

PER SERVING:
Calories: 383 | Fat: 22 g | Protein: 8 g | Sodium: 7 g | Fiber: 5 g

Carrot Ginger Soup

This is a colorful soup rich in antioxidants and phytonutrients. The pine nuts make it creamy and smooth, but you can also achieve this effect with cashews or young coconut meat.

INGREDIENTS | SERVES 2

1 cup carrot juice
1 cup cucumber, chopped
½ cup pine nuts
2 tablespoons fresh chopped cilantro
1 tablespoon fresh grated ginger
½ cup shredded carrots, for garnish

1. In a blender, add the carrot juice, cucumber, pine nuts, cilantro, and ginger and blend until smooth.

2. Garnish with the shredded carrots and serve.

PER SERVING:
Calories: 281 | Fat: 23 g | Protein: 6 g | Sodium: 22 mg | Fiber: 2 g

Simple Salsa

This is a basic, mild salsa. Most of the heat is in the seeds of the jalapeño, so if you want a mild salsa, discard the seeds. This is a good recipe to serve with burritos and tacos for a Mexican theme.

INGREDIENTS | SERVES 4

4 cups tomatoes, diced

½ cup white or red onion, diced

2 teaspoons salt

2 fresh jalapeño peppers, diced

Stir all the ingredients together in a bowl. Chill the salsa in the refrigerator for 1 hour to let the flavors marinate.

PER SERVING:

Calories: 43 | Fat: 0 g | Protein: 2 g | Sodium: 1,173 mg | Fiber: 3 g

Spicy Salsa

This spicier version of the Simple Salsa (above) uses cayenne pepper and garlic to add heat. Using fresh cayenne pepper in place of the powder creates a fresh flavor—use 1 tablespoon of the pepper, rather than the ½ teaspoon powdered. If you like hot foods, use a little habanero pepper and extra garlic.

INGREDIENTS | SERVES 4

4 cups tomatoes, diced

¼ cup white or red onion, diced

1 teaspoon salt

1 jalapeño pepper, diced

½ teaspoon cayenne pepper powder

1 teaspoon cumin

2 tablespoons lemon juice

1 tablespoon lemon zest

2 tablespoons cilantro, diced

1 clove garlic, minced

Stir all ingredients together in a bowl. Let the mixture sit for 10 minutes in the refrigerator so the flavors can marinate.

PER SERVING:

Calories: 48 | Fat: 1 g | Protein: 2 g | Sodium: 593 mg | Fiber: 3 g

Onions

Onions have been used in food preparation since the Bronze Age, 7,000 years ago. In contemporary raw foods cuisine, red onions, scallions, shallots, garlic, and chives are especially good complements because they are mild and flavorful. Red onions have a pleasant sweetness and can be sliced paper thin in salads and vegetable dishes, while other varieties can be served diced or minced.

Mango Salsa

*A sweeter version of salsa, which is good served with wraps and with Mexican pâté.
This salsa can also be used as a dip with slices of vegetables such as cucumber, celery, or zucchini.*

INGREDIENTS | SERVES 2

½ cup tomato, diced
1 cup fresh mango, seeded and diced
¼ cup white or red onion, diced
¼ cup diced cucumber
¼ teaspoon salt
½ tablespoon minced jalapeño pepper
1 tablespoon lime juice
2 tablespoons minced fresh cilantro

Stir all the ingredients together in a bowl and let the mixture sit for 10 minutes in the refrigerator to marinate.

PER SERVING:

Calories: 77 | Fat: 0 g | Protein: 1 g | Sodium: 296 mg | Fiber: 3 g

Mango Salsa

Mango salsa is refreshing, with a pleasant balance of sweet and spicy flavors. The mango provides a flavorful alternative to spicy salsa.

Tomato and Corn Salsa

This is a delicious sauce that goes well with a Mexican theme, good served with burritos and tacos, or as a salad dressing. Remember to choose white sweet corn for this recipe, which has a better flavor raw than the yellow variety.

INGREDIENTS | SERVES 4

3 cups cherry tomatoes, chopped in halves
½ cup sweet corn, cut fresh off cob
½ teaspoon salt
1 tablespoon jalapeño pepper, minced
1 tablespoon fresh ginger, minced
1 tablespoon lime juice
1 clove garlic, minced
¼ cup chopped fresh cilantro
1 tablespoon olive oil

In a large bowl, stir together all ingredients until chunky.

PER SERVING:

Calories: 71 | Fat: 4 g | Protein: 2 g | Sodium: 300 mg | Fiber: 2 g

Guacamole with Cilantro and Cumin

This is a nutritious food that is delicious served with burrito wraps, flax crackers, and as a dip for sliced vegetables.

INGREDIENTS | SERVES 4

2 cups avocado

1 clove garlic, minced

2 tablespoons lemon juice

¼ teaspoon salt

⅛ teaspoon cayenne pepper powder

1 teaspoon cumin

½ cup tomato, diced

¼ cup red or white onion, diced

2 tablespoons chopped fresh cilantro

1. Using a mortar and pestle, or a fork, mash the avocado with the minced garlic, lemon juice, salt, cayenne, and cumin. Alternately, you can prepare the guacamole in a bullet blender and pulse it until you get the desired texture.

2. Add tomato and onion to avocado mixture and stir together; garnish with fresh cilantro leafs.

PER SERVING:

Calories: 132 | Fat: 11 g | Protein: 2 g | Sodium: 8 mg | Fiber: 6 g

Raw Burritos

Although burritos originated in Mexico almost a hundred years ago, like pizza they've become great American standards. In raw food cuisine, you can create burrito wraps with young coconut meat or cabbage leaves. Traditional toppings you'll find in the book include salsas such as tomato, tomato and corn, or mango. Fillings seasoned with sun-dried tomatoes and jalapenos are ideal and include the Mexican pate, cashew almond pate, and spicy pate. Good replacements for sour cream include almond yogurt and sunseed cheese.

Tahini

This is a quick and easy way to make your own tahini in less than a minute. When you grind the seeds fresh, the flavor is improved. Fresh tahini can be used in salad dressings, as a spread in wraps, in sauces, and in any recipe that calls for tahini.

INGREDIENTS | SERVES 1

2 tablespoons sesame seeds

1 teaspoon sesame or olive oil

Pinch of salt (optional)

Pinch of cayenne, Italian seasoning, or raw chocolate (optional)

1. Grind the seeds to a powder in a coffee grinder or spice mill. Continue grinding until the seeds stick together and adhere to the walls of the grinder.

2. Remove from the grinder, add a small amount of oil (just enough to become smooth and creamy), stir with a fork, and add any desired seasoning.

PER SERVING:

Calories: 143 | Fat: 13 g | Protein: 3 g | Sodium: 2 mg | Fiber: 2 g

Tahini

Tahini is a paste made with sesame seeds, similar to a nut butter. Sesame seeds are high in protein and healthy fats, and are one of the richest sources of calcium available. For a nice variation in color, use black sesame seeds.

Zucchini Hummus

Zucchini replaces the traditional garbanzo beans in this recipe. It is good served as a dip for flax crackers and as a spread in sandwiches or burritos.

INGREDIENTS | SERVES 4

2 cups zucchini, peeled and sliced

1 clove garlic

4 tablespoons Tahini (above)

2 tablespoons lemon juice

2 tablespoons olive oil

1 teaspoon paprika, for garnish

2 tablespoons parsley, for garnish

1. In a food processor with the *S* blade, process the zucchini, garlic, tahini, lemon juice and olive oil until smooth.

2. Place in a serving bowl and garnish with the paprika and parsley.

PER SERVING:

Calories: 160 | Fat: 14 g | Protein: 4 g | Sodium: 19 mg | Fiber: 2 g

Garbanzo Bean Hummus

This is a delicious hummus pâté made with sprouted garbanzo beans. Macadamia nuts make a great substitution for the garbanzo beans. Inspect the garbanzos after soaking and discard any that are still hard. This recipe is good as a spread on flax crackers and a condiment in burrito wraps.

INGREDIENTS | SERVES 4

1 cup garbanzo beans
¼ cup Tahini (page 138)
1 clove garlic, minced
¼ cup lemon juice
1 tablespoon jalapeño pepper, minced
½ teaspoon cumin
½ teaspoon salt
¼ cup olive oil, as needed for consistency

1. Soak the garbanzo beans in 5 cups water for 12 hours. Drain and rinse.

2. Sprout the garbanzo beans for 12 hours. Rinse them a couple times during the sprouting process.

3. In a food processor with an *S* blade, process all ingredients except the olive oil. Gradually add the olive oil until the mixture becomes creamy.

PER SERVING:

Calories: 393 | Fat: 24 g | Protein: 12 g | Sodium: 315 mg | Fiber: 10 g

Garbanzo Beans

Garbanzo beans, also called chickpeas, are the traditional ingredient in hummus and falafel. They are a great source of protein and fiber and high in folic acid as well as the minerals molybdenum, manganese, copper, phosphorus, and iron. Garbanzos originated in the Middle East, where they are a staple food.

Baba Ganoush

A good recipe to serve with any of the falafel recipes in Chapter 12 and Tabouli Salad (page 94). Soaking the eggplant in salt water softens it and creates a texture similar to roasted eggplant. Another popular method for softening the eggplant is to slice it into thin strips, freeze it overnight, and thaw.

INGREDIENTS | SERVES 4

2 cups eggplant, sliced thin

3 tablespoons lemon juice

2 tablespoons Tahini (page 138)

1 clove garlic, minced

1 teaspoon cumin

½ teaspoon black pepper

Salt to taste

1 teaspoon paprika, for garnish

1 teaspoon olive oil, for garnish

2 tablespoons fresh chopped parsley, for garnish

Baba Ganoush

Baba ganoush is a popular Middle Eastern pâté and dip made from eggplant and spices. It is a wonderful complement to hummus and has a similar texture.

1. Place eggplant strips in a bowl or casserole dish and cover with 2 cups salt water. Add 1 teaspoon salt for every cup of water. Soften the eggplant by soaking it overnight in salt water in the refrigerator for 6 to 12 hours.

2. Drain the eggplant.

3. Place the eggplant, lemon juice, tahini, garlic, cumin, black pepper, and salt in a food processor with an *S* blade, and process until smooth.

4. Pour mixture into serving bowls, sprinkle on paprika and drizzle a little olive oil on top. Garnish with fresh parsley.

PER SERVING:
Calories: 59 | Fat: 4 g | Protein: 2 g | Sodium: 8 mg | Fiber: 2 g

CHAPTER 9

Pâtés and Nut Butters

Cashew Almond Pâté

This is a good pâté to serve with the Gazpacho Soup (page 125) and Tomato, Basil, and Flax Crackers (page 107). Fresh tahini or sunflower seeds make a good substitute for the almond butter. You could substitute cilantro for parsley. This recipe is also delicious made with just the cashews alone.

INGREDIENTS | SERVES 4

2 cups cashews, soaked but crunchy

¼ cup soaked almonds or almond butter (optional)

¼ cup sun-dried tomatoes, soaked

1 tablespoon Italian seasoning

2 tablespoons cilantro or parsley, minced

1 clove garlic, minced

1 tablespoon jalapeño pepper, minced

¼ cup lemon juice

Soak the cashews for 3 hours, or soak them in the fridge so they're still crunchy. Process all ingredients in a food processor until smooth and creamy.

PER SERVING:

Calories: 392 | Fat: 29 g | Protein: 13 g | Sodium: 150 mg | Fiber: 3 g

Cashews

Originating in Brazil, cashews are now cultivated worldwide, and more than 3 million tons are grown each year. These delicious nuts are high in healthy natural fats and low in cholesterol, so they serve as a good base for pâtés and creamed dishes. Cashews also provide a balance of protein to carb content and are a rich source of magnesium, phosphorus, and trace minerals.

Almond Garlic Pâté

This is a recipe for a basic raw pâté. You may substitute other nuts and seeds to vary the flavor. This recipe has many uses: as a spread on crackers or flatbread, a dip for celery sticks, or a filling in nori rolls, burritos, or wraps. This same recipe can be used to make crackers by dehydrating it.

INGREDIENTS | SERVES 2–4

2 cups almonds, soaked

1 cup cashews, soaked but crispy

¼ cup celery hearts or fennel bulb, chopped

4 tablespoons red or white onion, or scallions, chopped

2 tablespoons lemon juice

2 cloves garlic

¼ teaspoons salt

Soak the almonds and cashews in water for 8 to 12 hours. Blend all the ingredients together in a food processor using the *S* blade, or homogenize it using a heavy-duty juicer.

PER SERVING:

Calories: 521 | Fat: 44 g | Protein: 19 g | Sodium: 151 mg | Fiber: 11 g

Pâté

This is high-protein staple on a raw foods diet. This basic pâté will stay fresh for a week in the refrigerator because the salt and lemon juice help preserve it. Take the pâté to work with a salad for a satisfying lunch. When you are ready to use the pâté, take out 1 cup and keep the rest in the refrigerator. Mix 1 cup of the pâté with your favorite spices for a different flavor at each meal.

Zesty Italian Walnut Pâté

This pâté is good served with the Greek Salad (page 146).
Almond butter is a good substitute for the tahini.

INGREDIENTS | SERVES 4

2 tablespoons sesame seeds, ground
fresh, or raw tahini

1 teaspoon olive oil

2 cups walnuts, soaked

¼ cup sun-dried tomatoes

½ cup red bell pepper, chopped

¼ cup raw olives, pit removed

4 tablespoons cilantro

1 tablespoon Italian seasoning

¼ teaspoon salt

2 cloves garlic

Sun-Dried Tomatoes

In Italy before modern canning and food production, tomatoes were sun dried for use during the winter. It takes 20 pounds of fresh tomatoes to produce just 1 pound of sun-dried tomatoes, which explains the concentrated flavor they impart to foods ranging from salads to pasta sauces. If you have a dehydrator, during tomato season you can cost-effectively prepare your own sun-dried condiments.

1. Soak the walnuts for 6 to 10 hours. Soak the sun-dried tomatoes for 4 hours, reserving the soak water.

2. To make the tahini, grind the sesame seeds in a coffee grinder. Transfer the ground seeds to a food processor and blend with olive oil.

3. In a food processor, process walnuts and tahini with the *S* blade until smooth.

4. Add all remaining ingredients to the food processor and process until smooth. Pour in a ¼ cup of the soak water from the sun-dried tomatoes for a more intense tomato flavor.

PER SERVING:

Calories: 432 | Fat: 41 g | Protein: 10 g | Sodium: 294 mg | Fiber: 6 g

Heirloom Tomatoes with Spicy Pâté

Serve these tomato stacks with the Carrot Ginger Soup (page 134) and a side of Mashed Taters (page 220). If you don't have heirloom tomatoes on hand, you can make this recipe in a ramekin, layering the Pâté with cherry tomatoes, large slicing tomatoes, or sweet sugar plum tomatoes that are sliced in half.

INGREDIENTS | SERVES 4

½ cup sesame seeds (ground) or sunflower seeds (soaked)

½ cup almonds, soaked

4 sun-dried tomatoes, soaked and chopped

½ tablespoon jalapeño pepper, minced

2 tablespoons lemon juice

1 tablespoon basil, minced

2 cups heirloom tomatoes, sliced thick

1. Place all the ingredients, except the heirloom tomatoes, into a food processor with an *S* blade and process until smooth.

2. Place a layer of tomato slices onto a plate. Place a scoop of the pâté onto each tomato slice. A good option is to serve this with Tomato, Basil, and Flax Crackers (page 107) or Italian Crackers (page 109).

PER SERVING:
Calories: 248 | Fat: 18 g | Protein: 13 g | Sodium: 47 mg | Fiber: 4 g

Heirloom Seeds

There are thousands of heirloom fruit and vegetable plants that are not sold in stores. The fruits have a short shelf life and go bad a few days after picking. To find affordable heirloom produce, you'll either want to shop your local farmers' market or grow them yourself. The company Seeds of Change has one of the largest collections of heirloom seeds available for purchase.

Greek Salad with Macadamia Nut Pâté

A traditional Greek salad is simply cucumber, tomato, onion, olive, and feta cheese. In this recipe, the macadamia nut pâté replaces the feta cheese. If you are not vegan, you could use feta or a raw organic cheese. The macadamia pâté can also be dried in the dehydrator at 115°F for 2 hours for a drier consistency.

INGREDIENTS | SERVES 2

½ cup macadamia nuts

2 teaspoons Italian seasoning

1 cup cucumber, thinly sliced

1 cup tomato, chopped

½ cup red onion, sliced thin

¼ cup kalamata olives

2–4 tablespoons olive oil, to taste

Olives

Olives are nutrient-rich fruits rich in oleic acid, vitamins A and E, calcium, and magnesium.

1. Process the macadamia nuts and Italian seasoning into small chunks or a dense nut meal using a food processor with the *S* blade. The goal is to achieve a texture similar to crumbled feta cheese.

2. Place the sliced cucumber on a large plate. Put the tomato, onion, and olives on the cucumber slices.

3. Top the salad with the macadamia pâté and drizzle with olive oil.

PER SERVING:

Calories: 415 | Fat: 41 g | Protein: 4 g | Sodium: 152 mg | Fiber: 6 g

Mexican Pâté

This is a great pâté to serve with other Mexican cuisine, including tacos and burritos. Fresh chili peppers may be used in place of the chili powder.

INGREDIENTS | SERVES 4

2 cups soaked sunflower seeds

1 cup corn, fresh cut off cob

¼ cup red or white onion, diced

2 tablespoons lime juice

½ teaspoon oregano

½ teaspoon cumin

½ teaspoon chili powder

¼ teaspoon salt, to taste

1 cup tomato, diced

Grind the sunflower seeds in a food processor until smooth. Add the remaining ingredients, except the tomatoes, and process until chunky. Add the tomatoes and pulse briefly.

PER SERVING:

Calories: 320 | Fat: 25 g | Protein: 12 g | Sodium: 159 mg | Fiber: 6 g

Sweet Corn

Corn is the most widely grown crop in America. Sometimes called maize, it is a cereal grain that is a staple crop in many cultures with uses as both a food and a biofuel. Sweet corn is delicious raw, eaten right off the cob or sliced off the ear and included in vegetable dishes and salads. When making dehydrated crackers or tortillas, frozen corn works better than fresh.

Mushroom Pâté

Good substitutes for the crimini mushrooms include shiitake, maitake, reishi, or white button mushrooms. If you don't have portobello mushrooms on hand, you can replace them with more crimini mushrooms. If you have mushroom allergies, you can replace the mushrooms with nuts and seeds.

INGREDIENTS | SERVES 4

1 cup almonds
¼ cup black sesame seeds
1 cup portobello mushrooms
½ cup crimini mushrooms
2 tablespoons nama shoyu
1 tablespoon grated ginger
1 teaspoon sage
1 teaspoon thyme
¼ teaspoon salt
Scant ¼ teaspoon cayenne pepper powder

1. Soak the almonds in water for 12 hours. Soak the black sesame seeds in water for 1 hour. Drain and rinse.

2. Process the almonds and sesame seeds in a food processor with an *S* blade until well broken down. Add remaining ingredients and process until well blended.

PER SERVING:

Calories: 427 | Fat: 36 g | Protein: 15 g | Sodium: 603 mg | Fiber: 9 g

Crimini Mushrooms

Crimini mushrooms are a nutritious food rich in selenium, zinc, B vitamins, potassium, copper, and phosphorus. They are also rich in phytonutrients, which help protect the body from disease.

Vanilla Almond Butter

This recipe is great on celery sticks with raisins. It works well in desserts with dates and carob powder. The nut butter can also be spread on flax crackers with the Apricot Jam (page 232).

INGREDIENTS | SERVES 6

2 cups almonds, soaked
2 tablespoons olive, sesame, or flax oil
½ teaspoon salt
1 teaspoon vanilla extract

1. Homogenize the almonds in a masticating juicer. Alternatively, process the almonds in a food processor with an *S* blade until the almonds stick to the walls.

2. Gradually add in the olive oil, salt, and vanilla until creamy.

PER SERVING:

Calories: 296 | Fat: 26 g | Protein: 10 g | Sodium: 194 mg | Fiber: 6 g

Almond Butter

It is difficult to create the same smooth consistency and texture of the almond butter sold in stores. The companies that make almond butter use heavy-duty machines to homogenize the nuts. However, a food processor or masticating juicer will create a creamy nut butter that comes close to the texture of the store-bought variety.

Garam Masala Nut Butter

This nut butter is exceptional served with flax flatbread
and a glass of Basic Green Juice (page 40).

INGREDIENTS | SERVES 2

1 cup macadamia nuts

½ cup young coconut meat

4 tablespoons ground sesame seeds (optional)

½ teaspoon salt

1 teaspoon garam masala spice

½ teaspoon paprika or ¼ cup cilantro, diced

1. Place the macadamia nuts, young coconut meat, and sesame seeds if desired in a food processor with an *S* blade and process until the nut butter is well mixed and chunky.

2. Add the garam masala spice, salt, and either paprika or diced cilantro. Blend again and serve.

PER SERVING:
Calories: 496 | Fat: 51 g | Protein: 6 g | Sodium: 585 mg | Fiber: 6 g

Garam Masala

Garam Masala is a popular spice blend for Indian and Middle Eastern cuisine. The exact blend varies by country. It commonly includes cloves, cardamon, cinnamon, cumin, and star anise.

Black Pepper Cashew Butter

This is a good spread to use on flax crackers or sliced vegetables. It can also be used as a salad dressing when blended with water. Olive oil or flax oil is a good substitute for the sesame oil.

INGREDIENTS | SERVES 6

2 cups cashews, soaked

2 tablespoons sesame oil

½ teaspoon salt

1 teaspoon black pepper (to taste)

1 tablespoon agave nectar

Black Pepper

Black peppercorns are one of the most popular of all spices and are found on dinner tables throughout the world. This pungent spice originated in India and has been used as a seasoning for thousands of years. The peppercorns are the fruit or berries from the pepper plant, cultivated in black, white, red/pink, and green varieties. Peppercorns lose flavor and aroma after being ground into a powder, so freshly ground peppercorns have a stronger flavor.

1. Soak the cashews for at least 6 hours, drain, and rinse. For this recipe, you want the cashews to be quite moist so they provide a creamy texture.

2. Homogenize the cashews in a masticating juicer. Alternatively, use a food processor with an *S* blade. Process the cashews until they are smooth.

3. Stir in the sesame oil, salt, black pepper, and agave nectar.

PER SERVING:
Calories: 294 | Fat: 24 g | Protein: 8 g | Sodium: 199 mg | Fiber: 2 g

Pumpkin Seed Butter

*This butter is surprisingly good. It has a creamy, salty flavor
that makes an excellent vegetable dip.*

INGREDIENTS | SERVES 6

2 cups green pumpkin seeds, soaked
2 tablespoons olive oil
1 tablespoon agave nectar
½ teaspoon salt

Pumpkin Seeds

The seeds of the pumpkin are good
sources of the essential fats omega-6 and
omega-9. They are also high in vitamins A,
E, and C; the mineral zinc; and phytosterols. Phytosterols are plant phytochemicals
that have been found to help lower
cholesterol.

1. Soak the pumpkin seeds for 8 to 12 hours. Drain and
   rinse.

2. Homogenize the seeds in a masticating juicer.
   Alternatively, use a food processor with an *S* blade.
   Process the pumpkin seeds until they are smooth, and
   gradually add the olive oil while processing.

3. Add the agave nectar and salt to the food processor
   and blend until smooth, or stir with a fork.

PER SERVING:

Calories: 299 | Fat: 26 g | Protein: 11 g | Sodium: 202 mg | Fiber: 2 g

Coconut Butter

*You can make this spread using just the coconut meat and oil, for a lightly sweet flavor. The addition of
minced garlic produces a classic garlic butter. Both variations are good as a spread on crackers, flat
bread, or corn on the cob. Without the garlic, this can also be used in dessert recipes as a cream.*

INGREDIENTS | SERVES 4

½ cup coconut oil
2 cups young coconut meat
¼ teaspoon salt
1 teaspoon minced garlic (optional)

1. Place the jar of coconut oil in warm water until it
   becomes liquid.

2. Add all ingredients to a blender and blend together
   until smooth.

3. Place the mixture in a storage container and
   refrigerate for 1 hour until it becomes solid.

PER SERVING:

Calories: 137 | Fat: 15 g | Protein: 0 g | Sodium: 145 mg | Fiber: 0 g

Chocolate Hazelnut Spread

Use this spread for cakes and pies or as a tasty dip for fresh berries and bananas. It also works well on flax crackers or as a sandwich condiment. Other nuts can be substituted for the hazelnuts, including pistachios, macadamia nuts, and cashews. A pinch of cayenne powder adds just the right element of heat.

INGREDIENTS | SERVES 4

2 cups hazelnuts

2 tablespoons liquid coconut oil or cacao butter

Water to achieve desired texture

½ cup raw cacao powder

2 tablespoons agave nectar

1 teaspoon vanilla extract

½ teaspoon salt

Hazelnuts

Hazelnuts, also called filberts, are a nutritious nut rich in protein, beneficial fats, B vitamins, vitamin E, zinc, potassium, magnesium, and calcium. In the United States they are grown mostly in California and Washington.

1. Process the hazelnuts in a food processor with an *S* blade until they become a powder. Gradually add the coconut oil or cacao butter and continue processing until smooth. (These oils are usually in solid form, so they add stability to the spread.) You may need to add a little water to achieve a smooth consistency.

2. Add remaining ingredients and process until smooth.

PER SERVING:

Calories: 575 | Fat: 50 g | Protein: 13 g | Sodium: 294 mg | Fiber: 11 g

CHAPTER 10

Gourmet Vegetarian Yogurts and Cheese

Dairy Kefir

Kefir is a fermented milk beverage, similar to yogurt. It is good blended with fresh fruit and served in a tall glass, or in a bowl mixed with the Granola Bars (page 100). Store the kefir grain in dairy milk in the refrigerator. You may discard the milk that you store the grain in.

INGREDIENTS | SERVES 4

1 quart milk

1 package kefir grains

2 tablespoons agave nectar or raw honey

1 cup fresh blueberries

Kefir Grains

Kefir grain is a beneficial bacteria, or probiotic, that is used to culture milk. The culturing process predigests the milk to some degree and makes it easier to more fully digest the milk and assimilate the vitamins.

1. Fill up a glass jar with the milk. Place the kefir grain and agave nectar in the milk and put a cheesecloth over the jar opening. Use a rubber band to fasten the cheesecloth to the jar.

2. Let the milk mixture sit at room temperature for 12 hours.

3. After 12 hours, pour the milk through a strainer to strain out the kefir grains.

4. Place the strained milk into a blender and blend it with the blueberries until smooth.

PER SERVING:
Calories: 198 | Fat: 8 g | Protein: 8 g | Sodium: 98 mg | Fiber: 1 g

Almond Milk Kefir

Kefir grains can be used to culture nut milk, seed milk, and fresh juices.
This milk is good blended with fresh fruits or served with the Granola Bars (page 100).

INGREDIENTS | SERVES 4

1 quart Almond Milk (page 21)
1 package kefir grains
2 tablespoons agave nectar
1 cup strawberries

1. Pour the Almond Milk into a glass jar. Add the kefir grains into the milk and put a cheesecloth over the opening. Use a rubber band to fasten the cheesecloth to the jar.

2. Let the milk sit at room temperature for 12–24 hours. It cultures faster in the warm summer weather.

3. Pour the milk through a strainer to strain out the kefir grains.

4. Place the milk, agave nectar, and the strawberries in a blender and blend until smooth and serve.

PER SERVING:
Calories: 281 | Fat: 21 g | Protein: 8 g | Sodium: 11 mg | Fiber: 1 g

Dairy Yogurt

It's easy to make homemade yogurt with a good yogurt maker. Use organic whole milk so you can rest assured that it doesn't have hormones, pesticides, or sweeteners.

INGREDIENTS | SERVES 6

1 quart milk

1 teaspoon yogurt starter

3 cups fresh peaches, sliced

2–4 tablespoons agave nectar, to taste

½–1 teaspoon cinnamon, to taste

Dairy Yogurt

Yogurt has been eaten since ancient times, and it is often referenced in the Bible. It is an excellent source of probiotics, which help to maintain a healthy balance of flora in the digestive tract. In some cases, it can be eaten by lactose-intolerant people. Yogurt is a good source of protein, vitamin A, and calcium.

1. Warm milk on the stove, but do not boil it. Remove it from the stove before it boils.

2. With a liquid thermometer, check the temperature. When the milk is between 98°F and 116°F, add the yogurt starter culture and stir until all the powder is dissolved.

3. Place the milk and culture in a yogurt maker and let it culture for 9 to 15 hours, until the mixture thickens to a pudding-like texture.

4. Pour the yogurt into serving bowls. Place the peaches on top. The unused yogurt can be stored in a glass or plastic container.

5. Drizzle the agave nectar and cinnamon on top of the peaches.

PER SERVING:

Calories: 150 | Fat: 6 g | Protein: 6 g | Sodium: 75 mg | Fiber: 1 g

Almond Yogurt

This yogurt is good blended in a shake, served with a salad, or wrapped in a nori roll or burrito. It is delicious mixed with seasonings such as herbs, spices, young coconut meat, dill, or chives. A good replacement for the miso is 1 teaspoon probiotic powder, or Rejuvelac.

INGREDIENTS | SERVES 2

2 cups raw almonds

2 cups water or young coconut water

½ teaspoon salt

1 tablespoon miso or 1 teaspoon probiotic powder

Probiotics

Probiotics are the good bacteria naturally found in the digestive tract. Benefits of eating probiotic foods include improved digestion and absorption of nutrients, fewer harmful bacteria, and increased levels of certain nutrients.

1. Soak the almonds in water for 12 to 24 hours. Drain the water and replace with fresh water after 6 hours.

2. Drain and rinse the almonds. Blend them with water or young coconut water, salt, and miso or the probiotic powder until creamy.

3. Place mixture into a yogurt maker, or use a glass jar and cover the opening with a cheesecloth. Fasten cheesecloth to the jar with a rubber band or string.

4. Let the mixture sit at room temperature for 6 to 8 hours, then serve.

PER SERVING:

Calories: 393 | Fat: 72 g | Protein: 33 g | Sodium: 1,152 mg | Fiber: 21 g

Seed Cheese

This is the basic recipe for cultured cheese. Once the cheese is made, you can blend in your favorite herbs and seasonings to improve the flavor. Nuts and seeds that produce a flavorful cheese include sunflower seeds, sesame seeds, green pumpkin seeds, almonds, macadamia nuts, pine nuts, and cashews.

INGREDIENTS | SERVES 2

1 cup sunflower seeds
1 cup water
1 teaspoon probiotic powder

Nut Yogurt

A probiotic starter culture contains billions of microscopic beneficial bacteria that pre-digests the nuts and creates a flavor similar to cultured yogurt or sour cream. Probiotics are considered beneficial because they are essential for healthy digestion.

1. Soak the sunflower seeds in 2 cups water for 6 to 8 hours. Drain and rinse.

2. Blend the sunflower seeds with 1 cup water and the probiotic powder.

3. Transfer the sunflower seeds to a glass jar. Let sit at room temperature for 8 to 12 hours. Bubbles will form.

4. The cheese will separate from the liquid whey. Pour out the whey. If you stop here, you have a usable cultured seed cheese that resembles conventional cheese, with a sour and tangy taste.

5. If you want a product that resembles a cream cheese, you'll want to add this last step. Put the cheese in a nut milk bag or sprout bag and squeeze out the remaining liquid. Hang the bag over the sink for 4 hours or longer to culture it. Then store the cheese in an airtight container in the refrigerator.

PER SERVING:

Calories: 409 | Fat: 36 g | Protein: 15 g | Sodium: 9 mg | Fiber: 6 g

Almond Cheese

The turmeric gives this a cheddar cheese color. The miso has beneficial bacteria that cultures the almonds and gives them a pleasant, tangy flavor. One teaspoon probiotic powder is a good substitute for the miso.

INGREDIENTS | SERVES 4

2 cups almonds
1 tablespoon miso
½ cup water
½ teaspoon turmeric
1 teaspoon nutritional yeast
1 tablespoon lemon juice

Nut Cheese

Culturing and fermenting nuts and seeds creates a rich, creamy texture and flavor that mimics dairy cheese.

1. Soak the almonds for 8 to 12 hours. Drain and rinse. Stir together the miso and water with a spoon.

2. In a food processor with an *S* blade, process the almonds until smooth.

3. Add the remaining ingredients and continue processing until smooth. Alternatively, you may homogenize all ingredients in a heavy-duty juicer.

4. The cheese may be eaten immediately. Alternatively, place the cheese in a glass jar and cover with a cheesecloth. Let it sit at room temperature for 4 to 6 hours to culture.

PER SERVING:

Calories: 426 | Fat: 36 g | Protein: 16 g | Sodium: 168 mg | Fiber: 9 g

Almond Cheese with Garlic and Dill

In this recipe, the almonds are prepared just as they begin to sprout, at a point of maximum life force in the plant. Any type of good probiotic powder from the vitamin department will work in this recipe.

INGREDIENTS | SERVES 4

2 cups almonds

1 clove garlic, minced

2 tablespoons dill, chopped

½ cup water

½ teaspoon probiotic powder

Almonds

Almonds are an excellent source of protein, fiber, calcium, and vitamin E. Raw almonds also tend to have a subtle cleansing effect and are highly valued for their health benefits.

1. Soak almonds in water between 12 to 16 hours. Drain water after 6 hours and replace with fresh water.

2. Drain and rinse almonds. Place them in a food processor with the garlic, dill, water, and probiotic powder and process with the *S* blade until smooth.

3. Place mixture into a glass jar and cover the opening with a cheesecloth. Use a rubber band to secure cheesecloth to the jar.

4. Let it sit at room temperature for 6 to 8 hours and then serve.

PER SERVING:

Calories: 412 | Fat: 35 g | Protein: 15 g | Sodium: 2 mg | Fiber: 9 g

Sunflower Seed Cheese Spread

Serve with sandwiches and burritos. You can eat it plain, or dehydrate for a few hours for a chewy texture. This is a good spread on crackers, wraps, nori rolls, or collard rolls. You can add 1 tablespoon minced fresh herbs such as dill, chives, oregano, tarragon, parsley, or cilantro or 1 teaspoon dried herbs.

INGREDIENTS | SERVES 4

2 cups hulled sunflower seeds
5 cups water
1 clove minced garlic
1 teaspoon probiotic powder
½ teaspoon salt

Seed Cheese

The seed cheeses will stay fresh in the refrigerator for up to one week. They are good served as a topping on crackers, pizza, and tomato stacks.

1. Soak the sunflower seeds in 3 cups water for 8 to 12 hours. Drain and rinse.

2. Blend the sunflower seeds with the remaining 2 cups water, the minced garlic, probiotic powder, and salt until creamy. If desired, you may also blend in your favorite spice or fresh minced herb.

3. Place this sunflower seed mixture into a yogurt maker, or place in a glass jar. Fasten a cheesecloth over the jar opening.

4. Let your cheese culture sit at room temperature for 6 to 8 hours.

5. The cheese and liquid whey will separate. Pour off the liquid whey and discard it. Place cheese into a nut milk bag and squeeze out the remaining liquid. Your culture will then be the texture of cream cheese. At this point you are ready to use it as a spread.

6. Store the cheese in an airtight container in the fridge.

PER SERVING:
Calories: 205 | Fat: 18 g | Protein: 7 g | Sodium: 151 mg | Fiber: 3 g

Sunflower Seed Cheese Spread with Jalapeño

This recipe is a variation on the basic recipe for Sunflower Seed Cheese Spread (page 161). By comparing them, you'll gain a sense of how you can vary fresh cuisine and also adapt it to the traditional palate of other cultures. You can add a little more dulse or diced vegetables such as red bell pepper.

INGREDIENTS | SERVES 4

2 cups sunflower seeds, soaked

¼ cup black sesame seeds (could be soaked if desired)

¾ cup pine nuts

1 tablespoon olive oil

Water to achieve the desired consistency

1 tablespoon diced jalapeño pepper, seeds removed

1 tablespoon nama shoyu

2 teaspoons dulse sea vegetables (flakes)

1. Grind the sunflower seeds, sesame seeds, pine nuts, and olive oil in a food processor. Gradually add the water and process until smooth. The water will determine the consistency—you want the spread to resemble a thick cream cheese.

2. Place the jalapeño, nama shoyu, and dulse into the food processor and process until ingredients are mixed well and still chunky.

3. This spread is ready to eat immediately and does not require culturing.

PER SERVING:

Calories: 665 | Fat: 61 g | Protein: 20 g | Sodium: 248 mg | Fiber: 8 g

Pine Nut Cheese

*This is a great recipe that can be made in less than 30 minutes.
You can serve this cheese with veggie burgers or pasta.*

INGREDIENTS | SERVES 4

2 cups pine nuts
½ cup cashews
¾ cup water
½ teaspoon salt
1 teaspoon nutritional yeast

Nutritional Yeast

Nutritional yeast is a popular condiment and supplement in the vegan diet because it contains all the essential amino acids and the full spectrum of B vitamins. It works well as a seasoning in vegan cheese substitutes, on popcorn, in scrambles, and mixed into trail mix. Nutritional yeast is available in most health food stores.

1. Process all ingredients in a food processor until smooth.

2. You can use this spread right away, and it has a texture that resembles cream cheese. If you want it to taste more like a hard cheese, spread the mix onto dehydrator trays and dry at 145°F for 1 to 2 hours.

PER SERVING:
Calories: 550 | Fat: 53 g | Protein: 13 g | Sodium: 295 mg | Fiber: 3 g

Cashew Sour Cream

*This is delicious served with wraps, sandwiches, taco salad, collard wraps, and chile con carne.
To achieve a more tart flavor, the blended cream can be mixed with 1 tablespoon miso,
Rejuvelac, or ½ teaspoon probiotic powder. Let the cream sit at room temperature for 6 to 8 hours.*

INGREDIENTS | SERVES 2

1 cup cashews, soaked
1 cup water
2 tablespoons lemon juice
½ teaspoon garlic powder
½ teaspoon onion powder

Garlic and Onion Powder

Garlic and onion are essential seasonings in many recipes. The dry powder is less pungent than fresh and should be used when you don't want their flavors to overwhelm the recipe.

In a food processor or high powered blender, blend all ingredients into a thick and smooth cream. Add a little more water if needed.

PER SERVING:
Calories: 373 | Fat: 29 g | Protein: 12 g | Sodium: 9 mg | Fiber: 2 g

CHAPTER 11

Homegrown Sprouts and Cultured Foods

Chinese Kung Pao Almonds with Mung Bean Spouts

This is a great recipe that can be made in less than 30 minutes. This is essentially a mock stir-fry, a delicious, spicy dish seasoned with a raw version of traditional hoisin sauce. Garnish with diced scallions and julienned Asian vegetables of choice. This dish is good served with cauliflower rice.

INGREDIENTS | **SERVES 4**

1 cup almonds

¼ cup nama shoyu

¼ cup sesame oil

4 tablespoons chopped dates (optional)

½ tablespoon chopped fresh hot peppers (cayenne, jalapeño, chili)

½ clove garlic

1 tablespoon grated ginger

1 cup mung bean sprouts

1 cup additional chopped veggies (asparagus tips, chopped green or red bell peppers, celery, and cherry tomatoes)

¼ cup Jerusalem artichokes, sliced paper thin

Almonds

Almonds are a staple in the raw foods diet. They are rich in protein, healthy fats, vitamin E, magnesium, and calcium. California is the world's largest producer of almonds. The almond skin contains a bitter tannin, which is removed by soaking the almond in water. You can speed up the process of removing the tannins by soaking the almonds in warm water for one hour.

1. Soak the almonds for 8 to 12 hours in 4 cups of water. Drain and rinse.

2. Using a blender, prepare the hoisin sauce by blending together nama shoyu, sesame oil, dates, hot peppers, garlic, and ginger.

3. Using a food processor with an *S* blade, pulse the almonds until chunky.

4. In a bowl, stir together the almonds, mung bean sprouts, assorted veggies, artichokes, and prepared sauce.

5. Dehydrate mixture at 110°F for 3 hours and serve warm.

PER SERVING:

Calories: 359 | Fat: 31 g | Protein: 10 g | Sodium: 907 mg | Fiber: 6 g

Sprouted Moroccan Lentil Soup

To speed up prep time, use mung sprouts from the store in place of homegrown lentil sprouts, fresh raw almonds (without soaking them), and sun-dried tomatoes, available marinated in olive oil. This soup can be made with a chunky or smooth texture. Serve with couscous and salad.

INGREDIENTS | SERVES 2

½ cup sun-dried tomatoes, soaked

1 cup almonds, soaked

3 cups water

1 cup lentil sprouts

¼ cup dulse (optional)

2 tablespoons lemon juice

1 teaspoon cinnamon

1 teaspoon cumin

Pinch of salt

½ teaspoon turmeric

1 tablespoon miso (optional)

1 cup portobello or crimini mushrooms, diced

1. Blend the sun-dried tomatoes and almonds with 3 cups water until smooth. Add in the lentil sprouts, dulse, lemon juice, cinnamon, cumin, salt, and turmeric and blend until smooth. As an option, you could add 1 tablespoon miso at this point.

2. If you want the soup to have a chunky texture, save out ½ cup of the sprouted lentils.

3. Pour soup into serving bowls and stir in the diced Portobello (or reserved ½ cup whole lentil sprouts).

4. Garnish with fresh herbs such as cilantro or parsley.

PER SERVING:
Calories: 521 | Fat: 36 g | Protein: 23 g | Sodium: 383 mg | Fiber: 14 g

Cumin

Cumin is a culinary spice native to Syria, the Middle East, and India. It is a seed with a strong, spicy flavor popular in gourmet cuisine. It is commonly used in spice blends such as curry, chili powder, and garam masala.

Chipotle Sprout Wrap

This is a great recipe that can be made in less than 30 minutes. This is a delicious wrap served with guacamole and salsa. If you'd like you can add miso to the macadamias, or you could substitute a little salt or dulse sea vegetable in place of the miso.

INGREDIENTS | SERVES 4

1 cup macadamia nuts

2 tablespoons olive oil

1 tablespoon fresh chipotle pepper, or
1 teaspoon chipotle powder

2 tablespoons lemon juice

Water for blending

4 collard leaves, stemmed

1 cup mung bean sprouts

1 cup red bell pepper, sliced into strips

2 tablespoons minced fresh mint,
for garnish

1. Blend the macadamia nuts, olive oil, chipotle, and lemon juice together. Slowly add a little water until it blends into a creamy sauce.

2. To assemble the wrap, lay the collard leaves flat. Spread a layer of macadamia cream onto the leaves. Place some sprouts, red bell pepper, and mint on one end of the leaves and roll tightly.

3. This works well with different fresh herbs to replace the mint, such as minced cilantro, parsley, or rosemary. You could also garnish the wrap with julienned carrots and jicama for some extra crunch.

PER SERVING:

Calories: 329 | Fat: 32 g | Protein: 4 g | Sodium: 10 mg | Fiber: 5 g

Mung Bean Sprouts

Also called Chinese bean sprouts, these are the most popular sprouts in the world. They are readily available in most grocery stores. Mung beans are a protein-rich legume high in the minerals zinc, calcium, iron, magnesium, and potassium, and in vitamins A, B, C, and E. Mung sprouts can also be grown at home right in your kitchen.

Pecan Sprout Loaf

This is a good recipe to serve on a bed of lettuce with crudités.

INGREDIENTS | SERVES 4

½ cup cabbage sprouts, mung sprouts, or other sprouts
½ cup alfalfa sprouts
1 cup pecans
1 tablespoon tamari
¼ cup of red or white onions, chopped
¼ cup sweet bell pepper, chopped
¼ cup celery hearts, chopped
Water for blending

1. To use cabbage sprouts in this recipe, soak the cabbage seeds for 8 to 12 hours and sprout them for 3 days. Prepare the alfalfa sprouts in the same way.

2. Soak the pecans for 2 to 4 hours. Drain and rinse.

3. Grind the pecans and sprouts together in a food processor with the tamari.

4. Add the onion, bell pepper, and celery to the food processor. Briefly process with enough water to help the ingredients stick together in a loaf.

5. Form the ingredients into a loaf or into croquettes, and dehydrate at 145°F for 2 hours. Then turn down the heat to 110°F and continue dehydrating for 12 hours.

PER SERVING:
Calories: 205 | Fat: 20 g | Protein: 4 g | Sodium: 258 mg | Fiber: 3 g

Sprout Pie with Herbs

Slow bake and serve in casserole dishes and garnish with fresh parsley.

INGREDIENTS | SERVES 2

1½ cups raw pecans

2 tablespoons liquid coconut oil

1 tablespoon Italian seasoning

1 tablespoon miso

½ clove garlic, minced

½ teaspoon salt

1 cup diced fresh vegetable mix (zucchini, red bell pepper, carrots, onion, asparagus tips)

1 cup Black Sesame Seed Gravy (page 227)

1 cup small sprouts (fenugreek, alfalfa, clover, lentil)

Fenugreek

Fenugreek has culinary uses as both an herb (the leaves and sprouts) and as a spice (made from the seeds). A nutritious sprout, fenugreek contains about 30 percent protein, iron, niacin, calcium, and vitamin A. This herb has some medicinal uses and is popular as a digestive aid. The seed is a popular spice in Indian cuisine.

1. Prepare the pie crust in a food processor. Using the *S* blade, process the pecans until they break down and begin to stick to the walls of the food processor.

2. Into the food processor add the coconut oil, Italian seasoning, miso, minced garlic, and salt with the pecans and process until they are well mixed.

3. Press the pecan mixture into two small casserole dishes to create a crust.

4. Mix the vegetables with ½ cup gravy. Fill each casserole dish with ½ cup diced vegetables. Top the vegetables with sprouts and then drizzle on the remaining ½ cup gravy.

5. Dehydrate for 3 to 4 hours and serve warm. Garnish with fresh herbs.

PER SERVING:
Calories: 740 | Fat: 70 g | Protein: 14 g | Sodium: 1,291 mg | Fiber: 13 g

Sprout Burgers

These sprout burgers taste good with the Mustard Sauce (page 229) or the French Fries with Ketchup (page 197). You can serve them on crackers or bread, or roll them in a cabbage leaf. If you don't have nama shoyu, you can substitute 1 teaspoon salt or 1 tablespoon miso.

INGREDIENTS | SERVES 6

2 cups sunflower seeds, soaked

2 tablespoons flaxseed, ground

½ cup mixed sprouts (alfalfa, fenugreek, mung, lentil, green pea)

¼ cup celery, chopped

¼ cup red or white onion, chopped

4 tablespoons agave nectar

1 clove garlic, minced

1 tablespoon nama shoyu

1 tablespoon Italian seasoning

1. Using a food processor with an *S* blade, mix all ingredients together. Leave some texture and chunks in the mixture.

2. Form the mixture into 4 to 6 burger patties and dehydrate at 110°F for 4 hours. Flip over burgers and continue to dehydrate for 2 to 4 more hours.

PER SERVING:
Calories: 323 | Fat: 26 g | Protein: 11 g | Sodium: 160 mg | Fiber: 5 g

Nama Shoyu

This is a raw and unpasteurized soy sauce. It has a rich, salty flavor and is delicious with Asian meals. It does contains a little wheat so it is not appropriate for those with gluten intolerance.

Fennel Sprout Cakes

The fennel and mustard sprouts give these cakes a pleasant tang, balanced out by the mayonnaise. Try using organic celery; it is often more flavorful than conventional celery.

INGREDIENTS | SERVES 6

2 cups sprouted buckwheat

1 tablespoon sprouted mustard seeds or
1 teaspoon mustard powder

½ cup ground flaxseed

1 clove garlic, minced

1 cup celery, diced

1 cup fennel, diced

2 shallots, minced

3 tablespoons fresh minced dill, or
1 tablespoon dried

¾ cup Cashew Mayonnaise (page 88)

1. In a food processor, combine the buckwheat sprouts, mustard, flax, and garlic and process until smooth.

2. In a large bowl, mix together all the ingredients except the mayonnaise. Form into small patties and dehydrate at 110 degrees for 6 hours. Flip over and dehydrate another 2 to 4 hours.

3. Serve warm with the mayonnaise spread on each fennel cake.

PER SERVING:
Calories: 222 | Fat: 8 g | Protein: 8 g | Sodium: 59 mg | Fiber: 6 g

Alternative Preparation

You can also prepare these sprout cakes in the morning and have them for dinner. They can be dehydrated for 8 to 12 hours without turning them. That means if you put them in the dehydrator before you leave for work, they will be ready to eat when you get home. If you make them at bedtime, you'll have warm sprout cakes ready for breakfast.

Lentil Burgers

*These burgers are delicious served with a garnish of tomato slices, lettuce,
mint cashew cream, and dehydrated crackers. Fresh herbs are a good substitute
for the garam masala spice. You can substitute onions for the scallions.*

INGREDIENTS | SERVES 4

1 tablespoon coconut oil
2 cups lentil sprouts
¼ cup flaxseed, ground
¼ cup carrot, shredded
2 tablespoons olive oil
1 clove garlic
1 teaspoon garam masala powder
3 tablespoons lemon juice
¼ cup scallions

1. Warm the coconut oil to a liquid by placing the container in warm water.

2. Add all ingredients to a food processor with an *S* blade and process until the ingredients become a chunky pâté.

3. Form the pâté into burger patty shapes. Place them on dehydrator trays and dehydrate at 145°F for 2 hours. Flip over patties and continue dehydrating for 8 to 12 hours at 110°F.

PER SERVING:
Calories: 197 | Fat: 15 g | Protein: 6 g | Sodium: 15 mg | Fiber: 3 g

Cinnamon Apples in Sprouted Wheat Cups

You can dehydrate this crust while you're sleeping or while you're at work. This is a crispier crust, dehydrated for 8 to 12 hours—no flipping is required. Once the crust is done you're ready to prepare the filling, which takes less than 30 minutes.

INGREDIENTS | SERVES 4

1½ cups wheat berries, sprouted for 2 days

¼ cup raisins, currants, or chopped dates

1 teaspoon salt

1 teaspoon vanilla

Water to achieve the desired consistency

¼ cup goji berries

2 tablespoons agave nectar

1 teaspoon cinnamon

½ teaspoon nutmeg

2 cups peeled and grated apple

Sprouted Wheat

Sprouting wheat activates enzymes in the grain and brings the wheat to life. Sprouted wheat can help those who are underweight gain weight and build muscle. It is rich in vitamins B, C, and E and the minerals magnesium and phosphorus.

1. Prepare the sprouted wheat two days in advance.

2. Soak the raisins, currants, or chopped dates for 20 minutes.

3. To make a crust, mix together the sprouted wheat, salt, vanilla, and raisins. If you are making this dish in a juicer, use the blank plate for homogenizing. You probably won't need to add water. If you're making it in a food processor, gradually add water to create the consistency of dough, using the *S* blade until blended.

4. Spread a thin layer of the sprouted wheat dough onto a dehydrator tray with a nonstick sheet. Dehydrate at 145°F for 2 hours. Flip the dough over, score the batter into round shapes, and dehydrate for another 2 hours at 115°F.

5. Soak the goji berries for 20 minutes in water. Remove berries and set soak water aside. Blend the goji berries with the agave nectar, cinnamon, nutmeg, and ½ cup goji berry soak water until smooth.

6. Grate the apple and mix with the blended goji berries. Place the round wheat crust into dessert cups. Fill with the apple and goji berry mixture and serve.

PER SERVING:

Calories: 202 | Fat: 1 g | Protein: 5 g | Sodium: 590 mg | Fiber: 4 g

Sprout Medley with Green Goddess Dressing

This is a delicious fresh salad to serve with a gourmet entrée. A good substitute for nama shoyu is Bragg's Liquid Aminos. The dressing is good with finely chopped fresh herbs blended in, such as dill, chives, cilantro, or basil.

INGREDIENTS | SERVES 2

2 tablespoons Tahini (page 138)

2 tablespoons lemon juice

1 tablespoon nama shoyu

¼ cup olive oil

½ clove garlic, minced

½ teaspoon salt

⅓ cup water

1 cup green sunflower sprouts

2 cups microgreen sprouts (alfalfa, clover, broccoli, arugula, cabbage, cress, and radish sprouts)

½ cup celery hearts, diced

½ cup red cabbage, shredded fine

1. To make the salad dressing, blend together the tahini and lemon juice. Gradually add the nama shoyu, olive oil, garlic, salt, and ¾ cup water.

2. Rinse the sunflower greens and arrange them in salad bowls. Top with the microgreen sprouts, diced celery hearts, and shredded red cabbage.

3. Drizzle the dressing over the salad and serve.

PER SERVING:

Calories: 114 | Fat: 8 g | Protein: 5 g | Sodium: 1,066 mg | Fiber: 3 g

Microgreen Sprouts

Microgreens start as tiny seeds and grow into little plants in a few days. They are high in protein, antioxidants, enzymes, vitamins, and phytonutrients. For this recipe you can use a mixture of microsprout varieties. Soak them for 8 to 12 hours and sprout for 2 to 3 days.

Simply Sauerkraut

This is the basic recipe for making raw sauerkraut. It works best using an appliance designed specifically for making sauerkraut. Fresh cabbage should have enough juice to make the brine. If your cabbage is dry, you may add extra liquid brine. The brine is made by stirring in 1 teaspoon salt into 1 cup water.

INGREDIENTS | SERVES 10

5 medium-sized heads cabbage

3 tablespoons salt

1 tablespoon caraway seeds

Raw Sauerkraut

Raw, cultured sauerkraut is delicious and tastes much better than the sauerkraut found in most supermarkets and restaurants. The sauerkraut in supermarkets is a bland mixture of cabbage and vinegar. When people say they don't like sauerkraut, they are usually referring to the cooked, soggy, vinegar-soaked cabbage. If you have never tasted real cultured sauerkraut, you are in for a treat! Raw sauerkraut can be found bottled in most health food stores.

1. Grate the cabbage using a cabbage slicer or food processor. Alternatively, use a knife to chop the cabbage into small chunks.

2. Place the cabbage into a large bowl and sprinkle the salt on top.

3. Massage or pound the salt into the cabbage. Use a wooden pounding tool or meat tenderizer to pound the cabbage. Alternatively, massage and squeeze the cabbage by hand. This works the salt into the cabbage, helping to release the juices and create a brine.

4. Mix the caraway seeds with the cabbage. Pack the cabbage into a sauerkraut maker or crock. Press down so there are no air bubbles.

5. Place a weight on top of the sauerkraut to keep it submerged in the brine. Seal the container. As the cabbage cultures, it will create some gas bubbles and air pressure will build. Make sure there is a way for the air pressure to escape.

6. Let the sauerkraut sit at room temperature for 4 to 5 days. The sauerkraut will be ready when the activity stops and there are no more air bubbles. If you are using a Harsch crock, it will take about 4 weeks to completely culture.

PER SERVING:

Calories: 116 | Fat: 1 g | Protein: 6 g | Sodium: 2,175 mg | Fiber: 12 g

Sweet Sauerkraut

Fresh sauerkraut is delicious and full of flavor. It is a good side dish served with salads and entrées. It is also good as a condiment in wraps and sandwiches.

INGREDIENTS | SERVES 10

5 heads green cabbage

2 cups carrots, grated

3 tablespoons salt

2 tablespoons caraway seeds

Traditional Sauerkraut

Sauerkraut is an ancient method of food preservation and a standard in German cuisine. It is a good source of beneficial bacteria (probiotics), which are found naturally in the digestive tract, as well as vitamin C. There is a popular health regimen, the Budwig Diet, that recommends drinking one glass of sauerkraut juice daily.

1. Process the cabbage by grating, shredding, or chopping. Good tools to use include a food processor with the grating blade, a mandolin slicer, a heavy-duty juicer, or a knife.

2. Mix the grated cabbage and carrots with the salt. Massage and squeeze the salt into the vegetables. Another method is to pound the cabbage with a kitchen tool. This process draws the juice out of the cabbage to form a brine.

3. Mix together the caraway seeds with the cabbage and carrots. Pack the mixture into a sauerkraut crock pot, sauerkraut maker, or similar container with an airlocked lid, designed to minimize bacteria during the fermentation process. Using this type of container makes it unnecessary to skim the brine daily, an essential step in traditional recipes. Place a weight on top to keep the cabbage covered in the brine.

4. Place lid on the crock or jar and let it sit for about 5 days. If you are using a traditional sauerkraut crock pot, you may let it sit for longer, up to 4 weeks. The mix should culture at about 65 to 75°F.

5. If the cabbage is dry, you may need to add more brine into the crock or jar after a couple days. You can make more brine by mixing 1 teaspoon salt into 1 cup water, and pour this into the sauerkraut.

PER SERVING:

Calories: 133 | Fat: 1 g | Protein: 6 g | Sodium: 2,190 mg | Fiber: 12 g

Dill Pickles

These pickles have a mild, tasty flavor, echoing the subtle sweetness of the apple cider vinegar. You could substitute a wide variety of vegetables for the pickles.

INGREDIENTS | SERVES 8

6 tablespoons salt

½ gallon water

1 cup raw apple cider vinegar

4 pounds small pickling cucumbers

1 cup fresh dill leaf

2 tablespoons black peppercorns

½ cup pickling spice blend

The History of Pickles

Pickling is the process of fermenting a food to preserve it by soaking it in vinegar or brine. In Europe, vegetables commonly pickled include peppers, tomatoes, olives, eggplant, carrots, cauliflower, beets, and mushrooms. In Asia, nontraditional pickles include mangoes, papaya, pineapple, and ume plum, as well as garlic, ginger, and shallots.

1. Make the brine by dissolving the salt in a half gallon of water. Stir in the apple cider vinegar.

2. Mix the whole cucumbers with the dill, peppercorns, and pickling spice blend. Place mixture into a glass 1 gallon jar.

3. Pour the brine over the cucumbers. Add more apple cider vinegar and fill to the top of the jar. It may take up to an extra ½ cup of vinegar. Make sure all cucumbers are covered in brine.

4. Place the jar of cucumbers in the refrigerator and let sit. They will be ready to eat after 2 days. They become more sour after 1–2 weeks.

PER SERVING:

Calories: 45 | Fat: 0 g | Protein: 2 g | Sodium: 1,752 mg | Fiber: 2 g

Pickled Vegetable Medley

This is a delicious snack when eaten alone, and it is a good addition to salads and burrito wraps.

INGREDIENTS | SERVES 4

4 tablespoons pickling spice blend
4 tablespoons salt
1 cup carrot, chopped
½ cup beets, chopped
1 cup daikon radish, chopped
1 cup celery root, chopped
3 cloves garlic, sliced
2 cups raw apple cider vinegar
Water to fill jar

Pickled Vegetables

The process of pickling not only preserves food, it also increases the content of B vitamins. Other vegetables that lend themselves nicely to pickling include onions, cauliflower, and various peppers. (Remember Peter Piper picked a peck of pickled peppers?)

1. Place the pickling spices and salt at the bottom of a 1 gallon glass jar.

2. Place the vegetables and garlic into the jar.

3. Pour in the apple cider vinegar, and then add water and fill to the top of the jar.

4. Place a lid on the jar and shake it to mix up the spices and salt.

5. Gently shake the jar every day. The pickled vegetables will be ready to eat in 7 days.

PER SERVING:
Calories: 30 | Fat: 0 g | Protein: 1 g | Sodium: 907 mg | Fiber: 1 g

Traditional Korean Kimchi

Variations of kimchi emphasize radishes, scallions, or cucumbers, and seasoning options include ginger, chocolate, and coffee. You can vary the spiciness of the dish to suit your taste.

INGREDIENTS | SERVES 10

4 cloves garlic
1 cup onion, chopped
4 fresh hot red peppers
2 dried hot red peppers
2 tablespoons gingerroot
1 tablespoon unpasteurized miso
4 heads green cabbage
½ daikon radish
3 tablespoons salt

Kimchi

This Korean dish dates back thousands of years and is first mentioned in Chinese writings that date to about 1000 BCE. Kimchi is a good source of probiotics, vitamin A, and vitamin C.

1. Prepare the kimchi sauce using a food processor, blender, or heavy-duty juicer. Blend the garlic, onion, hot peppers, ginger, and miso into a sauce.

2. Grate, shred, or chop the cabbage and daikon radish. Mix in the salt and squeeze or pound the cabbage to create the brine.

3. Mix the cabbage and daikon with the kimchi sauce.

4. Pack the kimchi into a 1 gallon glass jar or crock. Make sure there are no gaps or air pockets. Place a weight over the kimchi to keep it covered in the brine. Place lid over the opening that will allow the pressure to release.

5. Let the kimchi sit at room temperature. It will be ready to eat in 4 to 5 days. Place in smaller canning jars and store in the refrigerator.

PER SERVING:
Calories: 112 | Fat: 1 g | Protein: 6 g | Sodium: 2,227 mg | Fiber: 10 g

Pu-erh Tea

This tea is a healthy replacement for coffee. It is typically enjoyed in the morning or afternoons because it contains caffeine and may keep you awake if you drink it late at night. It can be used as a liquid base for smoothies and shakes.

INGREDIENTS | SERVES 2

3 cups water
2 pu-erh tea cakes

Pu-erh Tea

Pu-erh tea is made from a specific green tea plant that grows in Pu-erh County, China. It is a fermented and aged green tea. The tea is classified using a system that identifies the year and location of origin, similar to the classification of wine. There are some varieties that have been aged between ten and fifty years, and they may cost thousands of dollars for a single cake. This exotic tea is prized in Chinese culture for its therapeutic and medicinal properties.

1. Bring 3 cups water to a boil in a tea kettle.

2. Remove the kettle from the heat and allow the water to cool down for a couple of minutes.

3. Steep the pu-erh tea cakes in the hot water for 2 minutes. Pour into tea cups or coffee mugs and enjoy the tea warm.

PER SERVING:

Calories: 0 | Fat: 0 g | Protein: 0 g | Sodium: 0 mg | Fiber: 0 g

Kitchen-Made Rejuvelac

This fermented beverage, made from grains, was popularized by Dr. Ann Wigmore. Rejuvelac contains beneficial bacteria; it can be made with any sprouted hard grain, including wheat, rye, quinoa, or buckwheat. Rejuvelac can also be used as a starter culture to make seed cheese or as a liquid base for smoothies.

INGREDIENTS | SERVES 4

2 cups rye
6 cups water

Rejuvelac

Rejuvelac should taste like sour lemonade. Sometimes it will not culture properly because of factors in the environment. Avoid any batch that has mold on the seeds or bad bacteria in the air. If the batch goes bad and spoils, it will have a nasty smell and taste. Don't give up! Simply discard the batch and start over.

1. Soak the rye seeds and sprout them for 1–2 days.

2. Drain and rinse the rye sprouts. Place them into a half-gallon glass jar and fill the jar with water.

3. Fasten a cheesecloth over the opening of the jar with a rubber band.

4. Let the jar sit at room temperature for 2 days.

5. Pour the rejuvelac into a new jar, straining out the rye seeds. The rejuvelac will keep in the refrigerator for 2 or 3 days, but ideally it should be consumed within 24 hours.

6. The same rye seeds can be used to make a second batch. Fill the jar with fresh water and let it sit for 24 hours. Pour into a new container and discard the seeds.

PER SERVING:
Calories: 93 | Fat: 0 g | Protein: 1 g | Sodium: 8 mg | Fiber: 0 g

CHAPTER 12

Burgers, Wraps, and Sandwiches

Pesto Tomato Stack

This is a great recipe to serve in the summer when basil is plentiful. The walnuts can be replaced with hazelnuts or pine nuts. In place of the beets, you can use radishes for some extra flavor and a little heat.

INGREDIENTS | SERVES 2

2 large slicing tomatoes
1 cup walnuts, soaked
2 cloves garlic
⅔ cups olive oil
¼ cups fresh basil, minced
1 teaspoon salt
½ cup zucchini, sliced into rounds
¼ cup beets, shredded

Tomatoes

Tomatoes are prized for their high level of lycopene, a powerful antioxidant. Blending or juicing the tomato makes the lycopene more readily available. Heirloom tomatoes are gaining popularity because of their delicious flavor and meaty texture. These plants make a great addition to your summer garden.

1. Slice the tomatoes into thick slices, about a ½-inch thick.

2. For the pesto sauce, place the walnuts, garlic, olive oil, basil, and salt in a food processor and process until it becomes a chunky sauce.

3. Place 1 zucchini slice onto each tomato slice.

4. Scoop a tablespoon of pesto sauce on top of each zucchini slice. Garnish the pesto sauce with the grated beet.

PER SERVING:

Calories: 149 | Fat: 13 g | Protein: 2 g | Sodium: 166 mg | Fiber: 2 g

Raw Sushi Nori Rolls

These nori rolls are delicious dipped into nama shoyu sauce and wasabi or homemade horseradish sauce and are wonderful paired with miso soup.

INGREDIENTS | SERVES 2

2 sheets raw or roasted nori

¼ cup Almond Garlic Pâté (page 143) for each sheet

4 tablespoons microgreen sprouts (alfalfa, sunflower, clover, or radish) per sheet

2 tablespoons finely grated carrot per sheet or more

½ avocado, sliced

Nori

Nori is a nutritious sea vegetable high in minerals and vitamins that is prepared in thin sheets. Nori is used as the wrap for sushi, and the texture makes a perfect replacement for tortilla wraps. Like other sea veggies, nori is high in iodine content, as well as iron, calcium, vitamins A, B, and C, and carotene.

1. Lay 1 nori sheet flat on a sushi mat. Spread about ¼ cup of the pâté across one end of the nori. Add a layer of sprouts and top with the carrot and avocado.

2. Roll up the nori sheets tightly using the sushi mat. Just before the completing the roll, dip your finger in water and run it along the edge of the nori sheet to create a seal.

3. Cut the sushi rolls into 6 round pieces with a sharp knife (ideally with saw teeth) using a gentle see-saw motion. Repeat the process with the remaining nori sheet.

PER SERVING:

Calories: 194 | Fat: 16 g | Protein: 6 g | Sodium: 312 mg | Fiber: 6 g

Nori Protein Roll with Parsnip Rice

Serve this with a nama shoyu sauce or the Carrot Ginger Sauce (page 190). For the parsnip rice, you can substitute cauliflower, turnip, or butternut squash. You can also use a pumpkin spread, buttered onto the layer of parsnips, before you add the veggies.

INGREDIENTS | SERVES 2

1 parsnip, peeled and chopped
1 tablespoon lemon juice
2 tablespoons scallions, minced
2 teaspoons minced ginger
¼ teaspoon salt
2 nori sheets
¼ cup cucumbers in matchstick slices
¼ cup avocado in matchstick slices

1. Place the parsnip into a food processor and process until it becomes the consistency of rice.

2. Add the lemon juice, scallions, ginger, and salt to the food processor.

3. Lay the nori sheets flat on a bamboo sushi mat or cutting board. Spread ¼ cup parsnip rice along one edge. Place the matchsticked vegetables on top of the parsnips.

4. Tightly roll up the nori roll using your fingers or the sushi mat. Use a little water to wet one edge of the nori to help create a seal. Let it sit for 5 minutes and slice into 6 equal parts.

PER SERVING:
Calories: 64 | Fat: 3 g | Protein: 2 g | Sodium: 303 mg | Fiber: 4 g

Sunny Pickle Rolls

The Bubbies brand of pickles are raw and unpasteurized. They can be found in most health food stores and are perfect for this recipe. Honey or dates can be used in place of the agave nectar. This is a good pâté to spread on crackers or roll into cabbage leafs.

INGREDIENTS | SERVES 4

1 cup sunflower seeds, soaked
1 cup buckwheat, sprouted
½ cup cauliflower, chopped
½ cup pickles, chopped
¼ cup onion, chopped
3 tablespoons lemon juice
1 tablespoon ume plum vinegar or balsamic vinegar
½ teaspoon salt
2 teaspoons garlic, minced
1 tablespoon dill, minced
½ teaspoon cayenne pepper powder
2 tablespoons agave nectar
1 tablespoon Italian seasoning
4 nori sheets

1. Process the sunflower seeds and buckwheat in a food processor until well broken down.

2. Process all remaining ingredients, except the nori sheets, together in the food processor until they are well broken down but still chunky.

3. Lay a nori sheet flat on a bamboo sushi mat. Place two scoops of prepared pâté onto each nori sheet and use the bamboo mat to roll. Alternatively, roll by hand. Chop the nori rolls into quarters and serve.

PER SERVING:
Calories: 312 | Fat: 19 g | Protein: 11 g | Sodium: 463 mg | Fiber: 7 g

Pickles

Raw and unpasteurized pickles can be found in most health food stores. The pickles in the supermarket are usually cooked.

Oriental Spring Rolls

This quick recipe captures the flavor of spring rolls found in Asian restaurants. The wraps can be dipped in nama shoyu, the delicious Carrot Ginger Sauce (page 190), or the almond sauce from the Pad Thai with Almond Sauce (page 212). You can also use your favorite salad dressing.

INGREDIENTS | SERVES 4

4 large romaine lettuce leaves
¼ cup mint leaves
¼ cup cilantro leaves
½ cup mung bean sprouts
¼ cup walnuts, whole or large pieces
½ cup carrot, julienned
½ cup sliced avocado or julienned radishes

1. Lay the romaine lettuce leaves flat. Place a layer of mint and cilantro onto one side. Top with the mung beans, walnuts, carrot, and avocado.

2. Roll up the wraps tightly. Place a toothpick through the middle to hold it together. Serve with sauce.

PER SERVING:
Calories: 89 | Fat: 7 g | Protein: 2 g | Sodium: 18 mg | Fiber: 3 g

Silica

Silica is an important but underappreciated mineral found in foods such as horsetail, nettles, radishes, cucumbers, burdock root, oats, bell peppers, and tomatoes. Scientific studies have found that our bodies transform silica into calcium, so it plays a role in the health of bones, skin, connective tissues, cartilage, and ligaments. Silica speeds up the healing process for broken bones and may help prevent osteoporosis. Horsetail is the best source of silica and is widely available as an herbal supplement.

Coconut Wraps

This is a delicious Mexican dish that is good served with a scoop of Guacamole with Cilantro and Cumin (page 137) and Cashew Sour Cream (page 163). For extra flavor, you could include 2 tablespoons fresh minced herbs such as cilantro, basil, dill, tarragon, chives, or oregano.

INGREDIENTS | SERVES 4

2 cups young coconut meat

1 cup mango

¼ teaspoon salt

½ cup iceberg lettuce, shredded fine

1 cup Mexican Pâté (page 146)

1 cup Simple Salsa (page 135)

1. Prepare the burrito wraps the day before or in the morning. To make the wraps, blend together the young coconut meat, mango, and ¼ teaspoon salt.

2. Spread the burrito wrap mixture onto dehydrator trays with nonstick sheets. Dehydrate at 115°F for 4 hours.

3. Cut the burrito wraps into round tortilla shell shapes and lay flat on a dish.

4. To prepare each burrito, place a layer of iceberg lettuce and 2 tablespoons Mexican pâté onto each wrap. Place a heaping spoonful of salsa onto each wrap. The sweetness of the mango in the wrap is a delicious contrast to the spices in the pâté.

PER SERVING:

Calories: 110 | Fat: 7 g | Protein: 4 g | Sodium: 1,060 mg | Fiber: 2 g

Carrot Ginger Sauce

This is a delicious sauce to serve with wraps and tacos. It makes a good dipping sauce for vegetables and crudités platters. The sesame oil can be replaced with olive oil. The onion powder can be replaced with fresh onion or shallots.

INGREDIENTS | **YIELDS 2½ CUPS**

2 cups carrot juice
2 tablespoons onion powder
2 tablespoons ginger
2 tablespoons lemon juice
¼ cup nama shoyu
1 tablespoon sesame oil

Blend all ingredients until smooth.

PER CUP
Calories: 138 | Fat: 6 g | Protein: 4 g | Sodium: 1,440 mg | Fiber: 1 g

Ginger

Ginger is a thick, knotted root that originated in China. It has become a popular spice that is now used throughout the world. In addition to the flavoring it provides to meals, ginger is recognized as a medicinal herb. It is used to improve digestion, treat upset stomach, reduce inflammation, relieve congestion, and improve blood circulation. It is a warming spice and is excellent as a tea and condiment for cold winters.

Tacos with Guacamole

This is an easy-to-prepare recipe with a nice spicy and salty flavor. These tacos are delicious served with the Carrot Ginger Sauce above.

INGREDIENTS | **SERVES 4**

4 red or green cabbage leaves
1 cup Guacamole with Cilantro and Cumin (page 137)
1 cup soaked whole dulse

1. Lay the cabbage leaves flat on a plate.

2. Scoop a heaping spoonful of guacamole onto each cabbage leaf.

3. Place a layer of dulse on the guacamole.

4. Roll up the cabbage leaves into a burrito. Place a toothpick though the middle to hold them together.

PER SERVING:
Calories: 100 | Fat: 6 g | Protein: 3 g | Sodium: 123 mg | Fiber: 6 g

Jamaican Wrap Filling

This is a delicious wrap made with a traditional Jamaican jerk spice blend. Serve this filling wrapped in collard greens or romaine lettuce. Additional items you can include in the wrap are julienned vegetables and minced herbs.

INGREDIENTS | SERVES 2

¼ cup flaxseeds
1 cup almonds, soaked
¼ cup celery, chopped
½ tablespoon Jamaican jerk seasoning
½ tablespoon jalapeño pepper, minced and seeds removed
¼ teaspoon salt
½ clove garlic, minced
1 tablespoon olive oil
2 collard leaves
Cucumber, finely julienned
Sweet red pepper, finely julienned

Jerk Spice

Jamaican jerk seasoning is an aromatic blend of white onion, garlic, salt, sugar, all-spice, green onion, cayenne pepper, black pepper, thyme, nutmeg, cinnamon, sage, and habanero peppers (known for their heat). This blend makes a delicious marinade for eggplant and zucchini.

1. Grind the flaxseed to a powder in a coffee grinder.

2. Process the almonds, flax, celery, jerk seasoning, jalapeño, salt, garlic, and olive oil in a food processor with an *S* blade until smooth.

3. To serve this filling in a wrap, remove the stems from 2 collard leaves and cut them in half. Spread a layer of pâté onto each collard green. Lay a few pieces of cucumber and red pepper on the pâté.

4. Tightly roll up each collard green. Stick a toothpick through the middle to hold them together.

PER SERVING:
Calories: 602 | Fat: 51 g | Protein: 20 g | Sodium: 317 mg | Fiber: 16 g

Fresh Falafels

These falafels are made with almonds rather than garbanzo beans. Cabbage leaves serve as the wrap. A good substitute would be the Coconut Wraps (page 189). This recipe works especially well served with the Sprouted Moroccan Lentil Soup (page 167).

INGREDIENTS | SERVES 4

¼ cup sun-dried tomatoes

1 cup almonds

¼ cup celery

2 tablespoons lemon

4 tablespoons Tahini (page 138)

¼ cup olive oil

1 clove garlic

1 tablespoon minced parsley

1 tablespoon cumin

1 teaspoon coriander

4 cabbage leaves

1 cup Zucchini Hummus (page 138)

1. Soak the sun-dried tomatoes for 2 hours. Chop them into small pieces.

2. Prepare the falafel balls by processing all ingredients, except for the cabbage leaves and hummus, in a food processor until well mixed and slightly chunky. Pat them into little balls. They are ready to serve immediately.

3. Lay the cabbage leaves on a plate. Spread the hummus onto each leaf and place falafel patties on top. Roll up into a sandwich wrap.

PER SERVING:

Calories: 784 | Fat: 77 g | Protein: 13 g | Sodium: 101 mg | Fiber: 8 g

Falafel

Falafel is a traditional Middle Eastern food. It is usually deep fried in oil and made with a blend of garbanzo beans or fava beans and spices. Falafels are the fast food of Middle East, comparable to hot dogs in the United States.

Spiced Almond Falafels

This recipe is delicious served with pasta dishes and with salads.
These falafels are dehydrated and have a texture similar to cooked falafels.

INGREDIENTS | SERVES 4

2 cups almonds, soaked
1 garlic clove
2 tablespoons lemon juice
1 tablespoon sage
¼ teaspoon cayenne pepper powder
2 tablespoons liquid coconut oil

1. Using a food processor with an *S* blade, process all the ingredients together.

2. Form into little balls and dehydrate at 145°F for 2 hours. Turn down the temperature and continue dehydrating at 115°F for 12 hours.

PER SERVING:

Calories: 474 | Fat: 42 g | Protein: 15 g | Sodium: 1 mg | Fiber: 9 g

Heated Oils

Research shows that deep-fried foods clog the arteries and contain carcinogens. This recipe will give you all the flavor of deep-fried falafel without the unhealthy fats.

Raw Sandwiches

In this recipe, the eggplant takes the place of bread. You could also use store-bought raw crackers in place of eggplant.

INGREDIENTS | SERVES 2

1 eggplant
½ cup shredded iceberg lettuce
1 large tomato, sliced
½ cup Pine Nut Cheese (page 163) or your favorite pâté
½ cup sliced avocado or guacamole

1. Peel the skin off the eggplant, and cut it into toast-sized slices about 1-inch thick. Dehydrate at 145°F for 3 hours.

2. Spread a layer of the pine nut cheese on 1 eggplant slice and top with a slice of tomato.

3. Spread a thin layer of sliced avocado or guacamole on top.

4. Place a second slice of eggplant on top to complete the sandwich.

PER SERVING:

Calories: 602 | Fat: 52 g | Protein: 14 g | Sodium: 17 mg | Fiber: 16 g

Mock-Tuna Salad Sandwich

You can make a complete meal by combining these sandwiches with a small side salad or soup. The dulse and capers give this pâté a flavor reminiscent of tuna fish salad, without the fishy taste.

INGREDIENTS | SERVES 2

1 cup sunflower seeds, soaked

½ teaspoon mustard powder

¼ cup chopped celery

¼ cup chopped carrots

2 tablespoons chopped onion

1 clove garlic, minced

2 tablespoons lemon juice

1 tablespoon capers (optional)

1 tablespoon dulse flakes

4 raw Tomato, Basil, and Flax Crackers (page 107)

1. In a food processor with an *S* blade, process all ingredients, except the crackers, together. The resulting pâté should be well mixed and slightly chunky.

2. Lay four flax crackers onto a plate. Spread a thick layer of the pâté onto each cracker, and place a second cracker on the top to create the sandwich.

PER SERVING:
Calories: 729 | Fat: 58 g | Protein: 25 g | Sodium: 869 mg | Fiber: 21 g

Sandwiches

The sandwich is named after John Montagu, 4th Earl of Sandwich, who was an eighteenth-century English aristocrat. He wanted an easy snack to eat while playing card games and the sandwich was perfect. In raw cuisine, tasty sandwiches can be made with crackers or flatbreads. You can be creative and garnish them with many different types of pâtés, sauces, and vegetables.

Raw Foods Pizza with Sprouted-Grain Crust

There are many ingredients that can be used as toppings for this pizza. Some good toppings include olives, mushrooms, bell pepper, onion, basil, cilantro, parsley, rosemary, avocado, dulse, pesto, pineapple, zucchini rounds, and marinated vegetables.

INGREDIENTS | SERVES 4

2 cups buckwheat, sprouted

1 cup sunflower seeds, soaked

½ cup sun-dried tomatoes, soaked

1 tablespoon olive oil

2 tablespoons honey

¼ teaspoon cayenne pepper powder

1 tablespoon Italian seasoning

½ teaspoon salt

1 cup Tomato Marinara Sauce (page 226)

½ cup Pine Nut Cheese (page 163)

Pizza

The first recipe for pizza originated in Italy. The basic pizza is a round, flat bread topped with a tomato sauce and mozzarella cheese. It is one of the most popular foods in North America, and different regions of the United States specialize in unique recipes. New York style is a thin, flexible crust with minimal toppings. Chicago style specializes in a deep dish and doughycrust. California style features nontraditional ingredients such as a peanut sauce, bean sprouts, and carrots.

1. Make the pizza dough using a food processor with an *S* blade or a heavy-duty juicer with a masticating screen. Process the buckwheat, sunflower seeds, sun-dried tomatoes, olive oil, honey, cayenne pepper, Italian seasoning, and salt until ingredients are well mixed with small chunks. They should be mixed long enough to form a batter-like consistency.

2. Form the dough into rectangular shapes, about ¼-inch thick. Make the edges a little thicker to form a crust. Dehydrate at 145°F for 2 hours. Flip over the dough and continue dehydrating at 110°F for 4 hours.

3. Spread the tomato marinara sauce onto the crust. Scoop tablespoons of pine nut cheese onto the pizza.

4. Garnish the pizza with toppings of your choice. Dehydrate at 110°F for 2 hours or until warm.

PER SERVING:

Calories: 1,042 | Fat: 57 g | Protein: 33 g | Sodium: 1,051 mg | Fiber: 21 g

Corn on the Cob with Avocado Butter

This quick recipe is perfect for summer when corn is ripe and plentiful. Freshly picked corn on the cob is sweet and does not need to be cooked. However, if the corn has been sitting on the shelf for a long time, it becomes starchy and loses its flavor, so you want to be sure to buy fresh corn.

INGREDIENTS | SERVES 4

2 avocados

1 clove garlic, minced (optional)

4 ears of fresh sweet corn

½ teaspoon salt

½ teaspoon freshly ground black pepper

Corn on the Cob

Sweet corn is a variety of maize that has been bred to have a high sugar content. It has the best flavor when freshly picked in season during the summer and is a good source of vitamin B1, folate, vitamin C, and phosphorus. White sweet corn is excellent raw.

1. Remove the pits from the avocados and scoop out the flesh with a spoon. In a small bowl, mash together the avocado and garlic.

2. Peel the ears of corn. Spread the avocado-garlic butter onto the corn.

3. Sprinkle on salt and pepper to taste.

PER SERVING:
Calories: 239 | Fat: 16 g | Protein: 5 g | Sodium: 311 mg | Fiber: 9 g

French Fries with Ketchup

You can prepare this dish in 10–15 minutes if you use store-bought marinated sun-dried tomatoes. This is a good side dish to serve with veggie burgers. You can also use this raw ketchup on sandwiches and wraps. The jicama provides raw food enthusiasts with a healthy alternative to this American classic.

INGREDIENTS | SERVES 2

¼ cup sun-dried tomatoes, soaked
½ cup chopped fresh tomato
¼ cup chopped red bell pepper
1 tablespoon chopped dates
1 tablespoon apple cider vinegar
½ teaspoon salt
1 clove garlic, chopped
½ jicama, to serve as fries
1 cup olive oil
½ teaspoon paprika

1. To make the ketchup, place the sun-dried tomatoes, fresh tomato, red bell pepper, dates, apple cider vinegar, ½ teaspoon salt, and garlic in a blender and blend until smooth.

2. Slice the jicama into French fry–shaped strips. Lightly sprinkle salt onto the jicama strips.

3. Coat the jicama in olive oil and sprinkle the paprika on top. Serve the jicama fries on a plate with a side of ketchup.

PER SERVING:
Calories: 184 | Fat: 7 g | Protein: 3 g | Sodium: 729 mg | Fiber: 7 g

Ketchup and Fries

French fries may actually be from Belgium, and they're at least 300 years old. Despite their popularity, they have some drawbacks. Fries are a double whammy, due to their high glycemic rating and their high fat content (20 percent!). Ketchup fares a little better, but it's the sugar that will settle on your middle—all good reasons to explore raw food cuisine and find your own true comfort food.

Sliders

*These mini-burgers make good appetizers and snacks. They are good
served warm out of the dehydrator accompanied with jicama French fries,
fresh pickled cucumbers, and a chocolate shake.*

INGREDIENTS | SERVES 4

2 cups Veggie Burgers mix (page 199)

1 cup Apple Flax Bread mix (page 112)

½ cup Pine Nut Cheese (page 163)

4 tablespoons ketchup (from French Fries with Ketchup, page 197)

4 tablespoons Mustard Sauce (page 229)

½ cup sliced cherry tomatoes

¼ cup red onion, thinly sliced

Sliders

Sliders are miniature burgers made famous by White Castle restaurant. The first White Castle opened in 1921 in Wichita, Kansas, making them the oldest fast food burger restaurant chain in America.

1. Prepare the veggie burger and flax bread recipes according to the instructions.

2. Form the veggie burger mix into small patties measuring about 3 inches wide and ⅜-inch thick.

3. Use the flax bread recipe to create small buns measuring about 5 inches wide.

4. Dehydrate the veggie burgers and flax bread at 110°F for 12 hours.

5. Create a sandwich with the veggie burger in the middle of two pieces of flax bread. Garnish the burger with ketchup, mustard, pine nut cheese, sliced cherry tomatoes, and sliced onion.

PER SERVING:

Calories: 548 | Fat: 41 g | Protein: 17 g | Sodium: 1,210 mg | Fiber: 15 g

Veggie Burgers

These burgers make a good sandwich with flax crackers or cabbage leaves as the bun. Good condiments include the Black Sesame Seed Gravy (page 227), French Fries with Ketchup (page 197), Fresh Barbecue Sauce (page 227), or fresh sliced tomatoes.

INGREDIENTS | SERVES 4

½ cup flaxseed, ground

2 cups sunflower seeds (soaked), or walnuts (soaked), pecans, or hazel nuts

2 tablespoons lemon juice

¼ cup water as needed

1 cup diced carrot

¼ cup diced onion

4 tablespoons basil, minced

2 tablespoons dill, minced

1 tablespoon jalapeño pepper, minced

½ teaspoon salt

1 clove garlic, minced

1. In a food processor, use the *S* blade to process the flaxseed and sunflower seeds with the lemon juice and a little water to create a batter the consistency of creamy peanut butter.

2. Combine all ingredients in the food processor and process until well mixed and chunky. You may need to add a little extra water to make it easier to form the mixture into patties.

3. Place the patties on dehydrator trays and dry for 8 to 12 hours at 115°F.

PER SERVING:
Calories: 542 | Fat: 45 g | Protein: 19 g | Sodium: 327 mg | Fiber: 13 g

Maca Protein Burger

This is a delicious, protein-rich burger.
The maca, walnuts, and flaxseed are great sources of protein.

INGREDIENTS | SERVES 2

1½ cups walnuts, soaked
¼ cup flaxseed
2 cups chopped zucchini
½ cup chopped celery
1½ cups chopped crimini or portobello mushrooms, minced
½ cup chopped red onion
1 clove garlic, minced
2 tablespoons miso
1 cup water
2 tablespoons maca
1 tablespoon minced sage
1 teaspoon salt
3 tablespoons minced basil

1. Grind 1 cup walnuts to a powder in a food processor. Grind the flaxseed into a powder with a coffee grinder. Pour them into a large mixing bowl.

2. Briefly process the remaining ½ cup walnuts in a food processor. Add the zucchini, celery, mushrooms, onion, and garlic and process until well mixed and still chunky. Add this to the mixing bowl containing the ground flax and walnuts.

3. Stir the miso into 1 cup water. Pour into the mixing bowl.

4. Add all remaining ingredients to the mixing bowl and stir well. Form the mixture into burger patties, about ½-inch thick.

5. Dehydrate the patties at 145°F for 2 hours. Turn down heat to 110°F. Flip the patties and continue dehydrating for an additional 8 to 12 hours.

6. As an alternative, you can eat this immediately as a pâté or in patty form.

PER SERVING:
Calories: 418 | Fat: 29 g | Protein: 15 g | Sodium: 1,841 mg | Fiber: 13 g

Stuffed Red Bell Peppers

This is another good 10-minute recipe. It goes well with the Ginger, Fennel, and Pear Soup (page 132). Macadamia nuts or cashews make good substitutions for the pecans. You can also use your favorite pâté to stuff the peppers.

INGREDIENTS | SERVES 2

2 red bell peppers

½ cup pecans

¼ cup hemp or sesame seeds

¼ cup chopped red or white onion

1 tablespoon lime juice

½ tablespoon chopped jalapeño pepper

¼ teaspoon salt

½ teaspoon Mexican seasoning

½ cup sliced avocado

2 tablespoons cilantro

1. Cut the red bell peppers in half and remove the stems and seeds.

2. In a food processor, process the pecans, hemp seeds, onion, lime juice, jalapeño, salt, and Mexican seasoning.

3. Fill each red bell pepper half full with the prepared mixture and garnish with avocado slices and cilantro.

PER SERVING:
Calories: 408 | Fat: 33 g | Protein: 12 g | Sodium: 301 mg | Fiber: 10 g

CHAPTER 13

Entrées and Comfort Foods

Raw Pasta with Tomato Marinara

Quick prep: If you use store-bought marinated sun-dried tomatoes, this takes about 15 minutes. This recipe is good served with the Marinated Kale and Avocado Salad (page 85). In place of the parsley, basil, and oregano, you can substitute other spices you may have on hand.

INGREDIENTS | **SERVES 2**

¼ cup sun-dried tomatoes, soaked, or marinated sun-dried tomatoes
½ cup water for soaking
1 cup fresh tomatoes
½ cup red bell pepper
2 tablespoons minced onion
1 clove garlic
2 tablespoons olive oil
1 tablespoon minced fresh parsley
1 tablespoon minced basil
½ tablespoon oregano
¼ cup raw olives, chopped
2 medium zucchini

1. To make the marinara sauce, place all the ingredients, except the olives and zucchini, into a blender and blend until smooth. Blend in the fresh herbs last. Add the sun-dried tomato soak water if you need more liquid.

2. Process the zucchini into noodles using a spiral slicer. Alternatively, use a mandolin or a knife to create long, thin slices.

3. Place the zucchini noodles in a serving bowl and place a scoop of the tomato sauce on top. Garnish with olives and your favorite fresh herbs.

PER SERVING:
Calories: 150 | Fat: 9 g | Protein: 4 g | Sodium: 304 mg | Fiber: 5 g

Raw Pasta with Cream Sauce

Quick prep: Soak the noodles for 30 minutes, and prepare the sauce while they're soaking. Serve with the Raw Caesar Salad (page 81) and the Ginger, Fennel, and Pear Soup (page 132). You can substitute zucchini noodles in place of the kelp noodles. Garnish with diced red bell pepper and parsley.

INGREDIENTS | SERVES 2

1 cups cashews, soaked

¼ cup pine nuts

2 teaspoons raw honey

1 clove garlic

½ teaspoon allspice

¼ teaspoon black pepper

2 tablespoons lemon juice

1 teaspoon nutritional yeast (optional)

½ package kelp noodles

Kelp Noodles

These noodles are a raw packaged food available in many health food stores and online. They are made of kelp sea vegetables and have a neutral flavor, so they absorb the flavor of any sauce. Kelp is an excellent source of trace minerals, especially iodine, which is important in thyroid function and can affect energy and weight mastery.

1. To make a creamy sauce, blend all the ingredients except for the noodles in a blender until smooth.

2. Rinse the kelp noodles and soak them in water for 30 minutes. Alternatively, you can soften the noodles by covering them in olive oil and nama shoyu and soaking them for 30 minutes. This enhances the flavor.

3. Place a serving of kelp noodles into each serving bowl. Place a heaping spoonful of sauce on top of the noodles.

PER SERVING:

Calories: 609 | Fat: 52 g | Protein: 17 g | Sodium: 36 mg | Fiber: 5 g

Raw Vegetable Lasagna

Quick prep: Use the Macadamia Alfredo Sauce (page 207) or homemade cheese you have on hand. This is a raw version of the popular pasta dish. The noodles are made with thin strips of zucchini. It is especially good served with the Raw Caesar Salad (page 81).

INGREDIENTS | SERVES 2

2 medium zucchini

¼ teaspoon salt

1 cup Tomato Marinara Sauce (page 226)

1 cup Almond Cheese (page 159) or Macadamia Alfredo Sauce (page 207)

1 cup chopped spinach

2 large tomatoes, sliced

Mandolin Slicers

Mandolin slicers and potato peelers are invaluable tools in the kitchen. They allow you to create thin slices of vegetables and fruits. The width and thickness of the slices can be adjusted to add variety to your meals. The broadly cut vegetables are great used as lasagna noodles, fettuccini noodles, and stuffed ravioli. Many vegetables, such as eggplant and jicama, can be sliced super thin, marinated, and then dehydrated into crunchy chips.

1. Create the lasagna noodles by slicing the zucchini on a mandolin or with a knife into long, thin strips. Sprinkle the strips with a ¼ teaspoon salt.

2. In a square or rectangle glass baking dish, spread a thin layer of the marinara sauce onto the bottom.

3. Arrange a layer of the zucchini strips on top of the marinara. Top the zucchini with a thin layer of almond cheese, and then a layer of spinach, and then a layer of tomatoes. Repeat the process alternating layers until you reach the top.

4. Cover the lasagna with marinara. It is now ready to eat, or it can be warmed in the dehydrator at 145°F for 1 hour.

PER SERVING:

Calories: 543 | Fat: 40 g | Protein: 21 g | Sodium: 765 mg | Fiber: 14 g

Macadamia Alfredo Sauce

Quick prep: This sauce only takes a few minutes to prepare. It provides a good alternative to cheese in noodle-type dishes, in wraps, nori rolls, and on sandwiches as a spread.

INGREDIENTS | SERVES 2

¾ cup macadamia nuts
½ cup pine nuts
1 teaspoon agave nectar
2 tablespoons lemon juice
½ teaspoon salt
½ teaspoon black pepper
2 teaspoons minced garlic (optional)
½ cup water for blending

In a blender, blend together all ingredients until smooth. Gradually add the water as the sauce is blending. Add just enough water to help it blend into a thick sauce.

PER SERVING:

Calories: 603 | Fat: 61 g | Protein: 9 g | Sodium: 586 mg | Fiber: 6 g

Pesto Lasagna

Quick prep: Use the Macadamia Alfredo Sauce (above) or homemade cheese you have on hand. This is a good recipe to serve with a green salad, such as the Romaine with Tangerines or Oranges (page 80). You could also try adding a layer of marinated portobello mushrooms or dehydrated eggplant strips.

INGREDIENTS | SERVES 2

2 medium zucchinis
¼ teaspoon salt
½ cup Cilantro Pesto (page 226)
½ cup Pine Nut Cheese (page 163)
¼ cup raw olives, for garnish

Pesto

Traditionally made by hand in a marble mortar with a wooden pestle, this dish can be created with mint and basil or cilantro. Other variations include the use of almonds or walnuts in place of pine nuts, and the addition of olives, sun-dried tomatoes, mushrooms, or lemon peel.

1. Create the lasagna noodles by slicing zucchini into long, thin strips with a potato peeler or mandolin slicer. Sprinkle the strips with a ¼ teaspoon salt.

2. Place a layer of zucchini on the bottom of a glass baking pan. Place a layer of pesto sauce on the zucchini. Place another layer of zucchini on the pesto. Place a layer of pine nut cheese, another layer of zucchini, and a final layer of pesto.

3. Sprinkle olives on top to garnish.

PER SERVING:

Calories: 821 | Fat: 82 g | Protein: 14 g | Sodium: 889 mg | Fiber: 5 g

Pasta Primavera

Quick prep: less than 30 minutes. Serve this dish with fresh spring vegetables, such as fresh pod peas or baby snow peas. Pettipan squash work well—these are the little round pale green squashes with a scalloped edge. Given their sweet, mild flavor, they can be sliced paper thin and used in layers in place of the zucchini.

INGREDIENTS | SERVES 4

3 medium zucchinis

½ cup sliced cherry tomatoes

¼ cup asparagus tips

¼ cup red bell pepper, sliced into thin strips

¼ cup carrots, grated or shredded

Pine Nut Sauce (below), as needed

1. Process the zucchini into noodles using a spiral slicer. Alternatively, grate the zucchini or slice into strips.

2. Toss the zucchini noodles with the chopped vegetables.

3. Pour the sauce over the noodles and vegetables and serve in pasta bowls.

PER SERVING:

Calories: 392 | Fat: 33 g | Protein: 11 g | Sodium: 316 mg | Fiber: 4 g

Pasta Primavera

Primavera is a word from the Romance languages that means the season of spring. Pasta primavera is a traditional pasta dish made with noodles, a cream sauce, and fresh vegetables.

Pine Nut Sauce

Quick prep: This is a raw cuisine version of a classic Mediterranean sauce for pasta. You could vary this sauce with whatever fresh herb is in season or with sun-dried tomatoes.

INGREDIENTS | SERVES 4

½ cup pine nuts

1 cup cashews, presoaked

2 tablespoons olive oil

1 clove garlic

½ teaspoon salt

2 tablespoons fresh herbs or 1 tablespoon dried herbes de Provence

Water for blending

Prepare the sauce by blending the pine nuts, cashews, olive oil, garlic, salt, and herbes de Provence. Add just enough water to help it blend into a cream.

PER SERVING:

Calories: 359 | Fat: 33 g | Protein: 8 g | Sodium: 295 mg | Fiber: 2 g

Stuffed Ravioli

Quick prep: less than 30 minutes. Make the pesto, make the pine nut sauce, slice the jicama, and serve. Thin strips of jicama make a good ravioli shell. Another good option for the shell is the Coconut Wraps (page 189).

INGREDIENTS | SERVES 2

½ jicama, peeled and sliced in thin strips
½ cup Cilantro Pesto (page 226)
¼ cup Pine Nut Cheese (page 163) or Pine Nut Sauce (page 208)
Raw olives to garnish (optional)

1. Peel the jicama and slice it into thin squares, about 4 inches by 4 inches. A mandolin slicer works great for this.

2. Place ½ tablespoon pesto in the middle of each jicama slice. Fold over the jicama and press together the edges to create the ravioli.

3. Place the raviolis onto a plate. Drizzle the pine nut cheese or pine nut sauce on top and garnish with olives.

PER SERVING:
Calories: 766 | Fat: 79 g | Protein: 11 g | Sodium: 732 mg | Fiber: 5 g

Indian-Style Curried Noodles

Quick prep: less than 30 minutes. This is a good dish to serve with the Thai Spice Crackers (page 104). Cashews or macadamia nuts make a good substitution for the young coconut.

INGREDIENTS | SERVES 2

1 cup young coconut meat
¼ cup dried coconut
½ cup young coconut water
1 teaspoon curry powder
¼ teaspoon turmeric
2 tablespoons minced fresh basil
½ package kelp noodles, soaked

1. In a blender, blend together the young coconut meat, dried coconut, young coconut water, curry, and turmeric until smooth. Add the basil last and pulse.

2. Separate the kelp noodles into serving bowls.

3. Pour the sauce over the noodles and stir to coat the noodles.

PER SERVING:
Calories: 96 | Fat: 6 g | Protein: 2 g | Sodium: 94 mg | Fiber: 4 g

Zucchini Pie with Italian Walnut Pâté

Quick prep: less than 20 minutes. This is a delicious pie that can be filled with many different types of pâtés and sauces. It can be dehydrated and served warm. Good garnishes include fresh herbs, Pine Nut Cheese (page 163), and a gravy sauce.

INGREDIENTS | SERVES 2

3 medium zucchinis
1 cup spinach
½ teaspoon salt
2 tablespoons lemon juice
1 cup Zesty Italian Walnut Pâté (page 144)
1½ teaspoons salt

1. Using a vegetable peeler, peel the zucchini into long, wide, and thin strips. Alternatively, use a knife to slice the zucchini into strips.

2. Soak the zucchini strips in a bowl with 1 cup warm water mixed with 1 teaspoon salt. Soak for 5 to 10 minutes to soften.

3. Mince the spinach and place into a bowl. Wilt the spinach by massaging in ½ teaspoon salt and lemon juice.

4. Place the zucchini strips into four ramekin bowls. Line the bowl with the strips in a single layer, about 1 inch overlapping. Let the top quarter of the zucchini strips hang outside the bowl, leaving the bottom inside the bowl.

5. Place a small layer of pâté into the bowl. Top with a single layer of spinach and a second layer of pâté.

6. Fold the zucchini strips over the filling to cover.

PER SERVING:
Calories: 243 | Fat: 21 g | Protein: 7 g | Sodium: 753 mg | Fiber: 5 g

Creamy Noodles

Quick prep: less than 30 minutes.
These noodles resemble Japanese egg noodles.

INGREDIENTS | SERVES 2

3 medium zucchinis
½ teaspoon salt
¼ cup macadamia nuts
¼ cup cashews
¼ cup water
½ tablespoon nutritional yeast
½ tablespoon nama shoyu
2 tablespoons lemon juice
1 clove garlic
½ teaspoon dried onion
⅛ teaspoon black pepper
½ cup asparagus tips
½ cup cherry tomatoes
1 tablespoon fresh tarragon, for garnish

Noodles

Cooked noodle dishes are easy to replicate in raw food cuisine. Raw kelp noodles are a healthy, mineral-rich food available at most health food stores. They can be softened up by marinating for a short time in your favorite marinade. A spiral slicer is perfect for making vegetable noodles. Good vegetables to use with the spiral slicer include onion, butternut squash, sweet potato, beet, zucchini, cucumber, carrot, turnip, and daikon radish.

1. Using a vegetable peeler, peel the skin off the zucchini and set aside. Peel the remaining inside of the zucchini into long, thin noodles and stop when you get to the center with the seeds. Set aside the centers.

2. Place the zucchini noodles in a big bowl. Sprinkle 1 teaspoon salt on top and stir.

3. To prepare the sauce, place the macadamia nuts, cashews, water, 1 cup of the zucchini centers, nutritional yeast, nama shoyu, lemon juice, garlic, dried onion, and black pepper in a blender or food processor and blend together.

4. Squeeze the noodles. Add any liquid that has collected beneath the salted noodles to the sauce in the food processor. Blend until it becomes a creamy sauce.

5. Toss the noodles with the sauce, asparagus tips, and cherry tomatoes.

6. Serve in pasta bowls and garnish with fresh tarragon leafs.

PER SERVING:
Calories: 259 | Fat: 20 g | Protein: 8 g | Sodium: 820 mg | Fiber: 5 g

Pad Thai with Almond Sauce

Quick prep: less than 30 minutes. Pad thai is a traditional dish from Thailand. This recipe uses a sesame seed tahini sauce in place of the peanut sauce. Good substitutions for the zucchini are jicama or kelp noodles. This recipe is good with a little curry powder or lemongrass blended into the sauce.

INGREDIENTS | SERVES 2

2 tablespoons lime juice

1 tablespoon Tahini (page 138) or freshly ground sesame seeds

1 tablespoon agave nectar or honey

2 tablespoons nama shoyu

1 clove minced garlic

½ tablespoon ginger

¼ cup sun-dried tomatoes, soaked

½ cup sun-dried tomato soak water

3 medium zucchinis

2 large carrots

½ cup mung bean sprouts

½ cup snow peas

¼ cup asparagus tips or pod peas in season

¼ cup finely sliced scallions

2–4 tablespoons minced cilantro, for garnish

1. To make the pad thai sauce, place the lime juice, tahini, agave nectar, nama shoyu, garlic, ginger, and sun-dried tomatoes in a blender and blend until smooth. Gradually pour in the sun-dried tomato soak water until it blends into a thick sauce.

2. Using a spiral slicer, make noodles with the zucchini and carrot. Alternatively, julienne or shred them.

3. Place the noodles, mung bean sprouts, snow peas, asparagus, and scallions on a large serving plate. Drizzle on the sauce and garnish with cilantro.

PER SERVING:
Calories: 207 | Fat: 5 g | Protein: 10 g | Sodium: 1,134 mg | Fiber: 9 g

Chiles Rellenos

Quick prep: 20 minutes. This is a spicy chili pâté that is good served with the Gazpacho Soup (page 125) and a garnish of Pine Nut Cheese (page 163).

INGREDIENTS | SERVES 2

½ cup jicama, peeled and chopped

¼ cup red onion, chopped

1 tablespoon olive oil

½ cup tomato, chopped

¼ cup sun-dried tomatoes, soaked

1 teaspoon chili powder

½ tablespoon minced garlic

¼ teaspoon salt

½ teaspoon oregano

¼ teaspoon cumin

2 tablespoons lime juice

½ cup water

1 yellow bell pepper

1 tablespoon minced cilantro, for garnish

1. To prepare the filling, add the jicama to a food processor and pulse until it becomes a rice consistency. Transfer to a large bowl and stir in ¼ cup onion and 1 tablespoon olive oil.

2. To prepare the sauce place the tomato, sun-dried tomato, chili powder, garlic, salt, oregano, cumin, lime juice, and water in a food processor and purée.

3. Slice the bell pepper in half. Remove the stems and seeds.

4. Fill each bell pepper half with a scoop of the filling. Pour the sauce over each bell pepper and garnish with fresh cilantro.

PER SERVING:
Calories: 213 | Fat: 15 g | Protein: 4 g | Sodium: 479 mg | Fiber: 6 g

Jicama Empanadas

*Quick prep: less than 30 minutes. These empanadas can be served fresh,
or they can be dehydrated and served warm.*

INGREDIENTS | SERVES 2

½ jicama
4 tablespoons lime juice
4 tablespoons olive oil
1 teaspoon cumin
½ teaspoon salt
1 cup walnuts
2 tablespoons green pumpkin seeds
1 tablespoon onion powder
½ clove garlic, minced
½ teaspoon cinnamon
½ tablespoon jalapeño pepper, diced
1 tablespoon fresh minced oregano or
1 teaspoon dried

1. Prepare the empanada shell by slicing the jicama with a mandolin slicer or cheese grater. Cut the jicama into long, thin slices.

2. Prepare a dressing by stirring together the lime juice, olive oil, ½ teaspoon cumin, and salt. Brush each jicama slice to lightly coat them with the dressing.

3. Prepare the filling by blending together the walnuts, pumpkin seeds, onion powder, garlic, remaining ½ teaspoon cumin, cinnamon, jalapeño, and oregano.

4. Lay the jicama slices flat. Place a small scoop of the filling onto one half of each jicama slice. Fold over the jicama to create a pocket. Serve immediately, or dehydrate for 2 hours at 145°F and serve warm.

PER SERVING:
Calories: 541 | Fat: 51 g | Protein: 11 g | Sodium: 590 mg | Fiber: 8 g

Taco Salad

Quick prep: To bring out the flavor, cut a head of lettuce in half and then slice off thin layers, which creates fine ribbons of the lettuce that are ideal for wraps or pocket sandwiches.

INGREDIENTS | SERVES 2

2 cups shredded iceberg lettuce

1 cup Mexican Pâté (page 146)

1 cup chopped tomato

1 cup avocado, sliced

½ cup corn, cut fresh off the cob

1 cup Simple Salsa (page 135)

¼ cup Cashew Sour Cream (page 163)

1. On salad plates, place a layer of lettuce.

2. Top with Mexican pâté, tomato, avocado, corn, and salsa.

2. Place a scoop of Cashew Sour Cream on top and serve.

PER SERVING:

Calories: 454 | Fat: 31 g | Protein: 14 g | Sodium: 690 mg | Fiber: 13 g

Iceberg Lettuce

Sometimes called crisp head lettuce, iceberg is a dense, tight head that resembles cabbage. Bred to remove the bitterness from the lettuce, it is one of the most popular lettuce varieties because of its mild taste and crunchy texture. Although it is low in nutrients compared to other nutrient-dense leafy green vegetables, iceberg lettuce is a natural refrigerant (cooling food), so it is ideal for hot summer dishes.

Lemon Parsnip and Parsley Rice Pilaf

Quick prep: less than 15 minutes. Processing parsnips gives them a similar texture to rice. This dish also works well with cauliflower or jicama used in place of parsnip. This "rice" is especially good in nori rolls and wraps.

INGREDIENTS | SERVES 2–4

2 medium parsnips
1 clove garlic, minced
2 tablespoons olive oil
2 tablespoons lemon juice
2 tablespoons parsley
½ teaspoon salt

1. Peel the parsnip and chop it into smaller chunks.

2. Pulse the parsnip and garlic in a food processor with the *S* blade until it has the consistency of rice.

3. Add the olive oil, lemon juice, parsley, and salt and pulse until well mixed.

PER SERVING:
Calories: 226 | Fat: 14 g | Protein: 2 g | Sodium: 597 mg | Fiber: 7 g

Rice

Rice is a food that is better consumed cooked, and it is a great food to eat if you are not 100 percent raw. Parsnip and cauliflower make the perfect substitute for rice because they have a similar taste and texture when processed in a food processor. Parsnip or cauliflower pilaf has many uses, including stuffing for nori rolls, as a bed for vegetables and curry sauce, and in standard rice and sprouted bean dishes.

African Tomato and Almond Wat Stew

This hearty stew requires some advance preparation. Made with traditional Ethiopian spices, this dish can be garnished with fresh parsley and served with a side of flax flatbread and a glass of young coconut water.

INGREDIENTS | SERVES 4

1 cup lentils, sprouted
1 cup sun-dried tomatoes, soaked
½ cup pine nuts
2 tablespoons olive oil
1 teaspoon salt
½ tablespoon Berber spice
3 cups water
½ cup zucchini, chopped
¼ cup celery, minced
1 cup tomato, chopped
¼ cup almonds, soaked
2 tablespoons lemon juice

1. Prepare the stew base by blending together the sun-dried tomatoes, pine nuts, olive oil, salt, Berber spice, and water.

2. Prepare the vegetables for the stew. Chop the zucchini into cubes. Dice the celery into small pieces.

3. Mix the stew base, lentils, zucchini, celery, whole almonds, and lemon juice together in a large bowl and serve.

PER SERVING:
Calories: 292 | Fat: 23 g | Protein: 9 g | Sodium: 877 mg | Fiber: 4 g

Ethiopian Cuisine

Ethiopian food is popular in the vegetarian community because it has many meat-free, plant-based meals. Berber is a spice blend commonly used in Ethiopian dishes and is available at most spice stores. *Wat* is the name for the hearty Ethiopian stew traditionally eaten with sourdough flatbread called *injera*.

New Orleans Beans and Rice

Some advanced preparation is required to sprout the lentils and soak the sun-dried tomatoes. The result is a spicy entrée reminiscent of New Orleans or Creole cuisine. Jicama or cauliflower are good substitutions for the parsnips.

INGREDIENTS | SERVES 2

¼ cup sun-dried tomatoes, soaked

2 tablespoons onion

1 clove garlic

2 tablespoons lemon juice

2 teaspoons miso

1½ teaspoons fresh jalapeño pepper

¼ cup red bell peppers

¼ cup celery

½ teaspoon salt

¼ teaspoon black pepper

1 teaspoon thyme

1 cup parsnips, peeled and chopped

½ teaspoon salt

1 cup sprouted lentils

1. To prepare the sauce, blend together the sun-dried tomato, onion, garlic, 1 tablespoon lemon juice, miso, jalapeño, red bell pepper, celery, salt, black pepper, and thyme. Add just enough sun-dried tomato soak water to create a thick sauce.

2. Process the parsnips with ½ teaspoon salt and 1 tablespoon lemon juice in a food processor with the *S* blade. Using the pulse function, process them just enough to make the mixture look like rice.

3. Make a bed of parsnip rice on a plate. Pour the sauce on top of the parsnip rice, and sprinkle the sprouted lentils on top.

PER SERVING:
Calories: 133 | Fat: 1 g | Protein: 6 g | Sodium: 844 mg | Fiber: 5 g

Parsnips

Parsnips are nutritious root vegetables that are delicious raw. They are good substitutions for starchy foods like rice, pasta noodles, and mashed potatoes. They are in the same family as carrots and are a good source of complex carbohydrates, fiber, potassium, and beta-carotene.

Dirty Rice (Traditional Southwestern Dish)

This is a raw food version of traditional dirty rice, which has a dark brown color. The parsnip mixed with the tahini gives this dish the same hue and texture of dirty rice. This dish is good served with the Sprouted Moroccan Lentil Soup (page 167) and a side salad.

INGREDIENTS | SERVES 4

1 cup portobello mushrooms, cubed

½ cup olive oil

½ cup nama shoyu

½ cup Tahini (page 138)

1 tablespoon miso

¼ teaspoon cayenne pepper powder

2 tablespoons lemon juice

2 cloves garlic

¾ cup water

2 medium parsnips

½ cup red bell pepper, finely chopped

½ cup celery, finely chopped

2 tablespoons parsley

¼ cup scallions, sliced thin

½ teaspoon fresh-ground black pepper

1. Place the cubed portobello mushrooms into a large bowl. Marinate them in olive oil and nama shoyu for 3 hours. As an alternative, you can dehydrate the mushrooms to richen the flavor. Dehydrate at 110°F for 8 to 12 hours.

2. Make a sauce by blending together the tahini, miso, cayenne pepper, lemon juice, garlic, and water until smooth.

3. Peel the parsnip and chop into smaller chunks. Pulse them in a food processor with the *S* blade until it creates a rice-grain consistency.

4. In a mixing bowl, toss together all ingredients until well mixed. Top with freshly ground black pepper.

PER SERVING:

Calories: 504 | Fat: 42 g | Protein: 10 g | Sodium: 2,001 mg | Fiber: 8 g

Dirty Rice

This is a popular dish served in the American South, especially in the Cajun regions of southern Louisiana and Mississippi. The portobello mushrooms are a hearty substitute for the traditional chicken.

Shepherd's Pie with Mashed Taters

This entrée is reminiscent of traditional comfort food. The dehydrator will help the mashed cauliflower taters form a crust, similar to that of a cooked shepherd's pie. The mushrooms are marinated in olive oil and nama shoyu. The leftover olive oil and nama shoyu may be saved and used as a salad dressing.

INGREDIENTS | SERVES 4

1 cup portobello mushrooms
½ cup olive oil
½ cup nama shoyu
1 cup macadamia nuts
2 cups cauliflower, chopped
¼ cup olive oil
1 clove garlic
1 teaspoon salt
¼ teaspoon cayenne pepper powder
1 teaspoon rosemary
2 teaspoons nutritional yeast
1 cup asparagus tips
½ cup chopped carrots
½ cup chopped onion
1 tablespoon lemon juice
1 cup Black Sesame Seed Gravy (page 227)
1 teaspoon sweet paprika

1. Chop the portobello mushrooms and place into a large bowl. Marinate them in olive oil and nama shoyu for 3 hours. Use the portobello mushrooms as is, or you may place them in a dehydrator and dehydrate at 110°F for 4 to 8 hours.

2. In a food processor, process the macadamia nuts until smooth. Add in the cauliflower, olive oil, garlic, ½ teaspoon salt, cayenne, rosemary, and nutritional yeast. Continue processing until smooth. Set aside.

3. Chop the asparagus tips, carrots, and onion into small chunks. Sprinkle ½ teaspoon salt and lemon juice onto the chopped vegetables.

4. Stir the black sesame seed gravy in with the chopped vegetables and mushrooms.

5. Scoop the vegetable mixture into casserole serving dishes. Spread a layer of the cauliflower mixture on top. Garnish with paprika.

6. Serve immediately, or warm in the dehydrator at 145°F for 3 hours.

PER SERVING:
Calories: 703 | Fat: 44 g | Protein: 8 g | Sodium: 799 mg | Fiber: 8 g

Spinach Pie

Quick prep: Chop and salt the spinach. If you make the crust with almond meal like a raw torte, rather than dehydrating it, you can prepare this dish in less than 30 minutes.

INGREDIENTS | SERVES 4

2 cups chopped spinach
1 teaspoon salt
1 cup almonds, soaked
¼ cup flaxseed, ground
1 tablespoon honey
2 tablespoons liquid coconut oil
½ cup pine nuts
¼ cup onion
1 garlic clove, minced
½ teaspoon nutmeg
2 tablespoons lemon juice
2 tablespoons nama shoyu

1. Remove any thick stems from the spinach. Roll the spinach leaves and slice them into small pieces. Sprinkle the salt onto the spinach. Squeeze and massage the spinach to create a wilting effect. Drain any excess liquid.

2. Prepare the crust by placing the almonds in a food processor and blending until ground into small pieces. Add the ground flaxseed, honey, and liquid coconut oil and continue processing until well mixed. The crust in this recipe can be dehydrated for 8 to 12 hours for a crispy texture.

3. Press a thin layer of the crust on the bottom of a casserole pan.

4. Place the spinach in a food processor with the pine nuts, onion, garlic, nutmeg, lemon juice, and nama shoyu. Briefly pulse until ingredients are well mixed but still chunky.

5. Spread out a layer of the spinach mixture into the pan, and top with a layer of the crust.

PER SERVING:
Calories: 465 | Fat: 41 g | Protein: 13 g | Sodium: 758 mg | Fiber: 9 g

Mushroom and Walnut Tartlets

Quick prep: less than 30 minutes. The cashews may be replaced with soaked sunflower seeds or young coconut meat. The chives and rosemary could be replaced with your favorite fresh or dried herbs.

INGREDIENTS | SERVES 4

1 cup walnuts

½ cup Brazil nuts

2 tablespoons liquid coconut oil

1 teaspoon salt

1 cup cashews

2 tablespoons olive oil

1 clove garlic, minced

2 tablespoons lemon juice

2 tablespoons tamari

1 tablespoon chives, chopped

½ tablespoon rosemary, chopped

½ teaspoon black pepper

½ cup crimini mushrooms, sliced thin

½ cup hearts of celery, sliced thin

Celery

Celery sticks have tough strings that can be difficult to chew. Removing the strings will make the celery more enjoyable to eat. To remove the strings, make a small cut at the top of the celery stalk and peel it back. The strings should come off easily with the knife. You may also use a vegetable peeler. If you want a gentle flavor or softer texture, use celery hearts in the recipe.

1. To prepare the crust place the walnuts, Brazil nuts, liquid coconut oil (place container in warm water to melt), and salt in a food processor and process until smooth.

2. Press the crust into small ramekin serving bowls.

3. In a food processor, process the cashews until well broken down. Gradually add the olive oil, garlic, lemon juice, and tamari. Process until smooth. Add the fresh herbs and black pepper last and briefly pulse to mix.

4. Place a layer of sliced mushrooms and thinly sliced celery in each ramekin bowl. Fill with the blended cashew sauce and serve.

PER SERVING:

Calories: 616 | Fat: 58 g | Protein: 14 g | Sodium: 1,100 mg | Fiber: 5 g

Fresh Ratatouille

This is a delicious, slow-baked stew prepared in the dehydrator that can be served as an entrée, a side dish, or as a filling in a collard wrap burrito.

INGREDIENTS | SERVES 2

½ medium eggplant

1½ teaspoons salt, divided

4 tablespoons olive oil

¼ cup red bell pepper

¼ cup sun-dried tomatoes, soaked

2 cloves garlic

4 tablespoons onions, diced

1 tablespoon herbes de Provence

1 cup tomatoes, thinly sliced

1 cup zucchini, thinly sliced

½ cup yellow or red bell peppers, thinly sliced

½ cup yellow summer squash, thinly sliced

1. Slice the eggplant into thin round slices, sprinkle with 1 teaspoon salt, and brush with olive oil. Dehydrate at 115°F for 12 hours.

2. Prepare the sauce in a food processor with the *S* blade. Process the red bell pepper, sun-dried tomatoes, garlic, onion, ½ teaspoon salt, and herbes de Provence until well mixed but still chunky.

3. Toss the sliced vegetables and eggplant together with the sauce and place into a casserole dish.

4. Serve as is, or dehydrate at 145°F for 2 hours and serve warm.

PER SERVING:
Calories: 198 | Fat: 14 g | Protein: 4 g | Sodium: 447 mg | Fiber: 5 g

Ratatouille

Ratatouille is a vegetable and herb stew, originated in France, that is prepared with different combinations of tomatoes, squashes, and spices, depending on the region. The three most popular ways to serve ratatouille include as a tossed stew, in a layered casserole, or as an arrangement of the vegetable rounds. (This delicious traditional dish was featured in the 2007 animated Walt Disney film of the same name.)

CHAPTER 14

Sweet and Savory Sauces

Cilantro Pesto

This is a great sauce to spread on crackers and wraps. To use this combination as a sauce on veggie noodles, thin the texture by blending in ¼ cup water.

INGREDIENTS | SERVES 4

1 cup fresh basil
1½ cups fresh cilantro
2 cloves garlic, minced
4 tablespoons olive oil
1 teaspoon salt
1 cup pine nuts

1. Using the *S* blade on a food processor, process the basil, cilantro, garlic, and salt until the basil is chopped.

2. Add in the pine nuts and olive oil. Process until smooth. Use a spatula to scrape the sides of the food processor bowl. Do not overprocess—there should still be small chunks of basil and pine nuts in the sauce.

3. Pesto will stay good for a couple of days in the refrigerator.

PER SERVING:
Calories: 351 | Fat: 37 g | Protein: 5 g | Sodium: 586 mg | Fiber: 2 g

Tomato Marinara Sauce

A delicious sauce to serve with almond meat balls, veggie noodles, or the Raw Vegetable Lasagna (page 206).

INGREDIENTS | SERVES 4

1 cup sun-dried tomatoes
2 cups water, for soaking
2 cups tomatoes, chopped
1 cup red bell pepper, chopped
2 tablespoons olive oil
2 cloves garlic, minced
¼ cup raisins, currants, dates, or chopped apples
1 tablespoon Italian seasoning
½ teaspoon cayenne pepper powder
½ teaspoon salt

1. Soak the sun-dried tomatoes in 2 cups water for 2 hours.

2. Blend all the ingredients together in a blender with 1 cup of the soak water until smooth.

PER SERVING:
Calories: 158 | Fat: 8 g | Protein: 4 g | Sodium: 581 mg | Fiber: 4 g

Fresh Barbecue Sauce

A rich and spicy sauce, this recipe is good served as a condiment on veggie burgers and as a marinade for diced vegetables. It can also be mixed with a flax cracker batter and dehydrated to make BBQ crackers. The spices in this recipe can be replaced with a store-bought barbecue seasoning blend.

INGREDIENTS | SERVES 4

1 cup sun-dried tomatoes, soaked
1 dried chipotle pepper, soaked
2 tablespoons maple syrup
1 cup tomato, chopped
2 tablespoons apple cider vinegar
½ teaspoon salt
1 teaspoon nama shoyu
1 clove garlic
2 teaspoons chili powder

Blend all ingredients with ½ cup sun-dried tomato soak water in a blender until smooth.

PER SERVING:

Calories: 80 | Fat: 1 g | Protein: 3 g | Sodium: 664 mg | Fiber: 3 g

Maple Syrup

Maple syrup is a mineral-rich, amber sap harvested from maple trees. While it is not raw, it is still used in raw gourmet cuisine because it is a whole plant food with a delicious earthy flavor. Maple syrup is high in vitamins and in minerals such as zinc and manganese. It was first harvested by the North American Indians, who taught the European settlers how to tap the maple trees.

Black Sesame Seed Gravy

This is a delicious sauce served over mashed taters (see Shepherd's Pie with Mashed Taters, page 220).

INGREDIENTS | SERVES 2

½ cup black sesame seeds
2 tablespoons finely sliced scallions, or minced red or white onion
1 tablespoon nama shoyu
1 cup chopped portobello mushrooms
1 clove garlic
1 tablespoon lemon juice
¼ teaspoon salt
Water for blending

1. Grind the sesame seeds into a powder with a coffee grinder or spice mill.

2. Blend all ingredients in a blender until smooth. Slowly pour in a little water until desired consistency is reached.

PER SERVING:

Calories: 228 | Fat: 18 g | Protein: 8 g | Sodium: 749 mg | Fiber: 5 g

Black Sesame Seeds

Black sesame seeds are higher in calcium and lower in fat than the white seeds. They are a good source of protein, zinc, phosphorus, and potassium.

Mole Sauce

This is a great recipe that can be made in less than 30 minutes. This traditional Mexican recipe has a good balance between sweet and spice. The sauce can be used as a dip, a salad dressing, and as a sauce for cabbage leaf rolls filled with Mexican Pâté (page 146).

INGREDIENTS | SERVES 6

2 tablespoons raw cacao or carob

1 tablespoon jalapeño pepper, seeds removed and minced

¾ cup banana, sliced

2 tablespoons onion, diced

1 tablespoon agave nectar

1 cup chopped tomato

1 tablespoon olive oil

½ teaspoon salt

½ teaspoon cinnamon

¼ teaspoon cloves

½ teaspoon oregano

½ cup avocado

1. In a blender, blend together the cacao, jalapeño pepper, banana, onion, agave nectar, tomato, olive oil, salt, cinnamon, cloves, and oregano. You could add a pinch of allspice if you'd like.

2. Add the avocado last and blend until the sauce becomes smooth and creamy.

PER SERVING:

Calories: 85 | Fat: 5 g | Protein: 1 g | Sodium: 197 mg | Fiber: 3 g

Mole Sauce

Mole sauce is widely used in Mexican cuisine in an endless number of variations. The mole sauce with which Americans are most familiar is mole poblano, made with hot chili peppers, onions, and ground nuts, which combines sweet and spicy seasonings such as chocolate with cinnamon, cumin, and oregano.

Mustard Sauce

This is a spicy condiment great for burgers and wraps. The mustard seeds can be blended immediately after soaking for 8 hours, or they can be sprouted for 3 days after soaking. If you don't have mustard seeds, you may substitute 1 teaspoon mustard powder.

INGREDIENTS | SERVES 6

½ cup mustard seeds
½ cup cashews
¼ cup lemon juice
3 tablespoons agave nectar
1 tablespoon nama shoyu
¼ teaspoon turmeric powder
1 tablespoon apple cider vinegar

1. Soak the mustard seeds for 8 to 12 hours. Soak the cashews for 2 hours. Drain and rinse.

2. In a blender, blend all ingredients until smooth.

PER SERVING:
Calories: 164 | Fat: 9 g | Protein: 6 g | Sodium: 153 mg | Fiber: 3 g

Apple Cider Vinegar

Apple cider vinegar is an unpasteurized vinegar that has many culinary and medicinal uses. It usually contains a beneficial bacteria described as "Mother of Vinegar." This pleasant-flavored, mild vinegar helps to restore the body to a more alkaline pH, which may help prevent illness.

Green Bean Spread

This is a delicious spread to use on crackers and wraps.

INGREDIENTS | SERVES 2

2 cups green beans
½ cup cashews
1 teaspoon blue-green algae
½ tablespoon Italian seasoning
½ teaspoon minced garlic
¼ teaspoon salt

Blend all ingredients into a smooth purée.

PER SERVING:
Calories: 223 | Fat: 15 g | Protein: 9 g | Sodium: 314 mg | Fiber: 5 g

Salt

There are three types of salt commonly used in raw food cuisine: Celtic Sea Salt, Himalayan salt, and Real Salt. They are about 80 percent sodium chloride and contain over fifty trace minerals that are used by the body. These salts help keep us hydrated, replenish minerals, and maintain a healthy sodium-potassium balance. Common table salt is processed with chemicals, and all the trace minerals are removed.

Olive Tapenade Spread

This is a good spread to serve with breads and crackers. It can also be used as a condiment in burrito wraps, sandwiches, and spring rolls.

INGREDIENTS | SERVES 4

1½ cups raw olives, pitted
½ cup walnuts
4 tablespoons capers
2 tablespoons olive oil
1 tablespoon lemon juice

Place all ingredients in a food processor and pulse until well mixed. The spread should be chunky, not completely puréed.

PER SERVING:
Calories: 216 | Fat: 22 g | Protein: 3 g | Sodium: 684 mg | Fiber: 3 g

Tapenade

Tapenade is a paste made mainly from olive and capers that originated in southeastern France. It is a popular appetizer commonly served with bread and crackers and as a stuffing in entrées.

Mint Cashew Cream

*Serve the sauce with a veggie burger, as a spread on crackers,
or as a dip for a crudités platter. Olive oil can be substituted for the avocado.*

INGREDIENTS | YIELDS 2 CUPS

1 cup cashews
½ cup avocado
¼ cup fresh mint
1 teaspoon minced garlic
½ teaspoon salt
3 tablespoons lemon juice
½ teaspoon apple cider vinegar
½ cup water

Blend all ingredients, except the water, in a blender or food processor until creamy. Gradually add just enough water to help the ingredients blend.

PER CUP:

Calories: 438 | Fat: 35 g | Protein: 14 g | Sodium: 597 mg | Fiber: 5 g

Strawberry Date Sauce

*This is another version of strawberry sauce that is great served with desserts
or breakfast foods. The dates help add a thick texture and sweet flavor.*

INGREDIENTS | SERVES 2

2 cups strawberries
½ cup dried dates
Water for blending

Blend all ingredients in a blender. Add just enough water to help it blend into a smooth sauce.

PER SERVING:

Calories: 146 | Fat: 0 g | Protein: 1 g | Sodium: 2 mg | Fiber: 5 g

Apricot Jam

This is a sweet sauce that is good as a spread on raw crackers. It can be spread on celery sticks with almond butter for a satisfying snack. It can also be used as a filling for breakfast crepes.

INGREDIENTS | SERVES 4

2 cups dried apricots
2 tablespoons lemon juice
⅓ cup water, for blending

1. Soak the dried apricots in water for 15 minutes.

2. Place all the ingredients except the water in a blender and blend together until it becomes a thick sauce. Gradually add the water until desired consistency is reached.

PER SERVING:

Calories: 159 | Fat: 0 g | Protein: 2 g | Sodium: 7 mg | Fiber: 5 g

Date Paste

Date paste is used in many raw food recipes. It is an excellent sweetener and adds a nice texture to breakfast and dessert dishes.

INGREDIENTS | YIELDS ½ CUP

1 cup dried dates

Dates

Dates are a sweet fruit harvested from palm trees. They originated in the Middle East and have been a staple food in Middle Eastern cuisine for thousands of years. There are many different varieties available, ranging in texture from soft or semidry to dry. The most popular is the medjool date because it is large, sweet, and has a long shelf life.

1. Soak the dates in water for 4 to 6 hours. Remove the pits.

2. In a blender or food processor, process the dates until smooth.

PER SERVING:

Calories: 490 | Fat: 1 g | Protein: 4 g | Sodium: 5 mg | Fiber: 13 g

Raspberry Sauce

A creamy berry sauce that tastes great on brownies or ice cream or as a dressing for fruit salad. You can substitute other types of berries or fruits in place of the raspberries.

INGREDIENTS | SERVES 4

2 cups raspberries
1 cup young coconut meat
¼ cup young coconut water

In a blender or food processor, blend the raspberries with the young coconut meat and young coconut water until smooth.

PER SERVING:
Calories: 54 | Fat: 1 g | Protein: 1 g | Sodium: 16 mg | Fiber: 4 g

Cake Frosting

This is a delicious sauce to use with desserts such as cakes and pies. The cashews can be replaced with other creamy foods such as young coconut meat, macadamia nuts, pine nuts, or avocado. The coconut oil can be replaced with lecithin or psyllium husk powder.

INGREDIENTS | YIELDS 2 CUPS

2 cups cashews, soaked
½ cup orange juice
¼ cup honey
2 teaspoons vanilla extract
3 tablespoons liquid coconut oil
½ teaspoon salt

Using a high powered blender or a food processor, blend all ingredients together until smooth.

PER CUP:
Calories: 1,073 | Fat: 78 g | Protein: 25 g | Sodium: 600 mg | Fiber: 5 g

Cranberry Sauce

This is a wonderful recipe to serve during the holidays when fresh cranberries are in season. It is a good condiment served on sandwiches, salads, and burrito wraps. You can vary this recipe by using 1 cup oranges and omitting the apple.

INGREDIENTS | SERVES 4

1 cup dried dates
3 cups cranberries
1 cup walnuts
½ cup chopped orange
½ cup chopped apple
1 teaspoon cinnamon
1 teaspoon ginger juice

1. Soak the dates in water for 30 minutes. Remove pits and chop into small pieces.

2. Blend all ingredients together in a food processor until slightly chunky smooth.

PER SERVING:
Calories: 372 | Fat: 19 g | Protein: 6 g | Sodium: 4 mg | Fiber: 10 g

Cranberries: Not Just for Thanksgiving Anymore

The humble cranberry has been getting a lot of buzz in the scientific journals lately. The effects of cranberries on health are being studied in kids, seniors, pregnant woman, and folks of all ages—from the Mayo Clinic to Rutgers, and from Chile to Finland. The main benefit of cranberries still seems to be prevention and control of bladder infections. Since the ideal juice is unsweetened, you might want to experiment with your favorite recipes to see how low you can get the sugar content and still have a great flavor.

CHAPTER 15

Cookies, Bars, and Other Treats

Fudge Truffles

These are delicious candy truffles with a rich, chocolate flavor. Some good ingredient substitutions include maca powder, cayenne pepper powder, mesquite powder, vanilla, and mint. You can substitute walnuts, almonds, or cashews for the macadamia nuts.

INGREDIENTS | SERVES 6

1½ cups macadamia nuts
¾ cup dates, pitted and chopped
4 tablespoons liquid coconut oil
5 tablespoons raw carob powder
2 teaspoons cinnamon
1 teaspoon vanilla extract
¼ cup hemp seeds

1. Process the macadamia nuts in a food processor until smooth. Add the dates and continue processing.

2. Add the coconut oil, carob, cinnamon, and vanilla to the mixture. Continue to process until smooth.

3. Form the batter into little balls and roll them in the hemp seeds until well covered.

4. Place the truffles into the freezer for a minimum of 1 hour to help the coconut oil set.

PER SERVING:
Calories: 184 | Fat: 12 g | Protein: 5 g | Sodium: 3 mg | Fiber: 5 g

Date Brownies

Brownies make a healthy and satisfying snack. They are delicious with a few dried berries mixed in. You can use this basic recipe to create new flavors by adding different seasonings, such as pumpkin pie spice, nutmeg, cinnamon, or mesquite.

INGREDIENTS | SERVES 4

2 cups almonds
1 cup dried dates
1 teaspoon salt
½ cup carob powder
½ cup walnut halves

1. Blend the almonds in a food processor until they are well broken down and still chunky.

2. Mix in the dates, salt, and carob powder. Continue processing until well mixed.

3. Press the brownie batter into a square pan. Gently press the walnuts into the top

4. Place the pan into the freezer for 1 hour until it hardens. Slice into small squares.

PER SERVING:
Calories: 378 | Fat: 24 g | Protein: 8 g | Sodium: 585 mg | Fiber: 8 g

Walnut Pecan Brownies

This brownie recipe is ideal with a cream berry sauce spread on the top (see Raspberry Sauce, page 233).
You can substitute other types of berries or fruits in place of the raspberries.

INGREDIENTS | SERVES 6

2 cups walnuts

2 cups pecans

1 cup dried dates

½ cup carob powder

½ tablespoon cinnamon

4 tablespoons raw honey or agave

½ teaspoon salt

½ cup coconut oil, melted

Raspberry Sauce (page 233)

Raw Honey

Raw honey is known for its high mineral content and unique nutrients. Although some vegans do not use honey, a few of these recipes include honey in small amounts. You can usually find locally produced honey at farmers' markets or health food stores. Buying local gives you an opportunity to purchase honey from a producer you trust, who treats his bees with love and kindness.

1. Blend the walnuts and pecans in a food processor until they are well broken down and still chunky. Do not over process.

2. Mix in dates, carob powder, cinnamon, honey, salt, and melted coconut oil. Continue processing until well mixed.

3. Press the brownie batter into a square pan. Pour a layer of the raspberry sauce on top.

4. Place the pan into the freezer for 1 hour until it becomes hard. Slice into small squares.

PER SERVING:

Calories: 707 | Fat: 61 g | Protein: 10 g | Sodium: 198 mg | Fiber: 11 g

Raw Chocolate Bars

These are delectable chocolate candies made with raw cacao butter. They're fun to pour into candy molds to make unique shapes like hearts and stars. Some additional ingredients you could use include cinnamon, cayenne, maca, goji berries, nuts, coconut, honey, and orange.

INGREDIENTS | SERVES 4

½ cup cacao butter
¾ cup raw cacao powder
½ teaspoon salt
1 teaspoon vanilla extract
3 tablespoons agave nectar

Raw Cacao Butter

Cacao butter is the pure oil from the cacao bean that is a white color. The butter is solid at room temperature, but it melts easily with a little heat. Cacao butter can be used in many recipes including cheesecakes, truffles, and smoothies.

1. Melt the cacao butter in a small saucepan on the stove. Gently warm it over low heat until it becomes a liquid.

2. In a large bowl, stir all ingredients together. Place the bowl of ingredients in the freezer for a few minutes to help the mixture begin to harden up.

3. Remove from the freezer and shape into chocolate bars. Place in the refrigerator until they are solid.

PER SERVING:
Calories: 364 | Fat: 29 g | Protein: 4 g | Sodium: 596 mg | Fiber: 5 g

Chocolate Apricot Bars

This is a rich dessert and should be cut into small servings. The agave nectar may be replaced with sucanat, a natural dry sweetener that mixes with cacao butter a little better than the liquid agave.

INGREDIENTS | SERVES 6

½ cup cacao butter

1 teaspoon vanilla extract

¼ cup agave nectar

¼ cup cacao powder

¼ cup carob powder

½ cup almond butter

¼ teaspoon salt

3 tablespoons dried apricots

Sucanat

Sucanat is a great sweetener to use in raw gourmet meals. It is a natural sugar made from pure cane juice. It is a good alternative to processed white sugar. Sucanat can be used in raw desserts, especially raw chocolates, as a lighter alternative to dates and agave.

1. Warm the cacao butter in a small saucepan on the stove. Warm it to a liquid over a low temperature. Stir frequently with a spatula until it melts.

2. Place all ingredients in a food processor and process until smooth.

3. Place wax paper or a nonstick sheet onto a shallow, rectangular baking pan. Pour the mixture into the pan and spread smooth.

4. Place the pan in the freezer for 20 minutes to help it set.

5. Remove from freezer and cut into small rectangular bars.

PER SERVING:
Calories: 371 | Fat: 31 g | Protein: 4 g | Sodium: 102 mg | Fiber: 3 g

Indian Almond Chai Bars

This snack is a delicious, healthy comfort food with a soothing, warming effect. You can make the recipe with a dried chai seasoning blend or a liquid chai tea.

INGREDIENTS | SERVES 4

2 cups almonds
½ cup flaxseed
1 cup water
1 teaspoon chai spice blend
1 cup goji berries
½ cup date paste
4 tablespoons agave nectar

Chai Spice

This tasty spiced tea is traditionally a blend of herbs that include cardamon, cinnamon, ginger, star anise, peppercorn, and cloves. The chai spices are steeped or boiled to make an herbal tea, which is then flavored with a sweetener and cream or milk. Chai is popular in India and Asia, enjoyed for its flavor as well as its therapeutic health benefits.

1. Soak the almonds for 12 hours in water. Grind the flaxseed to a powder.

2. To make the tea, bring 1 cup water to a boil. Let it cool for 1 minute and then steep the chai spice blend in the water for 5 minutes. Strain and discard the spice blend but reserve the liquid. Alternatively, you can use chai tea bags instead of the dried chai spice blend.

3. In a food processor, process all ingredients with the chai tea liquid until well mixed but still chunky.

4. Form the mixture into rectangular bar shapes.

5. Dehydrate the bars at 145°F for 2 hours. Flip over the bars and continue dehydrating at 115°F for 12 hours.

PER SERVING:
Calories: 705 | Fat: 44 g | Protein: 23 g | Sodium: 9 mg | Fiber: 20 g

Figgy Bars

These are delicious bars that can be served for breakfast or dessert, when you're traveling, and for snacks. You may also use ground whole almonds instead of almond flour.

INGREDIENTS | SERVES 5

1 cup flaxseed, ground
2 cups dried figs
¼ teaspoon salt
1½ cups almond flour
½ cup liquid coconut oil
½ cup dates

1. Remove the stems from the figs. Process the figs in a blender with the salt until they become the consistency of a thick paste.

2. In a food processor, mix together the almond flour, coconut oil, ground flaxseed, and dates until they stick together.

3. Form the resulting batter into a rectangular bar shape.

4. Spread a layer of the blended figs on top of the bars.

5. Dehydrate the bars at 145°F for 2 hours. Turn down the temperature to 110°F and dehydrate 8 to 10 hours.

PER SERVING:
Calories: 697 | Fat: 49 g | Protein: 14 g | Sodium: 141 mg | Fiber: 18 g

Goji Berry Bars

This snack is the perfect answer to food cravings. They are a solid source of protein, carbs, and fats and will sustain your energy levels for many hours. Sunflower seeds are a good substitution for the oats. Good substitutions for the honey include ¼ cup agave nectar or ¼ cup maple syrup.

INGREDIENTS | SERVES 4

1 cup goji berries
1 cup dried figs
¼ cup raisins or currants
1 cup rolled oats
¼ cup liquid coconut oil
¼ cup almond butter
4 tablespoons raw honey
½ teaspoon salt
1 tablespoon cinnamon

Goji Berries

Goji berries, sometimes called wolfberries, are one of the most nutrient-rich fruits on earth. They contain 18 amino acids, 21 trace minerals, vitamin E, and many B vitamins. They are also one of the most antioxidant-rich of all foods, containing about three times more antioxidants than blueberries.

1. Soak the goji berries, figs, raisins, and oats in water for 20 minutes to reconstitute.

2. Remove the stems from the figs. Warm the coconut oil to a liquid by placing the container in a bowl of warm water for a few minutes.

3. Process all the ingredients together in a food processor until well mixed.

4. Form the batter into squares. Refrigerate for a minimum of 1 hour to help the coconut oil solidify. Alternatively, dehydrate the bars for 12 hours at 115°F.

PER SERVING:
Calories: 621 | Fat: 25 g | Protein: 11 g | Sodium: 302 mg | Fiber: 13 g

Almond-Cranberry Thumbprint Cookies

These are good snacks for traveling. You could substitute other dried fruits for the figs, including prunes, dates, raisins, or apricots.

INGREDIENTS | SERVES 4

¼ cup flaxseed
1 cup rolled oats
1 cup dried figs
½ cup dried cranberries
¼ cup almond butter
¼ cup orange juice

Oats

Oats are nutritious grains rich in fiber and complex carbohydrates. There are a few ways to eat them raw. They can be ground into a powder using a coffee grinder or blender. They can be soaked in water overnight to soften and eaten immediately. Whole raw oat groats can be soaked and sprouted for two to three days.

1. Grind the flaxseed and rolled oats into a powder using a coffee grinder or heavy-duty blender.

2. Soak the figs in water for 20 minutes. Chop off the stems.

3. In a food processor, process the figs, dried cranberries, almond butter, oat groats, and flaxseed powder until well mixed. Gradually add the orange juice.

4. Form the mixture into cookie patties and make an indent in the center of each cookie with your thumb. Dehydrate for 2 hours at 145°F. The cookies taste good both after dehydrating for 2 hours or after dehydrating for another 12 hours at 115°F.

PER SERVING:
Calories: 378 | Fat: 16 g | Protein: 8 g | Sodium: 10 mg | Fiber: 10 g

Orange Almond Macaroons

This is a great low-carb treat. They are also good made with raw cacao or carob powder.

INGREDIENTS | SERVES 4

1 cup almonds
½ cup cashews
½ cup pine nuts
½ teaspoon salt
¼ cup orange juice
1 teaspoon vanilla extract
½ cup liquid coconut oil, for blending
2 cups dried coconut

Vanilla Essence

After the seeds are scraped out of the vanilla bean, place the bean into a glass of drinking water. Let them soak for a half hour to give the water a delicious vanilla flavor. The vanilla beans may be composted after soaking.

1. Process the almonds in a food processor until they are ground into small chunks. Set them aside.

2. In a food processor, process the cashews, pine nuts, and salt until smooth. Gradually add the orange juice and vanilla extract. Gradually pour in the melted coconut oil as it's blending until the batter takes on the consistency of almond butter or chunky peanut butter.

3. Pour the dried coconut and ground almonds into the batter and pulse until it is well mixed and chunky.

4. Form into macaroon-shaped blobs. Serve the macaroons as is, or dehydrate at 145°F for 3 hours.

PER SERVING:

Calories: 742 | Fat: 70 g | Protein: 15 g | Sodium: 305 mg | Fiber: 11 g

Chocolate Chip Cookies

These cookies can be eaten immediately, or dehydrated overnight for a crunchy cookie that will store for a couple of weeks. The cookies also work well with pine nuts, cashews, and cacao powder.

INGREDIENTS | SERVES 4

1 cup steel cut oats
¼ cup flaxseed
2 cups macadamia nuts
1 teaspoon vanilla extract
½ cup dried dates
½ cup liquid coconut oil
½ cup raw cacao nibs

Carob Versus Cacao

Carob has been used for years in the raw foods community as a chocolate replacement. Raw foods author David Wolfe first brought raw cacao to the United States in 2004. They are both nutritious foods and can be used interchangeably in raw cuisine. Carob has a slightly sweeter, silky smooth texture and is used more often because it is significantly less expensive. Both of these foods should be eaten in small amounts as condiments or seasonings rather than as staple foods.

1. Grind the oats and flaxseed into a powder using a coffee grinder.

2. Process the macadamia nuts in a food processor until they become a powder. Do not over process.

3. Mix in the oats, flaxseed, vanilla, dates, and liquid coconut oil and process until you achieve a creamy texture comparable to smooth peanut butter.

4. Stir in the cacao nibs by hand. Form into cookie shapes and dehydrate at 145°F for 2 hours.

PER SERVING:
Calories: 875 | Fat: 76 g | Protein: 11 g | Sodium: 23 mg | Fiber: 17 g

Chocolate Strawberries, Variation 1

Carob powder may be substituted for the cacao, or use a half cacao-half carob mixture. For a thicker sauce, the coconut oil may be replaced with cashews, young coconut, or cacao butter.

INGREDIENTS | SERVES 6

½ cup dates

½ cup cacao powder

¼ cup liquid coconut oil

1 cup water, or more as needed

1 pint fresh strawberries

Chocolate Sauce

Blending raw cacao with a little sweetener and water makes a delicious sauce. It can be drizzled on cookies and cakes, blended with hot peppers to make a mole sauce, and added to smoothies for extra flavor and nutrition.

1. To make the chocolate sauce, first warm the coconut oil to a liquid by placing the container in a bowl of warm water for a few minutes. In a blender, blend all ingredients except strawberries until smooth. You may want to add a little more water.

2. Pour the chocolate sauce into a bowl. Press a toothpick through the stem of the strawberry and dip the berry into the chocolate sauce. Cover the bottom ⅔ of the strawberry in chocolate, leaving the green stem and a little red fruit showing.

3. Arrange the strawberries on a plate and freeze for 1 hour until the chocolate sauce hardens. Store in an airtight container in the refrigerator.

PER SERVING:

Calories: 178 | Fat: 11 g | Protein: 3 g | Sodium: 4 mg | Fiber: 5 g

Chocolate Strawberries, Variation 2

This is a yummy snack that will store in the refrigerator for about three days. You may want to try other fresh fruits in addition to the strawberries, such as banana slices, pineapple cubes, plums, or mangos.

INGREDIENTS | SERVES 6

¾ cup raw cacao powder

2 tablespoons carob powder

¾ cup liquid coconut oil

2 tablespoons maple syrup or agave nectar

1 teaspoon vanilla

½ teaspoon salt

1 pint strawberries

1. To prepare the chocolate sauce, first warm the coconut oil to a liquid by placing the container in a bowl of warm water for a few minutes. In a blender, blend all ingredients except the strawberries until smooth. You may need to add a tablespoon of water to help the ingredients blend.

2. Pour the chocolate sauce into a bowl. Press a toothpick through the stem of the strawberry and dip the berry into the chocolate sauce. Cover the bottom ⅔ of the strawberry in chocolate, leaving the green stem and a little red fruit showing.

3. Arrange the strawberries on a plate and freeze for 2 hours until the chocolate sauce hardens. Store in an airtight container in the refrigerator.

PER SERVING:
Calories: 338 | Fat: 29 g | Protein: 3 g | Sodium: 199 mg | Fiber: 6 g

CHAPTER 16

Divine Desserts

Piña Colada Ice Cream

This recipe updates a tropical classic by adding two more layers of rich flavor.

INGREDIENTS | SERVES 4

1 cup dates
2 cups cashews
½ cup young coconut meat
1 cup pineapple juice

Piña Colada

The piña colada is a traditional Spanish drink made with coconut cream, pineapple juice, and rum. Blending young coconuts with fresh pineapple juice creates a delicious beverage reminiscent of a tropical paradise.

1. Remove the pits from the dates.

2. Blend all ingredients together in a food processor or blender. Alternatively, homogenize the ingredients in a heavy-duty juicer.

3. There are three ways to freeze this ice cream. You can use an ice cream maker, simply following the directions supplied with the appliance. The second method is to place the ingredients in a bowl, cover with plastic wrap, and put it in the freezer. Stir the ingredients every few hours to help it freeze evenly. A third method is to freeze the mixture, and then chop it into chunks. Run the chunks through a heavy-duty homogenizing juicer or a high-speed blender.

PER SERVING:

Calories: 525 g | Fat: 29 g | Protein: 13 g | Sodium: 10 mg | Fiber: 6 g

Mango Ice Cream

This is a great dessert on a hot summer's day. The lecithin helps bind the coconut oil to the mango, which makes for a thick, creamy texture.

INGREDIENTS | SERVES 2

2 cups fresh mango, peeled and seeds removed

¼ cup liquid coconut oil

1 tablespoon lecithin

1. Melt the coconut oil by placing the container in a bowl of warm water for a few minutes. Place all the ingredients in a blender and blend together until smooth.

2. Place mixture into a small bowl and cover. Place in the freezer for 3 hours or until solid.

3. Process the frozen mixture through a blender, heavy-duty juicer, or food processor until smooth.

PER SERVING:
Calories: 368 | Fat: 30 g | Protein: 1 g | Sodium: 4 mg | Fiber: 3 g

Strawberry Ice Cream

A simple ice cream that does not require an ice cream maker, these delicious flavors will satisfy your desire for a cold, sweet dessert.

INGREDIENTS | SERVES 2

2 cups strawberries

¼ cup orange juice

Organic Strawberries

It is important to buy your strawberries organic, especially if you are serving them to children. In conventional agriculture, strawberries are sprayed with 300 pounds of pesticides per acre and in some testing had the highest level of endocrine disrupters of any produce.

1. Freeze the strawberries for 6 to 12 hours in an airtight plastic bag.

2. Blend the strawberries with the orange juice until smooth. Alternatively, homogenize the frozen strawberries and orange juice in a heavy-duty juicer and serve.

PER SERVING:
Calories: 67 | Fat: 1 g | Protein: 1 g | Sodium: 2 mg | Fiber: 3 g

Strawberry Vanilla Ice Cream

This is a smooth and creamy ice cream that can be served with desserts such as cakes, cookies, and pies. The lecithin holds the mixture together and creates the thick, ice cream consistency. Dates can be used instead of agave.

INGREDIENTS | SERVES 4

1 cup Almond Milk (page 21)
1 cup cashews
½ cup organic strawberries
4 tablespoons agave nectar
1 tablespoon lecithin
1 teaspoon vanilla extract
¼ teaspoon salt

Strawberries

Strawberries are sweet, nutritious, and have a low glycemic rating. They are rich in vitamins C and K, B vitamins, potassium, and phosphorus.

1. Add the Almond Milk and cashews into a blender and blend until smooth.

2. Add the remaining ingredients and blend together until smooth and creamy. Place into an ice cream maker and follow the manufacturer's directions. Alternatively, place the mixture in the freezer; stir the ice cream once an hour until frozen.

PER SERVING:

Calories: 290 | Fat: 21 g | Protein: 8 g | Sodium: 152 mg | Fiber: 1 g

Mint Chocolate Chip Ice Cream

Chocolate and mint are a classic combination. Good substitutes for the cashews include young coconut meat, macadamia nuts, or almond milk. If you like your ice cream sweet, add 1 to 2 tablespoons maple syrup or agave. If you cannot obtain fresh mint, 1 teaspoon peppermint extract will work.

INGREDIENTS | SERVES 2

2 tablespoons liquid coconut oil
1 cup cashews
⅓ cup dates
1 tablespoon cacao nibs
2 tablespoons fresh chopped mint

1. Warm the coconut oil to a liquid by placing the container in a bowl of warm water for a few minutes.

2. Place all the ingredients in a blender and blend until smooth.

3. Pour mixture into ice cream trays or molds. Freeze for 3 hours or until mixture becomes solid.

PER SERVING:

Calories: 585 | Fat: 44 g | Protein: 13 g | Sodium: 14 mg | Fiber: 6 g

Banana Vanilla Ice Cream with Blueberry Sauce

Frozen bananas make a rich ice cream. Other frozen fruits that work well in this recipe include mangoes, pineapple, and berries. A heavy-duty juicer with a homogenizing plate yields the best consistency. Some good homogenizing juicers include the Champion, Samson, Omega, Green Star, and Super Angel.

INGREDIENTS | SERVES 4

3 whole bananas
¼ cup young coconut meat
½ cup blueberries
½ cup young coconut water
½ teaspoon vanilla extract

Ice Cream

Dairy-based ice cream can be difficult to give up, but the raw vegan ice creams are so delicious that you will never crave dairy ice cream again! The raw versions are nutritious and will leave you full of energy. The raw ice creams are usually made with a base of bananas, coconut, or cashews, so they are exceptionally rich and creamy.

1. Peel ripe bananas and chop them into quarters. Place them in a plastic zip-top bag and freeze them for a minimum of 5 hours.

2. Homogenize the bananas in a heavy-duty juicer. Alternatively, process them in a food processor with the *S* blade until smooth and creamy.

3. Make a sauce by blending the coconut meat, blueberries, coconut water, and vanilla until smooth.

4. Scoop the frozen bananas into serving bowls and drizzle the blueberry sauce over the top.

PER SERVING:
Calories: 89 | Fat: 0 g | Protein: 1 g | Sodium: 32 mg | Fiber: 2 g

Chocolate Pudding

To make this delicous pudding, you can use a fresh vanilla bean instead of vanilla extract. This recipe is also good with maple syrup, which can be used as a substitute for the dates. You can also use a half cacao-half carob mixture. Good garnishes for this pudding include edible flowers and slices of banana.

INGREDIENTS	SERVES 4

1 cup avocado, pitted and chopped

¼ cup dates, pitted

¼ cup black mission figs

2 tablespoons cacao or carob powder

½ teaspoon vanilla extract

Blend all the ingredients in a blender or food processor until smooth. Serve in small bowls.

PER SERVING:

Calories: 118 | Fat: 6 g | Protein: 2 g | Sodium: 4 mg | Fiber: 5 g

Carob

Carob powder is made from the edible seed pod of the carob tree. It is an ancient food that has been used by humans for thousands of years. There are many references in the Bible to it, and it is also known as St. John's bread. Carob has a sweet taste that resembles chocolate, and it is often used as a chocolate substitute in recipes. Unlike chocolate, carob does not contain the stimulant caffeine or theobromine. It is a nutritious food rich in calcium, potassium, zinc, and B vitamins.

Coconut Cream

This sweet sauce is perfect for desserts. Use as a garnish on Pumpkin Pie with Almond Crust (page 262), Apple Pie (page 265), Key Lime Pie (page 263), Vegan Strawberry Cheesecake (page 268), or fresh berries. This recipe also works well with macadamia nuts, liquid vanilla extract, and liquid coconut oil.

INGREDIENTS | **YIELDS 2 CUPS**

1 cup young coconut meat
2 cups cashews
½ cup young coconut water
4 tablespoons agave nectar
½ teaspoon salt
Pulp from 1 vanilla bean
1 cup water (optional)

Blend all the ingredients in a blender until smooth. You may need to add in up to a cup of water in order to achieve a smooth texture.

PER CUP:

Calories: 878 | Fat: 62 g | Protein: 26 g | Sodium: 660 mg | Fiber: 6 g

Young Coconut

Fresh young coconuts are a nutritious superfood and a great source of vitamins, minerals, and healthy fats. The coconut water has been filtered through the tree for over 9 months, so it is a pure (delicious) source of carbohydrates for energy. In a very young coconut, the nut meat is almost the texture of pudding, so it is very digestible. The fats can be used topically to soothe and nourish the skin.

Coconut Pistachio Ice Cream

Some good complements to this recipe include fruits such as fresh cherries, sliced peaches, blackberries, or mangoes. You can also season this ice cream with ¼ teaspoon nutmeg and ½ teaspoon cinnamon.

INGREDIENTS | **SERVES 2**

1 cup young coconut meat
¼ cup dried coconut
¼ cup pistachios
½ cup dates, pitted

1. Place all the ingredients into a blender and blend until smooth.

2. Place in an ice cream maker and follow the manufacturer's directions. Alternatively, freeze in an airtight container, and blend or homogenize the frozen mixture until creamy.

PER SERVING:

Calories: 387 | Fat: 21 g | Protein: 7 g | Sodium: 7 mg | Fiber: 8 g

Cherry Chocolate Pudding

A smooth and creamy dessert, this recipe is made with real chocolate. You can substitute macadamia nuts in place of the young coconut. If cherries are out of season, frozen cherries will work well. You could also flavor this pudding with 1 tablespoon maple syrup (though not raw).

INGREDIENTS | SERVES 4

1 cup fresh cherries

¼ cup dates, loosely chopped

¾ cup young coconut meat

½ cup young coconut water

2 tablespoons raw cacao powder

1. In a blender or food processor, blend all the ingredients together, except the cherries.

2. Add the cherries last and briefly pulse until they are mixed in but still chunky. Pour into bowls and serve.

PER SERVING:
Calories: 130 | Fat: 3 g | Protein: 2 g | Sodium: 32 mg | Fiber: 3 g

Chocolate Pudding with Maca

This smooth, creamy pudding contains two superfoods: maca and cacao. You could substitute carob for the cacao. Edible flowers and sliced bananas make decorative garnishes.

INGREDIENTS | SERVES 4

1 cup banana

½ cup avocado

2 tablespoons cacao powder

2 teaspoons maca powder

½ teaspoon peppermint extract

Blend all ingredients together until smooth. Serve in small ramekin dishes.

PER SERVING:
Calories: 74 | Fat: 3 g | Protein: 1 g | Sodium: 2 mg | Fiber: 3 g

Raw Cacao

Cacao, a nut that grows on the tropical cacao tree, is one of the most nutritious foods on earth, containing more antioxidants than any other food. It contains high levels of nutrients that promote blissful and feel-good neurotransmitters, such as anandamide, serotonin, and dopamine.

Chia Strawberry Pudding

This smooth pudding can be served as breakfast or dessert. The chia seeds soak up the liquid to create a thick pudding. Carob powder is a good substitute for the cacao. You could also leave out the cacao for a simple strawberry pudding. The almond milk can be replaced with water or young coconut water.

INGREDIENTS | SERVES 2

1½ cups Almond Milk (page 21)
¼ cup chia seeds
3 tablespoons agave nectar
1 tablespoon raw cacao powder
½ teaspoon vanilla extract
½ cup strawberries sliced

Chia

Chia seeds are very nutritious. They are rich in the omega-3 fats, fiber, antioxidants, protein, and minerals. They are similar to flaxseed because they are gelatinous and can be used as a thickener in recipes such as puddings, shakes, sauces, and porridges.

1. In a large serving bowl, combine the Almond Milk and the chia seeds and let sit at room temperature for 10 minutes. Stir every few minutes to ensure the chia seeds are soaking up the liquid.

2. Cover the bowl and place it in the refrigerator for 4 to 8 hours to allow the chia seeds to continue to absorb the Almond Milk.

3. Remove from the refrigerator and stir in the agave, cacao, and vanilla. Pour the pudding into small serving dishes and garnish with strawberry slices.

PER SERVING:
Calories: 368 | Fat: 23 g | Protein: 10 g | Sodium: 13 mg | Fiber: 9 g

Pecan Torte

The rich chocolate flavor of this torte is delicious with a garnish of fresh strawberries and a scoop of cashew cream. You could substitute cashews or macadamia nuts for the avocado.

INGREDIENTS | **SERVES 6**

2 cups pecans

1 cup Date Paste (page 232) or chopped dates

½ teaspoon salt

1 banana

2 cups avocado

½ cup raw carob powder or raw cacao powder

2 tablespoons agave nectar

2 tablespoons liquid coconut oil

Tortes

The recipe for tortes originated in central Europe and consists of a round cake or bread, often made with nut meal, with a sweet icing. They often have layers of cake and icing and are popular as wedding cakes.

1. Prepare the crust by placing the pecans in a food processor and processing them until they are broken down into small chunks. Add the Date Paste and ¼ teaspoon salt and continue processing until the mixture sticks to the walls.

2. Press the pecan crust evenly into a torte pan or pie pan. Slice the banana into thin pieces and place on the crust in a single layer.

3. Prepare torte filling by blending the avocado, carob or cacao, agave, coconut oil, and remaining salt until smooth.

4. Pour the filling into the pan. Put the torte in the refrigerator to set for 1 hour. Serve cold.

PER SERVING:
Calories: 518 | Fat: 37 g | Protein: 7 g | Sodium: 208 mg | Fiber: 13 g

Strawberry Bundt Cake

This cake becomes solid when cooled in the refrigerator and is then brought to room temperature before eating to enhance the flavor. There are many different bundt cake designs to choose from. The Strawberry Date Sauce (page 231) is a great frosting for this cake.

INGREDIENTS | SERVES 6

¾ cup liquid coconut oil, divided
½ cup Almond Milk (page 21)
2½ cups cashews
3 cups strawberries
3 tablespoons lemon juice
4 tablespoons agave nectar
1 teaspoon vanilla extract
¼ teaspoon salt
3 tablespoons lecithin

1. Oil the bundt pan with 1 tablespoon coconut oil to help prevent it from sticking.

2. Blend all ingredients together until creamy. Blend the lecithin and coconut oil last to bind the oils with the other ingredients.

3. Pour the filling into a bundt cake pan. Place into the freezer for 2 hours to let set.

4. Turn the bundt cake upside down and remove the pan. Let it thaw at room temperature for 30 minutes to an hour before serving. Garnish with strawberry sauce.

PER SERVING:
Calories: 554 | Fat: 46 g | Protein: 11 g | Sodium: 9 mg | Fiber: 3 g

Papaya Pudding

The tahini adds a rich and creamy texture to this pudding. For the tahini, you can substitute avocado, young coconut meat, or cashews.

INGREDIENTS | SERVES 2

2 cups papaya
½ cup banana
2 tablespoons Tahini (page 138)
½ cup blueberries, for topping

1. Blend together the papaya, banana, and Tahini until smooth.

2. Pour into small serving dishes and garnish with blueberries or other types of sliced fresh fruit, berries, or mint.

PER SERVING:

Calories: 195 | Fat: 8 g | Protein: 4 g | Sodium: 16 mg | Fiber: 6 g

Lemon Icing Cake

This is a good dessert to serve with a strawberry or blueberry sauce. The almonds may be replaced with walnuts or pecans. The cake will store longer if the almonds are dehydrated after soaking. This cake looks great with a fresh fruit garnish.

INGREDIENTS | SERVES 4

2 cups almonds, soaked
½ cup cashews, soaked
1 cup dates
½ teaspoon salt
4 tablespoons agave nectar
3 tablespoons lemon juice
½ teaspoon lemon zest

1. In a food processor, process the almonds, dates, and salt until well mixed into a batter.

2. Form the batter into a round cake shape.

3. To make the icing, blend together the cashews, agave nectar, lemon juice, and lemon zest until smooth. Spread the sauce over the cake. Freeze the cake for 1 hour to help the sauce set. At this point it is ready to be served.

PER SERVING:

Calories: 657 | Fat: 43 g | Protein: 19 g | Sodium: 295 mg | Fiber: 13 g

Carrot Cake

This cake is a delicious dessert. The raisins can be soaked in water for 10 minutes to soften them up. Goji berries make a good substitute for the raisins. One cup almond flour can be added to this recipe for a lighter texture.

INGREDIENTS | SERVES 2

½ cup pecans
¼ cup dates
1 cup shredded carrots
1 teaspoon cinnamon
1 teaspoon grated ginger
½ teaspoon nutmeg
1 teaspoon orange zest
½ teaspoon salt
4 tablespoons raisins or currants
½ cup Cake Frosting (page 233)

1. Place the pecans in a food processor with an *S* blade. Process until they are ground fine.

2. Add the dates to the food processor and continue processing until smooth.

3. Add the carrots, cinnamon, ginger, nutmeg, orange zest and salt to the food processor and process until it becomes a chunky batter. Stir in raisins.

4. Place cake batter into a cake pan or casserole dish. Use a spatula to spread a layer of Cake Frosting on top.

PER SERVING:
Calories: 608 | Fat: 40 g | Protein: 10 g | Sodium: 779 mg | Fiber: 9 g

Pumpkin Pie with Almond Crust

A delicious holiday dessert, this pie provides the finishing touch to Thanksgiving dinner. The sugar pumpkin, also known as pie pumpkin, is the only member of the pumpkin family that can be eaten raw. If pie pumpkins are not in season, you can substitute yam, sweet potato, or butternut squash.

INGREDIENTS | SERVES 6

½ cup dry Irish moss

2 cups pecans

¾ cup dates

½ teaspoon cinnamon

1 cup water

4 cups pie pumpkin, peeled and chopped

½ cup agave nectar

2 tablespoons pumpkin pie spice

¼ teaspoon cayenne pepper powder

2 teaspoons ginger juice

¾ cup liquid coconut oil

1 cup Coconut Cream, for frosting (page 255)

Pie Pumpkin

Hard, starchy vegetables like pie pumpkin and butternut squash can be eaten raw by blending them into a soup or pâté. They can also be turned into noodles with a spiral slicer and softened by massaging sea salt into the noodles. Pie pumpkins, also called sugar pumpkins, are a nutritious food rich in vitamin A, vitamin C, folate, and potassium.

1. Prepare the Irish moss by rinsing it in cold water to remove any debris. Soak the Irish moss in water using a container with a lid. Fill the container to the top with water. Soak for 24 hours in the refrigerator or 3 hours at room temperature.

2. Prepare the crust by blending together the pecans, dates, and cinnamon in a food processor. Press the crust into a pie pan.

3. In a blender, blend the Irish moss with 1 cup water until completely smooth.

4. Add the pie pumpkin, agave nectar, pumpkin pie spice, cayenne pepper powder, and ginger juice to the blender. Blend until smooth. Add the coconut oil last and continue blending until smooth.

5. Pour the filling into the crust and refrigerate for 3 hours to set the pie. Garnish with scoops of Coconut Cream.

PER SERVING:
Calories: 732 | Fat: 61 g | Protein: 9 g | Sodium: 116 mg | Fiber: 7 g

Key Lime Pie

If key limes are not available, you can use regular limes. You could add a teaspoon of spirulina or spinach juice as a green food coloring. Avocados may be substituted for the cashews. Whipped Coconut Cream (page 255) makes a good garnish.

INGREDIENTS | SERVES 6

1½ cups pecans

½ cup dates

½ teaspoon cinnamon

¼ teaspoon nutmeg

½ teaspoon salt

1 cup young coconut

2 cups cashews

½ cup key lime juice

½ teaspoon vanilla extract

¼ cup agave nectar

¼ cup liquid coconut oil

2 tablespoons lecithin powder

Key Limes

Key lime pie is a traditional American dessert and is the official state pie of Florida. The key lime is a little more tart, bitter, and aromatic than regular limes. Key limes are yellow when ripe and have a thin rind. They received their name from the Florida Keys where they grow naturally and in abundance.

1. Prepare the crust by processing the pecans, dates, cinnamon, nutmeg, and salt in a food processor. Press the batter into a pie plate.

2. Prepare the filling by blending together the young coconut, cashews, key lime juice, vanilla, and agave nectar and blend until smooth. Start with a ¼ cup lime juice and gradually blend in more. Taste the filling as you make it and adjust it to your taste. You may prefer more lime juice or agave nectar. Blend in the liquid coconut oil and lecithin powder last.

3. Pour the filling into the crust and chill in the freezer for 2 hours to set the filling. You can serve it immediately, or keep it in the refrigerator where it will stay fresh when covered for up to 3 days.

PER SERVING:

Calories: 516 | Fat: 38 g | Protein: 10 g | Sodium: 200 mg | Fiber: 4 g

Pecan Pie

This is a delicious pie to serve during the holidays. The almond flour can be made with whole ground almonds or the almond pulp that remains after making Almond Milk (page 21).

INGREDIENTS | SERVES 4

3 cups almond flour
¼ cup dates
¼ cup liquid coconut oil
¾ cup pecans, plus ¼ cup for garnish
¾ cup bananas
3 tablespoons maple syrup or honey
¼ teaspoon salt
⅓ cup water as needed for blending

1. Prepare the crust by blending together the almond flour, dates, and coconut oil.

2. To prepare the filling, use a blender or food processor and blend together the remaining ingredients until smooth. Add just enough water to help it blend.

3. Press the crust into a pie pan or tart dish. Spoon the filling into the crust and spread smooth with a spatula. Press ¼ cup whole pecans into the top.

4. Cover the pie and place into the freezer for 2 hours. Serve immediately or transfer to the refrigerator.

PER SERVING:
Calories: 820 | Fat: 70 g | Protein: 20 g | Sodium: 177 mg | Fiber: 16 g

Apple Pie

Apple pie is an excellent dessert for a summertime picnic. You may warm it in the dehydrator for a couple of hours and serve warm. Fresh or dried figs are a good substitute for the dates. This is good served with a scoop of Coconut Cream (page 255) or vanilla ice cream.

INGREDIENTS | SERVES 6

½ cup raisins, or fresh blueberries or currants

1½ cups dates

2 cups almonds

½ teaspoon salt

3 cups apples, peeled and chopped

1 teaspoon cinnamon

1 teaspoon cardamon

2 tablespoons lemon juice

Raw Pie Crusts

These pie crusts can be made with any combination of nuts and dried fruits. The nuts work better as a crust when they are dry. They have an improved flavor when soaked and then dehydrated overnight.

1. Soak the raisins and dates in water for 20 minutes to reconstitute.

2. To prepare the crust, process the almonds, salt, and 1 cup dates in a food processor until a batter is formed. Press the batter into a 9" round pie pan.

3. To prepare the filling, blend together 1 cup apple, ½ cup dates, raisins, cinnamon, and cardamon until smooth.

4. Process the remaining 2 cups of apples in a food processor with the lemon juice. The apples should be chunky. Add in the blended filling and briefly pulse until it is well mixed together.

5. Pour the filling into the pie crust. Refrigerate or dehydrate for 2 hours and serve warm.

PER SERVING:
Calories: 435 | Fat: 24 g | Protein: 11 g | Sodium: 390 mg | Fiber: 11 g

Banana Pie

This is a good summer pie with a tasty blend of fruits and nuts. You can also garnish the icing with fresh berries or peach slices. Note that the avocado is completely disguised by blending it with the dates.

INGREDIENTS | SERVES 6

2 cups walnuts
½ cup Brazil nuts
2 cups dates, divided
½ teaspoon vanilla extract
½ cup dried coconut
3 cups bananas, sliced
1 cup avocado for frosting
½ cup carob
4 tablespoons water, for blending
1 cup peeled, sliced kiwi, for garnish
Dried coconut flakes, for garnish

1. Soak the walnuts for 6 to 12 hours in water. Rinse and drain.

2. Prepare the crust by processing the walnuts and Brazil nuts in a food processor with the *S* blade until they are well broken down. Add 1 cup dates, vanilla, and dried coconut and process until well mixed.

3. Press the crust into a 9" round pie pan; the crust will be about an inch thick.

4. Layer the sliced bananas into the pie pan. Chop ½ cup dates and sprinkle them onto the banana.

5. Blend together the avocado, carob, and remaining ½ cup dates. Add just enough water to help it blend into a cream (you might not need the whole 4 tablespoons).

6. Pour the avocado cream over the pie. Garnish with kiwi slices and dried coconut.

PER SERVING:
Calories: 669 | Fat: 41 g | Protein: 11 g | Sodium: 11 mg | Fiber: 15 g

Chocolate Peanut Butter Pie

Jungle peanuts are the only variety of peanut that really tastes good raw. If you don't have raw peanuts, you may substitute cashews, Brazil nuts, or pistachios. Other sweeteners that could replace the maple syrup include agave nectar or dried fruits such as dates or figs.

INGREDIENTS | SERVES 6

2 cups pecans

½ teaspoon salt

2 cups raw jungle peanuts

½ cup dates

¼ cup almond butter

½ cup cacao powder

4 tablespoons maple syrup

1 teaspoon vanilla extract

½ cup liquid coconut oil

2 tablespoons lecithin powder

Jungle Peanuts

Peanuts originated in South America and have been used as food for thousands of years. From a health perspective, many peanuts are contaminated with a toxic mold that contains aflatoxins. In terms of raw food cuisine, varieties of raw peanuts such as valencias are too starchy and bitter to be eaten raw. However, the raw foods author David Wolfe has found a source of wild heirloom peanuts growing in the Amazon jungle that are free from the aflatoxin mold and taste delicious.

1. Process the pecans, dates, and ¼ teaspoon salt in a food processor with the *S* blade to make the pie crust. Press it into a 9" pie pan.

2. Process the peanuts alone in the food processor until they begin to stick to the walls.

3. Add in the almond butter, cacao powder, ¼ teaspoon salt, maple syrup, and vanilla. Continue processing until well mixed. Add in the liquid coconut oil and lecithin powder last and process until the filling is well mixed.

4. Pour the filling into the crust and refrigerate for 2 hours to help the filling solidify.

PER SERVING:

Calories: 852 | Fat: 75 g | Protein: 20 g | Sodium: 207 mg | Fiber: 12 g

Vegan Strawberry Cheesecake

This luscious nondairy cheesecake will store for a few days covered in the refrigerator. Agave nectar is a good substitute for the honey. This recipe works well with other types of berries and fruits.

INGREDIENTS | SERVES 6

2 cups macadamia nuts

½ teaspoon salt

½ cup dates

1 teaspoon cinnamon

2 cups cashews

½ cup honey

2 tablespoons lemon juice

1 teaspoon vanilla extract

½ cup liquid coconut oil

2 tablespoons lecithin

1 pint organic strawberries

Cheesecakes

There are many variations possible with cheesecake. You can use different types of nuts and dried fruits for the crust. The filling has a base of cashew, coconut oil, and lecithin, which make it creamy and solid. Lecithin is usually made from soy and has both medicinal and culinary uses. It is popular in dessert recipes and is used as a thickener or emulsifier. Lecithin is available in the supplement aisle in most grocery stores. Healthforce lecithin powder is a high-quality brand.

1. Prepare the crust by processing the macadamia nuts in a food processor until they are broken down but still chunky.

2. Add ½ teaspoon salt, dates, and cinnamon and continue processing until well mixed.

3. Press the crust into a 9" springform pan. You could spread some dried coconut or coconut oil onto the pan first to prevent the crust from sticking.

4. Prepare the filling by blending the cashews, honey, lemon juice, and vanilla until smooth and creamy. Add the liquid coconut oil and lecithin and continue blending until well mixed.

5. Pour half of the filling into the springform pan. Blend the second half with the strawberries until smooth.

6. Pour the remaining filling into the springform pan. Use a chopstick to swirl the filling.

7. Place the cheesecake in the freezer for 2 hours to set. Remove the spring form and garnish with fresh berries. Let thaw for 30 to 60 minutes before serving.

PER SERVING:

Calories: 845 | Fat: 73 g | Protein: 12 g | Sodium: 203 mg | Fiber: 8 g

Chocolate Peach Cheesecake

The rich, nutty flavor of this cheesecake provides the ideal contrast to the peaches.

INGREDIENTS | SERVES 6

1 cup pecans

1 cup walnuts

½ cup dates

1 cup cashews

1 cup Almond Milk (page 21)

2 tablespoons agave nectar

¼ cup liquid cacao butter

1 tablespoon lecithin

2 cups fresh peaches

1. Process the pecans, walnuts, and dates in a food processor with the *S* blade until mixture sticks together. Press the crust into the bottom of a 6" springform pan.

2. For the filling, blend together the cashews, Almond Milk, agave nectar, melted cacao butter, and lecithin into a cream. Add the peaches and continue blending until smooth.

3. Pour the cashew-peach filling into the springform pan and place in the freezer for 2 hours. Let the cheesecake thaw for 30 to 60 minutes before serving.

PER SERVING:
Calories: 574 | Fat: 49 g | Protein: 11 g | Sodium: 5 mg | Fiber: 6 g

Mint Chocolate Cheesecake

This final recipe is a visual treat. A good substitute for the lecithin powder is Irish moss. The green superfood powder is optional and is used as a decorative touch. There are many different brands of superfood powder that will work, including Klamath algae, spirulina, and Vitamineral Green.

INGREDIENTS | **SERVES 6**

1 cup Brazil nuts

1 cup dried coconut

1 teaspoon salt

2 cups cashews

½ cup liquid cacao butter

4 tablespoons agave nectar

½ teaspoon vanilla extract

2 tablespoons liquid coconut oil

2 tablespoons lecithin powder

½ cup raw cacao powder

4 tablespoons fresh mint, chopped

½ teaspoon green superfood powder (optional)

Cacao Butter

Cacao butter is the concentrated oil from the cacao bean. It makes smooth and rich chocolate desserts and is high in healthy fats, antioxidants, and magnesium.

1. Prepare the crust by processing the Brazil nuts, dried coconut, and ½ teaspoon salt in a food processor with the *S* blade until smooth. Press the crust into a 9" springform pan.

2. Prepare the filling by processing the cashews, cacao butter, agave nectar, ½ teaspoon salt, and vanilla in a food processor until smooth. Wait until the ingredients are smooth and then add the coconut oil and lecithin powder. Divide this filling into two parts, each in a different bowl.

3. To first half of the filling batter, add cacao powder and pour on top of the crust in the springform pan.

4. To the second half, add the chopped mint and green superfood powder and pour on top of the first layer of filling.

5. Swirl the filling with a chopstick.

6. Place the cheesecake into the freezer for 3 hours until solid. Remove the springform pan. You may need to use a knife around the edge to gently free the cake from the form. Let it thaw for 30 minutes to 1 hour.

PER SERVING:

Calories: 737 | Fat: 66 g | Protein: 14 g | Sodium: 209 mg | Fiber: 8 g

APPENDIX A

Raw Foods Resources

Everything.com

This site is a great introduction to the series.

www.everything.com

Raw Food Website Resources

The Raw Diet Health Shop

Kitchen equipment and supplements for the raw foods lifestyle. Equipment offered includes blenders, juicers, food dehydrators, sprouters, and more.

http://store.therawdiet.com

Raw Foods Restaurants

A comprehensive list of raw food restaurants in the United States and Canada.

www.TheRawDiet.com/restaurants.html

Mike Snyder's Raw Foods Newsletter

Featuring a free eBook titled *Getting Started with the Raw Foods Diet*, a free e-mail course, and free information on the raw and living foods.

www.TheRawDiet.com

Sunfood Raw Foods Shop

A raw and living foods store with a large selection of raw foods, superfoods, raw chocolate, CDs, books, kitchen appliances, skin care products, and more.

www.TheRawDiet.com/sunfood.html

Raw Food Resources

A list of recommended resources on a variety of subjects including raw food health retreats, raw food doctors, raw food stores, raw gourmet foods, cultured foods, sea vegetables, sprouting, gardening, vegetarian nutrition, raising vegetarian children, and more.

www.TheRawDiet.com/resources.html

Raw Food Festivals

A list of raw food festivals and special events

www.TheRawDiet.com/events.html

Living Light Culinary Institute
Professional raw foods chef training.
www.RawFoodChef.com

Raw Foods Teacher Certification
Alissa Cohen's Raw Food Teacher Certification
www.RawTeacher.com

Jaffee Brothers
Raw nuts, seeds, and dried fruits
www.OrganicFruitsAndNuts.com

The Date People
Featuring over thirty-five different varieties of the world's most delicious
date fruits. Start with the sampler pack.
www.DatePeople.net

The Raw Food World
An excellent raw foods store that carries many raw foods, superfoods, and
hard to find ingredients including chia seeds, Irish moss, carob powder,
and kelp noodles.
www.TheRawFoodWorld.com

Raw Food Magazines
A comprehensive list of the best magazines and newsletters related to
vegetarian raw and living foods.
www.TheRawDiet.com/magazines.html

Health Coaching
Nancy Faass provides personalized coaching for transitioning to raw foods;
nutritional counseling on energy, mood, and food; and resources
for weight mastery.
www.MyPrivateHealthCoach.com

Soaking and Sprouting Guide

SOAKING AND SPROUTING CHART

Food	Soaking Time	Sprouting Time
Alfalfa	5 hours	5 days
Almonds	8 to 12 hours	Do not sprout
Barley	6 to 8 hours	5 to 7 days
Broccoli	6 to 12 hours	3 days
Buckwheat	15 to 45 minutes	24 hours
Chickpea / Garbanzo	8 to 12 hours	1 to 2 days
Cloves	5 hours	5 days
Cabbage	8 to 12 hours	3 days
Dulse sea vegetable	5 minutes	Do not sprout
Fenugreek	6 hours	5 days
Flaxseeds	6 to 8 hours	Do not sprout
Green Pumpkin Seeds	4 hours	24 hours
Hemp Seeds	Do not soak	Do not sprout
Lentils	8 to 12 hours	2 days
Mustard	5 hours	5 days
Macadamia	Do not soak	Do not sprout
Pecans	1 to 2 hours	Do not sprout
Pine Nuts	Do not soak	Do not sprout
Pistachio	Do not soak	Do not sprout
Quinoa	3 hours	24 hours
Radish	6 hours	5 days
Raisins	1 to 3 hours	Do not sprout
Rye	6 to 8 hours	5 to 7 days
Sesame Seeds	4 to 6 hours	Do not sprout
Sun-dried Tomatoes	3 to 4 hours	Do not sprout
Sunflower Seeds	4 to 6 hours	24 hours
Walnuts	1 to 2 hours	Do not sprout
Wakame sea vegetable	2 hours	Do not sprout
Wheat	6 to 8 hours	5 to 7 days
Leafy Green Sprouts		
Wheatgrass	8 to 12 hours	7 days
Sunflower, Unhulled	8 hours	7 days
Buckwheat, Unhulled	6 hours	7 days

APPENDIX C

Glossary

Agave: A cactus found growing in Mexico and the Southwestern United States. The agave cactus produces a sweet honey-like nectar. Agave is a popular natural sweetener in raw food cuisine because it is nutritious, it is vegan, and it has a similar taste and texture to honey.

Algae: A superfood that contains a high concentration of vitamins and minerals. It is a single celled plant similar to grass. It is harvested from fresh water and packaged in liquid, powder, or tablet form. The most common algae includes spirulina, chlorella, and Klamath blue-green algae from Klamath Lake, Oregon.

Antioxidants: Nutrients that help to slow down and prevent premature aging and degenerative diseases such as cancer. They are molecules that neutralize harmful free radicals in the body that result from pollution and infection. Most raw foods contain high amounts of antioxidants. The foods at the top of the antioxidant list include goji berries, raw cacao, prunes, acai berry, green tea, blueberries, algae, and mangosteen.

Aroma: An odor or scent detected by the olfactory sense. Raw gourmet foods have a delightful aroma that is created as foods are blended, juiced, and dehydrated. A pleasant aroma helps stimulate the appetite and increases enjoyment of the meal.

Blender: An essential kitchen tool for the raw food kitchen. It is used daily to make different types of foods including soups, smoothies, shakes, sauces, juices, and nut milk. A high power blender is needed to blend the hard vegetables, nuts, and seeds.

Buckwheat groats: Delicious, nutritious, and inexpensive grains. They are popular because they are easy to prepare and they add a crunchy texture to gourmet foods. They are usually prepared by soaking in water for fifteen to forty-five minutes and then sprouted for one day.

Caraway seeds: Spices used to add flavor to gourmet foods. They are commonly found in sauerkraut, soups, stews, sauces, breads, and salads. They can be found in the dried spice aisle of your local grocery store.

Coconut oil: An oil that has been extracted from coconut meat at low temperatures. It adds a delicious flavor and unique texture to gourmet foods. It is also used topically as a skin lotion.

Dairy: Foods made with the milk from cows and goats. Raw dairy is usually available as raw milk, raw cheese, yogurt, and kefir. Raw dairy is available directly from the farm and in some health food stores. Most of the recipes in this book use vegan milk, cheese, and ice cream made with nuts and seeds.

Dehydrator: A tool that replaces the oven in raw gourmet cuisine. Dehydration is a food preservation method that removes water from the food. This is done at low temperatures to preserve the enzymes and life force. It allows you to store fresh food for long periods of time. Dehydrating gives food a similar texture, appearance, and taste to the cooked foods. Dehydrated foods help to satisfy the emotional cravings for cooked comfort foods.

Enzyme: Biochemical catalysts, or chemicals that speed up the reaction between two substances. Enzymes are found in all living plants and animals. There are three types of enzymes: digestive, metabolic, and food enzymes. The human body makes digestive and metabolic enzymes, while food enzymes are found in raw and living foods. The food enzymes are destroyed when food is heated to high temperatures. Metabolic and digestive enzymes are popular supplements among raw foodists.

Essene: A Jewish religious group who lived from 200 BCE to 100 CE. They have become popular in recent times because of the discovery of the Dead Sea Scrolls. The Scrolls are a collection of the Essene religious documents preserved since ancient times. Some of the documents offer advice on eating a vegetarian diet along with raw foods. *The Essene Gospel of Peace* by Edmond Bordeaux Szekely is believed to be a modern translation of the Dead Sea Scrolls, and it contains numerous references to living foods. The most well know reference is the Essene Bread recipe, which uses sprouted grains and low temperature dehydration.

Fermentation: An ancient method of food preservation. It involves converting a food from one substance to another in a controlled environment. The food is converted through the use of beneficial, microscopic organisms such as probiotics or yeast. The fermentation process makes foods easier to digest and improves the flavor. Some popular fermented foods include sauerkraut, pickles, miso, kefir, cheese, kombucha tea, rejuvelac, and yogurt.

Fiber: An essential nutrient found in plant foods. There are two types of fiber, soluble and insoluble. Both forms are indigestible and are not absorbed into the bloodstream. Fiber helps to prevent constipation by moving foods through the digestive tract. Fiber also helps to maintain healthy cholesterol levels. Most raw foods are rich in fiber.

Flax: A nutritious food that is high in protein and essential fats. It is an excellent source of the Omega 3 fatty acids. Both the seed and the oil are used in many raw gourmet recipes. Flax seeds are gelatinous and they hold ingredients together. They are a common ingredient in crackers, breads, and pie crusts. Flax seed oil is used as an Omega 3 supplement, and it also makes a great addition to salad dressings and sauces.

Garlic press: A handy kitchen tool that is used to crush garlic cloves through tiny holes. Crushing the garlic helps to release the flavors and evenly distribute it through the recipe. The garlic press is also used to extract juice from ginger and onion.

Goji berries: A popular and delicious superfood. They are used extensively in the raw foods community because they are high in vitamins, minerals, antioxidants, and protein. Goji berries are delicious in many recipes including trail mix, sauces, smoothies, desserts, and salads. Most goji berries are imported from China, but they are also cultivated in the Southwestern United States.

Grater: A tool that has many uses in the raw foods kitchen. It can be used to create zest from the peel of citrus fruits, which often adds more flavor to a recipe than the juice. The grater can also be used on fruits and vegetables to make attractive cuts and textures.

Juicer: A tool used to extract juices from plant foods. Fresh juice is healthy because the nutrients are quickly absorbed into the body. Juice is also used to add flavor to gourmet recipes. There are many types of juicers available. Some juicers will only juice fruits and vegetables. Others will juice only citrus fruits or wheatgrass. Some juicers will make nut butters, pates, and ice cream along with juice.

Leafy greens: Foods such as lettuce, spinach, kale, celery, bok choy, beet tops, and sprouts. Leafy greens are important to eat on a raw foods diet because they are rich in protein, vitamins, minerals, antioxidants, and chlorophyll. Chlorophyll is similar in composition to the hemoglobin in human blood. Leafy greens are used in many recipes, especially green smoothies, soups, salads, and wraps.

Living foods: Foods that still contain their electrical life force energy. They are different than raw foods in that raw foods while not cooked, do not contain the same life force. Living foods include freshly picked fruits, vegetables, fermented foods, and sprouted grains, seeds, and nuts.

Locally grown: Foods have been grown and harvested close to home. These foods are fresh, taste delicious, are better for the environment, and are healthy. Foods that have been shipped from thousands of miles away become stale, lose their flavor, and they are treated with chemicals for a longer shelf life. Three ways to eat more locally grown foods are to plant your own fruit trees, plant a vegetable garden, and set up a kitchen sprout garden.

Mandolin: A kitchen tool that allows the user to make different types of cuts on fruits and vegetables. For example, it is excellent for making thin, wide cuts, or thin julienne style cuts. A mandolin adds to the enjoyment of eating because it makes the food look beautiful and professionally prepared. A mandolin is useful in making recipes like lasagna, ravioli, and marinated zucchini strips.

Nama Shoyu: A condiment made from soy beans. It is a raw and unpasteurized soy sauce used in many sauces and pates. It has a rich, salty flavor and is delicious with Asian meals. It does contain a little wheat so it is not appropriate for those with gluten intolerance.

Natural: Foods that are unprocessed and do not contain artificial additives or chemicals. Natural foods include whole fruits, vegetables, nuts, seeds, grains, and sea vegetables grown without chemical pesticides.

Nori: A nutritious sea vegetable high in minerals and vitamins that is prepared in thin sheets. Nori is used as the wrap for raw vegan sushi, also called Nori Rolls. The texture makes a perfect replacement for tortilla wraps in burritos. Like other sea veggies, nori is high in iodine content, as well as iron, calcium, vitamins A, B, and C, and carotene.

Nut milk: A milk made from nuts, seeds, or grains rather than soy or dairy products. Nut milk is a staple in a raw foods diet. It is similar to juice because the nuts are blended into a liquid and the fiber is strained out. Nut milk is a delicious beverage and is used in many different recipes, including smoothies, soups, sauces, and cakes.

Nut milk bag: An easy-to-use kitchen tool for making fresh vegan milks. It is a mesh bag that strains out the pulp from the nut milk. It is also used to make fresh fruit and vegetable juices with a blender.

Pasteurized: Foods that have been heated to high temperatures to kill off any harmful bacteria. The pasteurization process cooks the food, killing the enzymes and beneficial bacteria. Unpasteurized foods have not been heated and they still contain enzymes and beneficial bacteria.

Peeler: A tool used to slice vegetables into thin strips. It is handy for making pasta-like noodles out of zucchini and root vegetables. The thin slices are good for marinating and dehydrating for snacks.

Pickle: A method of food preservation that gives food a long shelf life. The pickling process involves marinating vegetables in a saltwater brine for an extended length of time. Raw pickles have not been pasteurized or cooked, and they are usually made without vinegar.

Protein: Built from amino acids. There are twenty amino acids that contribute to building protein in humans. The amino acids found in raw plant foods are easy to digest and assimilate. There are many raw plant foods that contain between eighteen and twenty amino acids, including algae, hemp seeds, sprouts, and goji berries.

Pulp: The fiber that is removed from foods when making juice or nut milk. Once removed, the pulp can be used in new recipes, or it can be tossed in the compost pile. The pulp from almond milk can be used to make dehydrated cookies and piecrusts. The pulp from carrot juice can be used to make a carrot cake.

Raw: Foods have not been cooked or heated. They contain all their original nutrients. Some raw foods must first be soaked before being eaten to soften them up and activate the life force. In general, raw foods have not been heated over 115°–120°F.

Raw honey: A natural sweetener known for its high mineral content and unique nutrients. Locally produced raw honey is found at farmers' markets and health food stores. When buying raw honey do a little research on the beekeeper to ensure the bees are treated humanely.

Root vegetables: Hearty vegetables that are usually grown in the ground. They store well without refrigeration for long periods of time. They are excellent sources of complex carbohydrates, which help sustain energy. Popular root vegetables include beets, carrots, parsnips, turnips, sweet potatoes and yams, as well as celery root, daikon and other radishes, fennel, ginger, Jerusalem artichokes, jicama, maca, and water chestnuts.

Sauerkraut: An ancient food preservation method. It involves grating and salting cabbage. The salt creates a brine with the sauerkraut juices. The cabbage cultures in the brine for an extended period of time, usually between one to four weeks. Sauerkraut is rich in vitamins, minerals, and is an excellent source of probiotics.

Spice mill: An essential kitchen tool. A spice mill allows the user to grind hard seeds into a fresh powder. The grinding process breaks down the food, making it easier to digest. This is especially important with flax seeds because they have a hard shell that is difficult to chew. The spice mill is also good for grinding herbs and spices into a powder, which helps to evenly distribute the seasonings throughout the entire recipe.

Spiral slicer: A kitchen tool that allows the user to make pasta or noodles from vegetables. The noodles can be combined with your favorite sauce or salad dressing. Most hard vegetables make good noodles, including zucchini, beets, and sweet potato.

Sprouter: A kitchen tool that allows the user to sprout seeds, nuts, and grains. In general, sprouts contain ten to thirty times more nutrients than vegetables. Sprouting seeds are inexpensive to buy, and they are easy to grow all year round. There are both manual and automatic sprouters available.

Superfood: Foods with an unusually high concentration of nutrients. They contain many essential nutrients in a small serving. For example, a conventional tomato in the supermarket may contain twelve minerals. A superfood like algae or wheatgrass juice may contain over seventy minerals. There are many whole superfoods that you can prepare at home, including sprouts, sea vegetables, and goji berries. A second form of superfood is a powdered blend containing a variety of different foods available in one bottle.

Supplement: A food or isolated nutrient added to the diet to make up for a deficiency. Supplements are added to the diet as insurance against deficiency. Some essential nutrients, like vitamin B12, are not found in raw foods and must be supplemented.

Texture: The feel and consistency of a food. Many raw gourmet foods mimic the texture and taste of familiar cooked foods. The unique textures are created with special tools, including the blender, food dehydrator, and spiral slicer. For example, zucchini noodle pasta has a similar texture to pasta made with flour, and dehydrated crackers have a similar texture and crunch to store bought crackers. Creating foods with a pleasing texture will increase your enjoyment of the meal.

Uncooked: Foods that have not been exposed to high temperatures. They are usually considered uncooked when the food temperature stays below 115°F. All nutrients and enzymes are preserved in the food.

Vegan: A person who eats only plant foods. A vegan does not consume any animal products. This means no fish, no eggs, no dairy, and no bee products. A vegan also avoids products made from animals, such as leather shoes and belts. This lifestyle choice is made both for the positive health benefits, and for a philosophy of nonviolence, love, and compassion for all animals.

Vegetarian: A person who does not eat animals. A vegetarian avoids meat-based foods and does not eat seafood, chicken, beef, or pork. A vegetarian may eat some foods made by animals, including eggs, dairy, and honey.

Warm foods: Foods that are served warm, but not cooked. Warm foods can be heated up to about 115°F and still be considered raw. Cookies and crackers can be warmed in the dehydrator. Soups can be warmed on the stove to 115°F. Blending soups and sauces for a few minutes in a high powered blender is another technique to warm up the food.

Whey: A by-product of making cultured cheese or yogurt. It is the liquid that remains after the food has been fermented or cultured. Whey is most commonly seen when making sunflower seed cheese. The whey can be discarded or mixed back into the cheese.

Whole grain: Grains that have not been processed. Whole grains have all their nutrients intact and are more nutritious than refined flour. Whole-grain foods in this book include muesli cereal, sprouted grain cereal, and other cereals, granola bars, trail mix, various types of slow-baked crackers, breads, including Essene bread, and pizza with sprouted-grain crust.

Index

The EVERYTHING Series!

BUSINESS & PERSONAL FINANCE

Everything® Accounting Book
Everything® Budgeting Book, 2nd Ed.
Everything® Business Planning Book
Everything® Coaching and Mentoring Book, 2nd Ed.
Everything® Fundraising Book
Everything® Get Out of Debt Book
Everything® Grant Writing Book, 2nd Ed.
Everything® Guide to Buying Foreclosures
Everything® Guide to Fundraising, $15.95
Everything® Guide to Mortgages
Everything® Guide to Personal Finance for Single Mothers
Everything® Home-Based Business Book, 2nd Ed.
Everything® Homebuying Book, 3rd Ed., $15.95
Everything® Homeselling Book, 2nd Ed.
Everything® Human Resource Management Book
Everything® Improve Your Credit Book
Everything® Investing Book, 2nd Ed.
Everything® Landlording Book
Everything® Leadership Book, 2nd Ed.
Everything® Managing People Book, 2nd Ed.
Everything® Negotiating Book
Everything® Online Auctions Book
Everything® Online Business Book
Everything® Personal Finance Book
Everything® Personal Finance in Your 20s & 30s Book, 2nd Ed.
Everything® Personal Finance in Your 40s & 50s Book, $15.95
Everything® Project Management Book, 2nd Ed.
Everything® Real Estate Investing Book
Everything® Retirement Planning Book
Everything® Robert's Rules Book, $7.95
Everything® Selling Book
Everything® Start Your Own Business Book, 2nd Ed.
Everything® Wills & Estate Planning Book

COOKING

Everything® Barbecue Cookbook
Everything® Bartender's Book, 2nd Ed., $9.95
Everything® Calorie Counting Cookbook
Everything® Cheese Book
Everything® Chinese Cookbook
Everything® Classic Recipes Book
Everything® Cocktail Parties & Drinks Book
Everything® College Cookbook
Everything® Cooking for Baby and Toddler Book
Everything® Diabetes Cookbook
Everything® Easy Gourmet Cookbook
Everything® Fondue Cookbook
Everything® Food Allergy Cookbook, $15.95
Everything® Fondue Party Book
Everything® Gluten-Free Cookbook
Everything® Glycemic Index Cookbook
Everything® Grilling Cookbook
Everything® Healthy Cooking for Parties Book, $15.95
Everything® Holiday Cookbook
Everything® Indian Cookbook
Everything® Lactose-Free Cookbook
Everything® Low-Cholesterol Cookbook

Everything® Low-Fat High-Flavor Cookbook, 2nd Ed., $15.95
Everything® Low-Salt Cookbook
Everything® Meals for a Month Cookbook
Everything® Meals on a Budget Cookbook
Everything® Mediterranean Cookbook
Everything® Mexican Cookbook
Everything® No Trans Fat Cookbook
Everything® One-Pot Cookbook, 2nd Ed., $15.95
Everything® Organic Cooking for Baby & Toddler Book, $15.95
Everything® Pizza Cookbook
Everything® Quick Meals Cookbook, 2nd Ed., $15.95
Everything® Slow Cooker Cookbook
Everything® Slow Cooking for a Crowd Cookbook
Everything® Soup Cookbook
Everything® Stir-Fry Cookbook
Everything® Sugar-Free Cookbook
Everything® Tapas and Small Plates Cookbook
Everything® Tex-Mex Cookbook
Everything® Thai Cookbook
Everything® Vegetarian Cookbook
Everything® Whole-Grain, High-Fiber Cookbook
Everything® Wild Game Cookbook
Everything® Wine Book, 2nd Ed.

GAMES

Everything® 15-Minute Sudoku Book, $9.95
Everything® 30-Minute Sudoku Book, $9.95
Everything® Bible Crosswords Book, $9.95
Everything® Blackjack Strategy Book
Everything® Brain Strain Book, $9.95
Everything® Bridge Book
Everything® Card Games Book
Everything® Card Tricks Book, $9.95
Everything® Casino Gambling Book, 2nd Ed.
Everything® Chess Basics Book
Everything® Christmas Crosswords Book, $9.95
Everything® Craps Strategy Book
Everything® Crossword and Puzzle Book
Everything® Crosswords and Puzzles for Quote Lovers Book, $9.95
Everything® Crossword Challenge Book
Everything® Crosswords for the Beach Book, $9.95
Everything® Cryptic Crosswords Book, $9.95
Everything® Cryptograms Book, $9.95
Everything® Easy Crosswords Book
Everything® Easy Kakuro Book, $9.95
Everything® Easy Large-Print Crosswords Book
Everything® Games Book, 2nd Ed.
Everything® Giant Book of Crosswords
Everything® Giant Sudoku Book, $9.95
Everything® Giant Word Search Book
Everything® Kakuro Challenge Book, $9.95
Everything® Large-Print Crossword Challenge Book
Everything® Large-Print Crosswords Book
Everything® Large-Print Travel Crosswords Book
Everything® Lateral Thinking Puzzles Book, $9.95
Everything® Literary Crosswords Book, $9.95
Everything® Mazes Book
Everything® Memory Booster Puzzles Book, $9.95

Everything® Movie Crosswords Book, $9.95
Everything® Music Crosswords Book, $9.95
Everything® Online Poker Book
Everything® Pencil Puzzles Book, $9.95
Everything® Poker Strategy Book
Everything® Pool & Billiards Book
Everything® Puzzles for Commuters Book, $9.95
Everything® Puzzles for Dog Lovers Book, $9.95
Everything® Sports Crosswords Book, $9.95
Everything® Test Your IQ Book, $9.95
Everything® Texas Hold 'Em Book, $9.95
Everything® Travel Crosswords Book, $9.95
Everything® Travel Mazes Book, $9.95
Everything® Travel Word Search Book, $9.95
Everything® TV Crosswords Book, $9.95
Everything® Word Games Challenge Book
Everything® Word Scramble Book
Everything® Word Search Book

HEALTH

Everything® Alzheimer's Book
Everything® Diabetes Book
Everything® First Aid Book, $9.95
Everything® Green Living Book
Everything® Health Guide to Addiction and Recovery
Everything® Health Guide to Adult Bipolar Disorder
Everything® Health Guide to Arthritis
Everything® Health Guide to Controlling Anxiety
Everything® Health Guide to Depression
Everything® Health Guide to Diabetes, 2nd Ed.
Everything® Health Guide to Fibromyalgia
Everything® Health Guide to Menopause, 2nd Ed.
Everything® Health Guide to Migraines
Everything® Health Guide to Multiple Sclerosis
Everything® Health Guide to OCD
Everything® Health Guide to PMS
Everything® Health Guide to Postpartum Care
Everything® Health Guide to Thyroid Disease
Everything® Hypnosis Book
Everything® Low Cholesterol Book
Everything® Menopause Book
Everything® Nutrition Book
Everything® Reflexology Book
Everything® Stress Management Book
Everything® Superfoods Book, $15.95

HISTORY

Everything® American Government Book
Everything® American History Book, 2nd Ed.
Everything® American Revolution Book, $15.95
Everything® Civil War Book
Everything® Freemasons Book
Everything® Irish History & Heritage Book
Everything® World War II Book, 2nd Ed.

HOBBIES

Everything® Candlemaking Book
Everything® Cartooning Book
Everything® Coin Collecting Book
Everything® Digital Photography Book, 2nd Ed.

Everything® Drawing Book
Everything® Family Tree Book, 2nd Ed.
Everything® Guide to Online Genealogy, $15.95
Everything® Knitting Book
Everything® Knots Book
Everything® Photography Book
Everything® Quilting Book
Everything® Sewing Book
Everything® Soapmaking Book, 2nd Ed.
Everything® Woodworking Book

HOME IMPROVEMENT

Everything® Feng Shui Book
Everything® Feng Shui Decluttering Book, $9.95
Everything® Fix-It Book
Everything® Green Living Book
Everything® Home Decorating Book
Everything® Home Storage Solutions Book
Everything® Homebuilding Book
Everything® Organize Your Home Book, 2nd Ed.

KIDS' BOOKS

All titles are $7.95
Everything® Fairy Tales Book, $14.95
Everything® Kids' Animal Puzzle & Activity Book
Everything® Kids' Astronomy Book
Everything® Kids' Baseball Book, 5th Ed.
Everything® Kids' Bible Trivia Book
Everything® Kids' Bugs Book
Everything® Kids' Cars and Trucks Puzzle and Activity Book
Everything® Kids' Christmas Puzzle & Activity Book
Everything® Kids' Connect the Dots
    Puzzle and Activity Book
Everything® Kids' Cookbook, 2nd Ed.
Everything® Kids' Crazy Puzzles Book
Everything® Kids' Dinosaurs Book
Everything® Kids' Dragons Puzzle and Activity Book
Everything® Kids' Environment Book $7.95
Everything® Kids' Fairies Puzzle and Activity Book
Everything® Kids' First Spanish Puzzle and Activity Book
Everything® Kids' Football Book
Everything® Kids' Geography Book
Everything® Kids' Gross Cookbook
Everything® Kids' Gross Hidden Pictures Book
Everything® Kids' Gross Jokes Book
Everything® Kids' Gross Mazes Book
Everything® Kids' Gross Puzzle & Activity Book
Everything® Kids' Halloween Puzzle & Activity Book
Everything® Kids' Hanukkah Puzzle and Activity Book
Everything® Kids' Hidden Pictures Book
Everything® Kids' Horses Book
Everything® Kids' Joke Book
Everything® Kids' Knock Knock Book
Everything® Kids' Learning French Book
Everything® Kids' Learning Spanish Book
Everything® Kids' Magical Science Experiments Book
Everything® Kids' Math Puzzles Book
Everything® Kids' Mazes Book
Everything® Kids' Money Book, 2nd Ed.
Everything® Kids' Mummies, Pharaoh's, and Pyramids
    Puzzle and Activity Book
Everything® Kids' Nature Book
Everything® Kids' Pirates Puzzle and Activity Book
Everything® Kids' Presidents Book
Everything® Kids' Princess Puzzle and Activity Book
Everything® Kids' Puzzle Book

Everything® Kids' Racecars Puzzle and Activity Book
Everything® Kids' Riddles & Brain Teasers Book
Everything® Kids' Science Experiments Book
Everything® Kids' Sharks Book
Everything® Kids' Soccer Book
Everything® Kids' Spelling Book
Everything® Kids' Spies Puzzle and Activity Book
Everything® Kids' States Book
Everything® Kids' Travel Activity Book
Everything® Kids' Word Search Puzzle and Activity Book

LANGUAGE

Everything® Conversational Japanese Book with CD, $19.95
Everything® French Grammar Book
Everything® French Phrase Book, $9.95
Everything® French Verb Book, $9.95
Everything® German Phrase Book, $9.95
Everything® German Practice Book with CD, $19.95
Everything® Inglés Book
Everything® Intermediate Spanish Book with CD, $19.95
Everything® Italian Phrase Book, $9.95
Everything® Italian Practice Book with CD, $19.95
Everything® Learning Brazilian Portuguese Book with CD, $19.95
Everything® Learning French Book with CD, 2nd Ed., $19.95
Everything® Learning German Book
Everything® Learning Italian Book
Everything® Learning Latin Book
Everything® Learning Russian Book with CD, $19.95
Everything® Learning Spanish Book
Everything® Learning Spanish Book with CD, 2nd Ed., $19.95
Everything® Russian Practice Book with CD, $19.95
Everything® Sign Language Book, $15.95
Everything® Spanish Grammar Book
Everything® Spanish Phrase Book, $9.95
Everything® Spanish Practice Book with CD, $19.95
Everything® Spanish Verb Book, $9.95
Everything® Speaking Mandarin Chinese Book with CD, $19.95

MUSIC

Everything® Bass Guitar Book with CD, $19.95
Everything® Drums Book with CD, $19.95
Everything® Guitar Book with CD, 2nd Ed., $19.95
Everything® Guitar Chords Book with CD, $19.95
Everything® Guitar Scales Book with CD, $19.95
Everything® Harmonica Book with CD, $15.95
Everything® Home Recording Book
Everything® Music Theory Book with CD, $19.95
Everything® Reading Music Book with CD, $19.95
Everything® Rock & Blues Guitar Book with CD, $19.95
Everything® Rock & Blues Piano Book with CD, $19.95
Everything® Rock Drums Book with CD, $19.95
Everything® Singing Book with CD, $19.95
Everything® Songwriting Book

NEW AGE

Everything® Astrology Book, 2nd Ed.
Everything® Birthday Personology Book
Everything® Celtic Wisdom Book, $15.95
Everything® Dreams Book, 2nd Ed.
Everything® Law of Attraction Book, $15.95
Everything® Love Signs Book, $9.95
Everything® Love Spells Book, $9.95
Everything® Palmistry Book
Everything® Psychic Book
Everything® Reiki Book

Everything® Sex Signs Book, $9.95
Everything® Spells & Charms Book, 2nd Ed.
Everything® Tarot Book, 2nd Ed.
Everything® Toltec Wisdom Book
Everything® Wicca & Witchcraft Book, 2nd Ed.

PARENTING

Everything® Baby Names Book, 2nd Ed.
Everything® Baby Shower Book, 2nd Ed.
Everything® Baby Sign Language Book with DVD
Everything® Baby's First Year Book
Everything® Birthing Book
Everything® Breastfeeding Book
Everything® Father-to-Be Book
Everything® Father's First Year Book
Everything® Get Ready for Baby Book, 2nd Ed.
Everything® Get Your Baby to Sleep Book, $9.95
Everything® Getting Pregnant Book
Everything® Guide to Pregnancy Over 35
Everything® Guide to Raising a One-Year-Old
Everything® Guide to Raising a Two-Year-Old
Everything® Guide to Raising Adolescent Boys
Everything® Guide to Raising Adolescent Girls
Everything® Mother's First Year Book
Everything® Parent's Guide to Childhood Illnesses
Everything® Parent's Guide to Children and Divorce
Everything® Parent's Guide to Children with ADD/ADHD
Everything® Parent's Guide to Children with Asperger's
    Syndrome
Everything® Parent's Guide to Children with Anxiety
Everything® Parent's Guide to Children with Asthma
Everything® Parent's Guide to Children with Autism
Everything® Parent's Guide to Children with Bipolar Disorder
Everything® Parent's Guide to Children with Depression
Everything® Parent's Guide to Children with Dyslexia
Everything® Parent's Guide to Children with Juvenile Diabetes
Everything® Parent's Guide to Children with OCD
Everything® Parent's Guide to Positive Discipline
Everything® Parent's Guide to Raising Boys
Everything® Parent's Guide to Raising Girls
Everything® Parent's Guide to Raising Siblings
Everything® Parent's Guide to Raising Your
    Adopted Child
Everything® Parent's Guide to Sensory Integration Disorder
Everything® Parent's Guide to Tantrums
Everything® Parent's Guide to the Strong-Willed Child
Everything® Parenting a Teenager Book
Everything® Potty Training Book, $9.95
Everything® Pregnancy Book, 3rd Ed.
Everything® Pregnancy Fitness Book
Everything® Pregnancy Nutrition Book
Everything® Pregnancy Organizer, 2nd Ed., $16.95
Everything® Toddler Activities Book
Everything® Toddler Book
Everything® Tween Book
Everything® Twins, Triplets, and More Book

PETS

Everything® Aquarium Book
Everything® Boxer Book
Everything® Cat Book, 2nd Ed.
Everything® Chihuahua Book
Everything® Cooking for Dogs Book
Everything® Dachshund Book
Everything® Dog Book, 2nd Ed.
Everything® Dog Grooming Book

Everything® Dog Obedience Book
Everything® Dog Owner's Organizer, $16.95
Everything® Dog Training and Tricks Book
Everything® German Shepherd Book
Everything® Golden Retriever Book
Everything® Horse Book, 2nd Ed., $15.95
Everything® Horse Care Book
Everything® Horseback Riding Book
Everything® Labrador Retriever Book
Everything® Poodle Book
Everything® Pug Book
Everything® Puppy Book
Everything® Small Dogs Book
Everything® Tropical Fish Book
Everything® Yorkshire Terrier Book

REFERENCE

Everything® American Presidents Book
Everything® Blogging Book
Everything® Build Your Vocabulary Book, $9.95
Everything® Car Care Book
Everything® Classical Mythology Book
Everything® Da Vinci Book
Everything® Einstein Book
Everything® Enneagram Book
Everything® Etiquette Book, 2nd Ed.
Everything® Family Christmas Book, $15.95
Everything® Guide to C. S. Lewis & Narnia
Everything® Guide to Divorce, 2nd Ed., $15.95
Everything® Guide to Edgar Allan Poe
Everything® Guide to Understanding Philosophy
Everything® Inventions and Patents Book
Everything® Jacqueline Kennedy Onassis Book
Everything® John F. Kennedy Book
Everything® Mafia Book
Everything® Martin Luther King Jr. Book
Everything® Pirates Book
Everything® Private Investigation Book
Everything® Psychology Book
Everything® Public Speaking Book, $9.95
Everything® Shakespeare Book, 2nd Ed.

RELIGION

Everything® Angels Book
Everything® Bible Book
Everything® Bible Study Book with CD, $19.95
Everything® Buddhism Book
Everything® Catholicism Book
Everything® Christianity Book
Everything® Gnostic Gospels Book
Everything® Hinduism Book, $15.95
Everything® History of the Bible Book
Everything® Jesus Book
Everything® Jewish History & Heritage Book
Everything® Judaism Book
Everything® Kabbalah Book
Everything® Koran Book
Everything® Mary Book
Everything® Mary Magdalene Book
Everything® Prayer Book

Everything® Saints Book, 2nd Ed.
Everything® Torah Book
Everything® Understanding Islam Book
Everything® Women of the Bible Book
Everything® World's Religions Book

SCHOOL & CAREERS

Everything® Career Tests Book
Everything® College Major Test Book
Everything® College Survival Book, 2nd Ed.
Everything® Cover Letter Book, 2nd Ed.
Everything® Filmmaking Book
Everything® Get-a-Job Book, 2nd Ed.
Everything® Guide to Being a Paralegal
Everything® Guide to Being a Personal Trainer
Everything® Guide to Being a Real Estate Agent
Everything® Guide to Being a Sales Rep
Everything® Guide to Being an Event Planner
Everything® Guide to Careers in Health Care
Everything® Guide to Careers in Law Enforcement
Everything® Guide to Government Jobs
Everything® Guide to Starting and Running a Catering
   Business
Everything® Guide to Starting and Running a Restaurant
**Everything® Guide to Starting and Running
   a Retail Store**
Everything® Job Interview Book, 2nd Ed.
Everything® New Nurse Book
Everything® New Teacher Book
Everything® Paying for College Book
Everything® Practice Interview Book
Everything® Resume Book, 3rd Ed.
Everything® Study Book

SELF-HELP

Everything® Body Language Book
Everything® Dating Book, 2nd Ed.
Everything® Great Sex Book
**Everything® Guide to Caring for Aging Parents,
   $15.95**
Everything® Self-Esteem Book
Everything® Self-Hypnosis Book, $9.95
Everything® Tantric Sex Book

SPORTS & FITNESS

Everything® Easy Fitness Book
Everything® Fishing Book
Everything® Guide to Weight Training, $15.95
Everything® Krav Maga for Fitness Book
Everything® Running Book, 2nd Ed.
Everything® Triathlon Training Book, $15.95

TRAVEL

Everything® Family Guide to Coastal Florida
Everything® Family Guide to Cruise Vacations
Everything® Family Guide to Hawaii
Everything® Family Guide to Las Vegas, 2nd Ed.
Everything® Family Guide to Mexico
Everything® Family Guide to New England, 2nd Ed.

Everything® Family Guide to New York City, 3rd Ed.
**Everything® Family Guide to Northern California
   and Lake Tahoe**
Everything® Family Guide to RV Travel & Campgrounds
Everything® Family Guide to the Caribbean
Everything® Family Guide to the Disneyland® Resort, California
   Adventure®, Universal Studios®, and the Anaheim
   Area, 2nd Ed.
Everything® Family Guide to the Walt Disney World Resort®,
   Universal Studios®, and Greater Orlando, 5th Ed.
Everything® Family Guide to Timeshares
Everything® Family Guide to Washington D.C., 2nd Ed.

WEDDINGS

Everything® Bachelorette Party Book, $9.95
Everything® Bridesmaid Book, $9.95
Everything® Destination Wedding Book
Everything® Father of the Bride Book, $9.95
Everything® Green Wedding Book, $15.95
Everything® Groom Book, $9.95
Everything® Jewish Wedding Book, 2nd Ed., $15.95
Everything® Mother of the Bride Book, $9.95
Everything® Outdoor Wedding Book
Everything® Wedding Book, 3rd Ed.
Everything® Wedding Checklist, $9.95
Everything® Wedding Etiquette Book, $9.95
Everything® Wedding Organizer, 2nd Ed., $16.95
Everything® Wedding Shower Book, $9.95
Everything® Wedding Vows Book, 3rd Ed., $9.95
Everything® Wedding Workout Book
Everything® Weddings on a Budget Book, 2nd Ed., $9.95

WRITING

Everything® Creative Writing Book
Everything® Get Published Book, 2nd Ed.
Everything® Grammar and Style Book, 2nd Ed.
Everything® Guide to Magazine Writing
Everything® Guide to Writing a Book Proposal
Everything® Guide to Writing a Novel
Everything® Guide to Writing Children's Books
Everything® Guide to Writing Copy
Everything® Guide to Writing Graphic Novels
Everything® Guide to Writing Research Papers
Everything® Guide to Writing a Romance Novel, $15.95
Everything® Improve Your Writing Book, 2nd Ed.
Everything® Writing Poetry Book